Bless Me Father, for I Have Sinned

To Luise,
Hope you enjoy
the book
All the best,

[signature]

Bless Me Father, for I Have Sinned

Memories of Yore

Armando and Fernando Garcia-Davila

McCaa Books · Santa Rosa

McCaa Books

McCaa Books
684 Benicia Drive #50
Santa Rosa, CA 95409

ISBN 978-17378683-0-9

First published in 2021 by McCaa Books,
an imprint of McCaa Publications.

Printed in the United States of America
Set in Minion Pro

Cover art by Luz Rameño of Siker Publicidar.
Cover and book layout by Waights Taylor Jr.

www.mccaabooks.com

Dedications

Armando dedicates this book
to Sister Marie Lucille.

Fernando dedicates this book to Jan, the best wife
a man could ask for, I love you honey, also for Ma
and Pa and for Antonio, Holly, Jacob, Katie, Cally,
Josh, Davila, Voytek, Aurora, Ana, Ken, Raul,
Anna Marie, Cory, Jamie, Garrett, Vinny, Jessica,
MacKenzie, Jordan, Carolyn, Bill, Kenny, Kim,
Stephen, Nicole, Natalie, Barbie, Kelly, Paige, Jenna,
Jake, Katie, Kyle, Mia, Martha, Wayne, Aaron,
Desiree, Peyton, Olivia, Adam, Anthony, Lynne,
Aiden, Mateo, Gabe, McKenzie, Mack, Eliana, Jacob,
Damien, Alicia, Tony, Armando, Emilio, Cecilia,
Carlos, Enrique, Mila, Carmen, Jim, Michelle, Pete,
Frances, and Carmelita. Whew, that's a load off my
mind.

Table of Contents

Forward

Fernando

"Mom, what was it like raising twins?"
Fernando
"Ay, sometimes I go to bed crying."
Carolina Garcia

MOST OF WHAT Armando and I have written in our stories is true. We used poetic license in the sequence of events to give the reminiscences a logical flow.

We attended St. Jude Academy for the first two years and St. Rita's Catholic Grammar School for the rest of our elementary education. Armando and I received enough sacraments during our primary-education years to guarantee us a shot at getting into heaven in the event of our untimely deaths.

By the time we reached age of five, Ma must have rejoiced when she walked us to our first day of kindergarten and could look forward to a few hours of peace. Between the ages of six months and five years, we had already put her through a lifetime of worry. Before my first birthday, and while living in a migrant worker camp, I swallowed some kerosene from a glass jar that Ma kept near the lamp. I had mistaken the clear liquid for water. While I spent a day in the hospital, my sister Martha spent the day on her knees praying for me. She likely regretted it a few years later when I sneaked into her bed one night and scared the hell out of her.

An exciting new world lay before Armando and me when we learned to walk. We climbed into the cab of dad's 1948 GMC work truck, somehow released the parking brake, and coasted out of the driveway and down a hill. My brother stood on the seat playing with the steering wheel. I sat on the floor pushing and pulling the clutch, brake, and accelerator pedals. Ma realized a moment too late that her house was unusually quiet and noticed that the front door was open. She stepped out to see one of the cuates standing inside the truck as it rolled away. She chased after, waving arms and screaming. The truck came to a stop when it turned into an embankment. Fortunately, it didn't turn in the other direction crossing a street heavy with traffic. Our Aunt Mary, Ma's sister—not to be confused with Aunt Mary, my father's sister—found our little adventure riotously funny.

On another occasion I stood on a ladder rung and dropped a half-pound lead weight on my twin to see what would happen. He cried and got a pot knot on the top of his head. Ma gave him a treat; I got a whack.

Armando and I played with an old quilt Ma had discarded in our backyard, which in and of itself was highly unusual as Ma rarely threw anything away. I wrapped him in the quilt, with his head out, and pushed him down a knoll. He laughed gleefully as he rolled until his head hit a piece of broken concrete protruding out of the ground. When he came to a stop, I grabbed the end of the quilt and rolled him out. He cried as blood pulsed from the wound. He came home from the emergency room missing a patch of hair and four neat cat-gut stitches that closed the wound.

When we climbed a rickety wood fence in our back yard, Armando grabbed a fence board, it gave way, and he fell nose first just as Pa was pulling into the driveway from his work shift. Pa saw blood flowing onto his chest. Pa ran to him, covered his nose with a handkerchief rushed him back to an emergency room. For the record, I did not push him off the fence.

Armando got mad after I took away the broom handle that was his rifle. He sunk his teeth into my shoulder blade. Ma had to pry him off as I screamed.

We got caught, with our neighbor Genie, playing with matches and nearly burned down his garage. Ma smacked our hands with the backside of her hairbrush; Genie got a whipping.

I shot my brother in the back with our neighbor Mikey's BB gun that he kept just inside their back door. The BB embedded itself into my brother's back. I begged him not to tell Ma, but he snitched.

When Ma called us for dinner, we raced, trying to get there first. I tripped my brother. He landed open mouth on the concrete stairs from the lower yard and knocked an impressive-sized chip out of one of his front teeth. It took Dr. Rover, our kindly and patient dentist, an afternoon to cap it.

This was an era before behavioral scientists and child psychologists or modern helicopter parents that hover over their children. Ma used her Old World system of threat, guilt, *El Cucuy*, (the Mexican boogie man), and the devil, as tools for keeping us under some semblance of control and discipline.

Our stories were written to give you an insight into what it was like growing up in this era. We sincerely apologize if we have offended any friend, classmate, neighbor or relative, whether they be Mexican, American, Chicano, gringo, gay, straight, transsexual, transvestite, bisexual, bilingual or bipolar, with our writing. If you feel slighted, know that it is unintentional. We will never, however, apologize to Sister Mary Constance the principal and Mother Superior of the convent at St. Rita's School. You will soon find out why.

Introduction
Fernando

IT WAS TWO THOUSAND FIVE HUNDRED and two steps from the front door of our home on Euclid Avenue in San Diego, California, to the plain red-brick entry of St. Rita's grammar school. I know this because my twin brother, Armando, and I made the daily trek with our older sister Martha for two years until she graduated. Armando and I then made this walk eight hundred and forty times. It should only have been seven hundred and sixty-eight times, but an extra year was added to our sentence since we both managed to flunk third grade. We did first and second grades at St. Jude Academy before moving to St. Rita's Parish.

We were all-weather trekkers: rain, fog, hot and humid, hot and dry, cold and rainy. A rarity was white frosty dew on roadside weeds during short cold snaps. Walking or riding bikes to school was the norm in the 1960s. A few kids took the school bus. I wondered what it would be like to ride on a bus. The daily twenty-five-cent two-way fare was beyond our family's means.

The walk took us downhill and past Horton Elementary School where our neighborhood friends went. The little pagans didn't have religion class in their school; they were fortunate to have my twin and me as neighborhood apostles to instruct them on the benefit of knowing the damning consequences of sin and the glorious rewards of heaven.

We walked past a large roadside billboard and decided whether the current advertisement merited a dirt-clod assault. Our targets included scantily clad women or ads promoting smoking or drinking. Mud grenades were preferred after a rare rain, as they stuck, making our attacks more effective.

We were moral crusaders rescuing an unsuspecting public from the devious entrapments of the devil that could result in one burning in the fires of hell for eternity. We were in the middle of doing our moral duty one morning when a driver pulled over long enough to yell, "Hey!" His misplaced admonishment was effective enough to stop us from meting out our just punishments. It was a relief to see him drive off. We shrugged our shoulders and left him to his grim fate.

We crossed Market Street, then on toward the railroad tracks, and past a Jehovah's Witness temple. Martha speculated once that they were like Communists. "I think they don't even vote," she said. I was not quite sure why not voting was wrong, but since she thought it important enough to bring up, it must have been unpatriotic and therefore sinful. The poor lost souls of Jehovah didn't have a chance of making it into heaven. Believers in any religion except Catholicism were doomed to limbo, or worse, in the afterlife. Limbo was a place of neither inconceivable suffering nor heavenly bliss where the poor slobs who weren't exposed to the truth, like us, went to experience eternal boredom.

My twin and I discussed a myriad of topics on our way to school. Who we thought was the prettiest girl in our class. Who were the nicest or meanest nuns. We wrestled with philosophical questions. If God is all-powerful, can He create a boulder so heavy that even He can't lift it? If you found a bag of food on the street and gave it to a poor person and the food was poisonous and he died, would you be virtuous or sinful?

Ma, Carolina Davila, was born on December 27, 1915, in Hermosillo, Sonora, just south of Arizona. She came to the United States at eighteen to help Aunt Helen with her children. Although Ma lived most of her life in the United States and developed a strong English vocabulary, she never lost her accent, so yellow was "jello" and him, was "heem." She also brought her Old-World healing methods. Ma applied a hot cloth to an ear for an infection and liberally applied Mentolato (Mentholatum) in nostrils, on chests, the bottom of your feet and on the forehead for colds or coughs. It was rubbed into arms and legs for sore muscles and into any bodily orifice in need of healing. After washing cuts with soap and water, she applied straight alcohol and ignored our screams, keeping a firm hold as we wriggled futilely. She used an enema bag filled with hot water and salt to cure my brother and me of worms. Ma believed drinking iced drinks or walking barefoot could cause a cold and not washing well could invite cancer, as could breathing in cat hairs and scratching scabs. The list was endless.

When we began to lose teeth, we put them under our pillows so El Raton, the tooth Mouse, would exchange them for a nickel.

Like many of her contemporaries, she lost her teeth at an early age. I was born when she was thirty-four and have no memory of her not wearing dentures. Having brought seven children into the world, she lost the figure of the slim young woman in her wedding picture. Ma, like the rest of her siblings, was a devout Catholic and had an undying devotion to Nuestra Señora de Guadalupe, as well as a handful of favorite saints.

Ma put a holy medal of St. Martin de Porres under our pillow when we got sick. Things weren't looking good for my cousin Tony Alvarez when he was born. My Aunt Helen, knowing that Ma had a profound faith, asked her to pray for Tony to survive. Ma got busy and prayed to St. Jude, the patron saint of lost causes and lo and behold Tony made it. Tony spent most of his life behind bars. Be careful what you pray for.

Ma had been taught by no-nonsense nuns in Mexico. No matter the cost, no matter the sacrifices that Pa and she had to make, Ma insisted on sending us to Catholic schools. She believed that Catholic education was superior to public school education. She was adept at mending torn school uniforms and making nutritious food on a commoner's wage and still found a way to contribute to the church.

With the church's strict stance on contraception, she and her sisters had large families. Ma bore seven children; her sisters Mary had fifteen, Emma had eight and Eva twelve. Interestingly, Ma, Mary and Emma all had identical twin boys.

Pa, Antonio Mendoza Garcia, was born in Mazatlán, Sinaloa, on September 16, 1913. In 1923, when his mother, Antonia, was abandoned by her husband, she decided to bring Pa and his two siblings to the United States. Pa was ten years old, his brother Sam twelve and their sister Maria fourteen when they made the seven-hundred-mile trek from Mazatlán into El Norte. Pa, born in a coastal city, never lost his love of the sea, loved to fish, and swim in the salty water. As long as Pa fished, we never went hungry.

When Grandma Antonia got to the Mexico-Arizona border, she was informed that in order to cross they had to prove that they had an intact family, that is, at a minimum, a male head-of-household and a wife. She found a man wanting to cross and they agreed that he'd pose as her husband. Afterward he went his way, and they went theirs. She enrolled her children in American public schools, and they quickly became bilingual.

My parents met shortly after Ma came to San Diego. She fell in love with the tall, handsome man from Sinaloa who had no fear of gringos. My father, out of respect, wrote a letter to his future in-laws in Sonora asking for their daughter's hand in marriage. They gave their blessing and Ma, and Pa were married in 1937 at Our Lady of Guadalupe Church in Logan Heights barrio, a few blocks east of downtown San Diego. Our brother, Tony, was born the following year, 1938, followed by our sisters, Ana, Carolyn, Martha, then Armando and me (Fernando), with our little sister, Carmen, who was born in 1953.

Pa opened a grocery store in Old Town. Tony's Market prospered for a few years, but he decided to sell his business and home and start a trucking company in Nogales, Arizona, hauling freight across the border. This business failed and he lost everything. He moved our family to work in the agricultural fields of Southern and Central California. He worked tirelessly long days, barely keeping our family fed. At one point he worked irrigating fields for a farmer. The farmer allowed Pa to move his family of eight into a water tower. Oblivious to the dire circumstances of our condition, my older siblings saw their humble dwelling as another adventure. Ma tired of following the crops, living in labor camps and her children bouncing from school to school, talked Pa into coming back to San Diego.

The post-war economy of the '50s and '60s was strong and jobs were plentiful. Pa landed a job working the graveyard shift, from midnight to eight in the morning, at a trucking company. He took on a Saturday afternoon job at the San Diego Union newspaper company delivering bundles of their Sunday morning edition to grocery stores, liquor stores, hotels, bowling alleys, and diners.

Mexican culture values hard work. A truly macho man fathers children and does a good job as a provider and role model. His life- long duty was tantamount to doing God's work. Pa never complained, always maintained a positive can-do spirit and never lost his sense of humor. All seven of us learned from his example and took pride in being able to add to the family's income. We all started working in our early teens. And this is how a family bordering on poverty pays tuitions for seven children to attend Catholic school.

The School Sisters of Notre Dame, headquartered in St. Louis, Missouri, was the order of nuns dedicated to teaching grammar schools. The Church considered California missionary country overrun by Mexicans, Filipinos, black people, mixed-race couples, the unbaptized, divorcees and the decadent Hollywood lifestyle. It was the sacred duty of these dogmatic Midwestern women of God to save California's children, who unbeknownst to them, were merrily skipping down the road to perdition. The nuns tasked themselves with imparting their value system on these unrefined people. The Sisters had no knowledge or appreciation of the cultures or mores of the children that they were to teach and indoctrinate.

My brother and I were two little brown-haired, brown-eyed power plants of energetic enthusiasm. We ran rather than walked and rambled more than talked. Our home was a brew of Californian pop culture and the chaotic festive Mexican culture of music, food, laughter and language that didn't mesh with the authoritarian discipline of a group of introspective Anglo-Saxon religious women who were hellbent on infusing us with the infallible teachings of the Church and what they deemed as acceptable behavior. A child would be severely admonished for merely uttering the word fart, or any other word having to do with bodily functions.

So, we invite you into the world of our home, neighborhood, friends and school where two cultures, one Midwestern American conservative, the other a hybrid of New World America and Old-World Mexico collided. Inasmuch as there is cataclysmic upheaval when continents collide in the natural world, there was dreadful disruption at St. Rita's Grammar School between the nuns and the Garcia twins. We hope you enjoy our side of the story.

1.

Kindergarten
Armando

A good teacher covers the material well.
A great teacher shows you, her stuff.

I WAS FIVE WHEN WE MOVED into the Logan Heights barrio
of San Diego, in the summer of 1954. Logan was a series of
small one- and two-bedroom custom-built houses. The neighborhood was a mix of Anglo and Black families, but mostly
Mexican-American. The Rodriguez family lived on one side
of our house on Acacia Street and the Gastelums on the other.
The Washington's, a Black family lived next door to them.

My older sister Carolyn told me that Fernando and I would
be starting school in September and how exciting it was going
to be.

"You are going to meet lots of kids," she said. A week later,
Ma dressed my brother and me, told Ana, our oldest sister, to
watch little Carmen, saying that we would be back before long.

"*Vamonos, cuatitos,*" (Let's go little twins,) Ma said.

"Are we going to school?"

"*Todavia no.*" (Not yet.) We walked to a big one-story building a few blocks from home. There was a white sign on the
front lawn with some black letters on it. We entered the door
and into a room that was filled with people sitting in chairs;
most of them were women with kids. Ma stopped in front of a
lady at a big desk, talked to her, then took us to chairs along the

wall, and had us sit on either side of her. She told us that we had to be quiet. Moments later a lady in a white dress and shoes opened a door and called out a name. She cradled a board with papers attached to it. A lady got up and reached for the hand of a little girl next to her and followed the lady in white through the door. My legs dangled off my chair. Ma sat quietly and looked at us, she looked sad. I got bored and wanted to get up.

"*Paciencia*," Ma whispered. I knew better than to challenge her. I looked at the big clock on the wall, I wondered why it was there. I had never seen such a big clock. I heard a girl cry from behind the door. The lady and the little girl that had gone in came out and walked out the door. The girl whimpered. The lady with the board and papers opened the door to our room with the big clock and called out, "Mrs. Garcia." Ma told us to follow her. The lady led us down a hall to a small room. The room had white walls and two long white lights on the ceiling; the room had a nasty smell that kind of stung my nose.

"*No quiero que lloran*," Ma said. I nodded but didn't understand why she told us not to cry. There was a bed on a tall stand in the room and a picture of an outline of a body showing its bones and another picture of a body showing the insides. I didn't like the way they looked.

A different lady in a white dress, stockings and shoes came into the room and said, "Good morning, Mrs. Garcia." She sounded nice.

"Goot morning," Ma replied. I didn't remember ever hearing Ma speak English.

"What are these two handsome boys names?"

"Dees is Armando and dees ees Fernando."

She smiled, "Hello, Armando, would you come here and sit on the bed for me?"

Ma told my brother to stay in his seat, walked me over, lifted me, and sat me on the bed. The lady took a cotton ball and wiped the top of my arm. It was cold and had the same

20

bad smell as the room. The lady turned to the table and picked something up from under a white cloth.

"Look at your mother, honey." I turned and felt a deep sting on my arm and wanted to cry but Ma told me not to. "All done," she said and put a round Band-Aid on my arm. She put me on the floor. I ran back to Ma and buried my face in her side; my arm hurt. The lady asked Ma to take my brother to her. He didn't want to go but she took him and put him on the bed. He didn't cry either. I saw Ma wipe a tear from his cheek. I wanted to cry for him. We walked out of the smelly room, down the hall and out the front door.

"Mami, why did we have to go there?"

"Because you had to go there before going to school." If we had to go there before going to school, then I didn't want to go to school.

A week later, on what would be our first day at school, Fernando and I rose from our Army surplus mats on the living room floor and stood naked not sure what to do. The blankets where Tony, our older brother, had slept were folded and sat in a corner of the room. Tony used the couch for his bed. Ana, Carolyn, Martha, and our cousin Ana Berta slept on twin beds in the second bedroom. Ma and Pa slept in the first bedroom with one-year-old Carmen in her crib.

Our sisters and cousin had gotten up earlier and were getting ready for the half-mile walk to St. Jude Academy. Ma was in the kitchen putting sack lunches together. Pa was at his job at the freight company. Tony was on the bus heading for St. Augustine High School.

The girls walked from their bedroom to the bathroom to an ironing board set up in the living room where they pressed the pleats in their school uniform skirts. On a trip between the rooms Martha, four years older than me, looked at Fernando and me, wrinkled her nose in disgust, "Yuck, would someone please dress them?"

"*Carolina*," Ma called.

"Mande?" Carolyn answered.

"*Vistelos*," she ordered.

"*Si, mami.*" Carolyn appeared from the bathroom, sighed and took our hands. She was patient with us. Carolyn was slim, had short dark hair, brown eyes and a slight gap between her two front teeth.

"Come on *cuatitos.*" Her hand was warm and felt good as she led us back to the dresser in her room. The house wasn't warm yet and the cold morning air gave me a chill.

Carolyn searched out underwear, t-shirts and socks from a drawer.

"You two are old enough to dress yourselves," she muttered. She helped us get dressed. A few minutes later the four girls left the house with their hair perfectly groomed and uniforms ironed.

Ma made Fernando and me scrambled eggs with *chorizo*, buttered toast and a glass of milk for our first day of school. After we ate, she took us to the bathroom and combed our hair with a neat part on the side.

"*Que guapos se ven,*" she said and kissed us on top of our heads. She walked us to school for the first and only time.

"You are going to behave yourselves."

"We will, Mami," I said.

"Do what the teacher tells you."

"*Si, Mami.*"

I had to take two steps for each of Ma's. She wore her navy-blue dress with puffy sleeves that ended at the elbow. The dress had small whit polka dots and reached below the knee. Ma had applied a dab of a pink-colored powder to her palm and rubbed it into her cheeks.

"Mami, where're our sisters?"

"They went to St. Jude."

"Can we go there too?"

"Not until next year."

I didn't know we were going to a different school. I learned later that Ma saved the tuition money she would have paid at Catholic school.

The front of Balboa school was a beehive of activity. Parents walked or dropped their kids off from cars. I held tight to Ma's hand. Most of the kids were older than us and we recognized a few from the rec center.

We walked to the end of the school and into a cavernous room. A lady with a red dress greeted parents and children as they entered. Unlike Ma, her short-sleeved dress showed her knees. She smiled when she saw us. I shrunk back. Boys and girls our age sat at munchkin-sized tables and chairs, some talked and giggled. Others sat quietly, some looked dazed. One boy sobbed in a lady's arms.

"Oh my goodness, twin boys. This is my lucky day." I looked up at her not sure what to do. The lady wasn't wearing a white dress or shoes and wasn't holding anything in her hand. She squatted and looked Fernando and me in the eye. I took a stepped behind Ma.

"I can tell by looking at you that you are well behaved boys."

"Oh, jes," Ma said, "berry good boyce."

The lady, still smiling, pointed to a table, "Find yourselves seats, please."

Ma walked us over. A boy was seated there and a girl with shoulder-length blonde hair sat across from him. I didn't want to let go of Ma but she grabbed my wrist, pulled my hand loose, and nudged us to our chairs. I saw Ma and the lady exchange a few words, ma turned, smiled and abandoned us. I turned to see if Fernando was still in the seat next to me.

After all the parents left the lady stood at the front of the room. "My name is Mrs. Smith and I will be your teacher. Welcome to your first day of school. We are going to have fun."

I sat not knowing what to do. Should I look around? Should I keep my eyes on the teacher? I ventured a glance at the blonde girl next to me. She was pretty and smiled. I looked away. The boy who had been sobbing settled down to sniveling. The teacher had hugged him. His mother wiped her eyes when she walked out. Fernando looked to me and whispered, "cry baby." I tried not laugh. Tony called us cry babies when we cried or whined. We didn't like being called that but today it sounded funny.

Things improved a lot when Mrs. Smith brought out a box of Graham Crackers and smell cartons of milk. Pa bought quart bottles by the case at a dairy. Mrs. Smith showed us how to fold down the top of the carton top to make a spout. The crackers and milk tasted good. Crybaby just looked at his snack sitting on the table. I wanted to take it but didn't.

Mrs. Smith told us we had to be quiet when she spoke. Her voice was soft and nice. After the snack she walked to a corner of the room and lifted the lid off of a big red wooden box and told us to take an instrument and sit in a circle on the carpet in the middle of the floor. I took a horn, my brother a tambourine. At her signal we played our instruments. I blew my horn and Fernando hit his tambourine against the floor. Seconds later Mrs. Smith asked us to stop and put them back in the box.

Children its time for recess. You may go out and play in the yard. When you hear the school bell, it will be time to come back in." Fernando and I raced out the door and were first to get to the swings. Some kids stood gawking not sure what to do. Others climbed monkey bars and used the slide. Blondie got on a swing next to me. I jumped off my swing and walked in front of her, "hi."

She smiled and said, "hi." I went behind her and pushed. When she got high enough, I walked back around and lay down just out of reach of her feet. They missed me by inches. Tony taught us that trick over the summer in the big kids' playground. Blondie laughed, it made me happy. The bell rang and we saw Mrs. Smith come to the door of the classroom and motioned to us.

Once inside she told us to sit on the carpet, Blondie sat next to me. The teacher brought out a book with a picture of a princess and a castle on the cover. She told us to be quiet and read us a story that was just an okay story. Tony told us really good stories about giants and monsters and heroes.

"Now children, I want everyone to lie down for a nap. Please be still and I will tell you when its time to get up." My brother lay next to me; we looked at each other, our noses nearly touched. When he turned his back to me his face was inches from crybaby's butt. He turned back to me and pinched his nose. I covered my mouth, but a laugh escaped. Mrs. Smith looked at us and put a finger to her lips.

A little later Mrs. Smith spoke softly and told us it was time to get up. "It's almost time to go home. You all did a wonderful job today on your first day of school. I am looking forward to seeing you tomorrow."

The noon bell rang. It was lunch time for the big kids and time for the kindergarteners to go home. "I think I like school," Fernando said.

"I really like school." We walked through our small front yard and into the house.

"Did you behave?"

"Yes Ma."

We told her about crybaby and how we didn't cry, about the Graham Crackers and the little milks and the swings and the musical instruments. I told Ma about blondie that sat next to me and that I found out her name was Julie Mills and I was going to marry her one day. I don't know why Ma laughed about it.

"Good boys, change your clothes and come back for lunch." By the end of the first week my brother and I settled into routine. We were a hit with the rest of the kids in our class. We roughed housed with the boys and were good at making the girls laugh, like we did with Ma and our sisters.

I lay on my mat that night thinking about Julie Mills. I wasn't sure how old I had to be before I could marry her, but I was willing to wait. I held hands with her on the playground the next day. It felt good holding her hand and making her laugh.

I saw her holding hands with a boy the following day. It made me mad. She tried to make it up by taking my hand but it over as far as I was concerned. I pushed Julie's hand away. When Mrs. Smith had the class lie on the rug in a circle for our daily nap, Julie lay just above me. I was next to Fernando. I felt something loose in my nose. I breathed in, it flapped up. I breathed out, it flapped down—up, down, up, down. I stuck my finger in and pulled out a green cornflake. I showed it to my twin then wiped it onto Julie's leg. She looked down and giggled. She must have thought I was tickling her. Fernando told me on the way home that she had it coming.

"And how is Julie?" Ma asked when we got home. My girlfriend was big news in our home.

"Okay," I said. I didn't want to tell her the bad news of the breakup. I wasn't sure why our sisters and brother thought it funny that I had a girlfriend.

One of Mrs. Smith's routines for us was an imaginary trip to Toyland. She had us form a circle as she said, "chug, chug, chug." We followed her, pumped our arms and marched, resembling a locomotive. We pulled the cord and tooted our steam whistles along the way. After a lap around the carpet, we arrived.

"Now children, let's build a tower." She began to stack imaginary blocks and invited us to do the same. The tower started on the floor and worked up and up past our heads until we could barely reach the top. It got so high that it became unbalanced, teetered until it came crashing down onto the rug. She fell along with the invisible blocks and we fell too.

After another trip to Toyland, my brother saw something he wanted to share with me. He made sure we were at the teacher's feet when the tower toppled. He nudged me and pointed up Mrs. Smith's dress. We saw nylons reach up to a girdle with snaps and big white underwear just like the ones on Ma's clothesline. We giggled. Mrs. Smith rose with a big smile, happy that my brother and I were having a good time.

Between Graham Crackers and milk, musical instruments, fairy tales and new friends, school turned out to be a lot of fun, not to mention we were learning a lot more than Ma could ever guess. At the end of the school year, we said good-bye to Mrs. Smith with sadness knowing that we would probably not be going to Toyland again.

2.

1st Grade – Missing Twin
Fernando

Blessed are they who mourn for they shall be comforted.
Jesus Christ

SUMMER CAME AND WENT, and the time for Armando and me to attend St. Jude Academy Catholic grammar school with out big sisters. Ana, the oldest, was light complected like Ma and had light brown hair, green-eyes and was the tallest of the girls. Ana and Carolyn, the next oldest, helped us put on our new corduroy pants white cotton shirts and navy-blue uniform sweaters.

The girls wore blue pleated skirts, white blouses, blue sweaters and black and white oxford shoes with white socks folded down at the ankle. Martha the next in line was the shortest of the three. She like Carolyn had darker skin, only Pa was darker. She handed us sack lunches containing bean burritos wrapped in waxed paper that Ma had made the night before and two chocolate chip cookies that Carolyn had baked. Ma gave Armando and me a nickel each for milk money.

After we saw our older sisters and cousin Ana Berta get ready and walk to St. Jude's each morning the previous year, we finally got to join them. Ma stood at the door.

"Adios, Mami," our sisters said.

"Adios, tia," Ana Berta said.

"Bye Ma," Armando and I said.

Ma watched us file out to the walk through the gate and to the sidewalk. The girls talked excitedly. I looked back; Ma held the Virgin of Guadalupe medallion that hung from her neck while she whispered a blessing. Only two-year-old Carmen was left home. Ma must have treasured a quiet house for the length of a school day.

Our sisters made us walk in front of them. The clear morning sky had patches of frothy white clouds. Carolyn and Martha gave us tips about attending the big kids' school. Ana and Ana Berta chatted a few paces behind.

"Do what the nuns tell you, and you'll be fine," Martha said as she took my brother's hand. Carolyn held mine as we crossed the busy street.

"What's a nun?" I asked.

"The nuns are the teachers, like Mrs. Smith was in kindergarten."

"Will we be going to Toyland?" Armando asked.

"No," Martha said, "you'll be learning your ABCs and numbers."

"Will we get Graham Crackers?"

"No, that's just for kindergarteners, you're in a big school now."

The big kids' school didn't sound like it was going to be very much fun.

WE WALKED UNDER A GIANT PALM TREE, alive with chattering birds. Its branches stretched into the street. The sidewalk was white with lumpy dried bird poop.

Don't talk or fool around during class to make kids laugh," Martha said, "there's time to have fun at recess."

"Will there be kids our age like kindergarten?"

"There'll be lots of kids your age to play with, just don't start playing until recess."

By the end of the third block my toes and heels started to sting from my new shoes. Except for Sundays, when we wore tennis shoes to church, we'd gone barefoot all summer. Even with the sting, I was too excited to give it much thought. When we finally got to school, I asked Martha, "Where are we going to meet to eat lunch?"

"You'll eat in your classroom and so will we." I didn't like we were not going to eat with my sisters.

The entrance to the school was like kindergarten, lots of kids getting dropped off; some rode bikes, and others walked, like us.

"When schools over, meet us at this corner, "Ana said. "Don't cross the street by yourselves."

It was a lot to remember, I hoped Armando was listening. We ascended the wide concrete steps of the single-story beige stucco building. A plain white cross hung over the open breeze-way. It was filled with big and small kids, all in blue-and-white uniforms, like us. Loud chatter echoed off the side walls. It was exciting and scary. I tightened my grip on Carolyn's hand.

Our sisters said hi to a lot of kids as we walked toward the end of the long hall. Ana led my brother past a room with a number 1A over the thick tan door. Carolyn led me into a room with a number 1B. My brother and I looked at each other as we separated. The far side of my room had a wall with big windows that let in lots of sunshine. I could see the wall of the church where we went to Mass on Sundays. Carolyn turned my hand over to a tall woman she called Sister Andrea. She was in a strange, long black dress that went all the way down to her black shoes. She had a thin black rope with a big cross at the end tied around her waist. Her hair, ears and neck were hidden by stiff white cloth. All that I could see was her pink cheeks, chin, and pointy nose. Her glasses were put together by shiny thin gold wires. Her eyes look really big. Below her chin was a white round bib like babies wore.

I didn't want to let go of Carolyn's hand, but she gently loosened my grip and said, "You'll be okay, cuatito," and left me. The lady in black pointed to a chair that had a little table on top.

"Sit here, young man."

I did as told. I was afraid to look around. I sat with my eyes to the front and waited. The classroom smelled like the wax that Ma used on the floors at home. Carolyn had told us how we were going to like first grade, but I was sitting in a room full of kids I didn't know, and I was alone without my brother. My cheeks and forehead got warm. I looked to either side and to the back of the room, hoping to see Armando but he wasn't there, and my sister was gone too.

The woman in black walked around, showing kids where to sit. Above the door was a cross with Jesus on it like the one we had at home. There was a big black board on the wall behind a big wooden desk in the front of the room. Over the black board were letters, one bigger and one letter smaller. I didn't see a toy box with horns and drums or a rug on the floor. The woman in black didn't seem nice like Mrs. Smith.

"Hey," said a boy sitting next to me in a loud whisper. I looked over. My name is Brian, your name is fart." He covered his mouth, laughing. My face got warmer.

I got up and walked behind the strange woman in black. She walked, I walked, she stopped, I stopped.

"You may sit here," she told a boy that she held by a shirt sleeve and made him sit in one of the chairs. A girl saw that I was walking and stopping with the woman and giggled. The woman turned around, "What are you doing young man? Go back to your desk."

"Where's my brother?" I said in a tiny voice.

"What did you say? Speak up."

"Where's my brother?"

"Sit at your desk."

31

My face got hot. It as hard talking. "Wh-wh-where's my brother?" Tears blurred the image of the woman.

"Your brother? Your brother? Is that what you're saying?"

She squatted and looked into my eyes. All I could see was her pink face and big eyes.

Your brother is in room 1A, the other first grade. It's right next door."

"Can, can I be with my brother? I think , he needs me."

She stared at me for a moment, "I'll see what I can do, but for now, I want you to go back to your desk."

"Can I go where he is?"

"Sit at your desk, and then we will see about your brother."

I went back to the chair, wiped my nose with my hand then wiped my hand on my new pants. The woman in black put a final girl into a chair, looked at me, then to the class. "Children, I want you to sit silently. You may take the tablets and pencils on your desks and draw pictures of your homes." Pencils and papers rustled. "I want to see your drawings when I come back. You must remain silent. Do you understand?" A few of the kids nodded, I sat still. She walked out the rear door and left it open. I heard girls whispering behind me.

"Will you be my best friend?"

"Okay."

"Hey," whispered Brian, "Your name is fart." Kids giggled. Everyone around me was drawing. I sat holding the pencil and stared at the tablet. I looked out the back door. The woman in black was in the hall talking to another woman in black then the other woman walked away and returned with Armando and handed him over. I was happy to see him. The woman brought him in.

"Brian, give this young man your desk, please." He stood and she sat my brother down. "Children, you are to remain silent for just a couple of more moments. I am proud of you for being so good while I was away. I can't wait to see your drawings when I return." She led fart boy out of the room.

"Hey," my brother whispered. I turned to look at him. He put his fingers in his nose, stretched his nose-holes apart, crossed his eyes and smiled, showing his missing front teeth. I laughed.

3.

1st Grade – Two Times Two
Fernando

Double your pleasure, double your fun.
Doublemint gum slogan of the sixties
Wrigley Company

THE BELL RANG FOR OUR FIRST ten o'clock recess in the first grade on our first day of school at St. Jude Academy. "Children, you may go out and play. When you hear the bell at the end of recess, you are to become silent and walk back to class. Do you understand? You are to be quiet as soon as the bell rings," said stoic Sister Mary Andrea.

Having had the same recess drill in kindergarten, I knew what to do except I didn't understand why we had to be quiet all the time. So far first grade wasn't any fun; we hadn't had milk and Graham Crackers, musical instruments, or nap time. Maybe after lunch we'll go on a train trip to Toyland. Although it would be hard to look up Sister Andrea's dress.

I walked with my twin out the back door of the classroom. Within seconds the playground was alive with screaming kids chasing each other and balls flying. Boys threw a ball at other boys standing inside a box painted with white lines on the ground. The boys in the box ducked, jumped and swerved side to side. In another part, there white balls attached to poles by a rope with kids hitting the balls in opposite directions. I didn't understand what they were doing. Bigger boys played basketball. A group of girls were playing jacks on the slick concrete surface of the breezeway like our big sisters did on our front porch. Other girls played jump rope. My brother and I stayed close together trying to find our sisters. I liked the noisy playground after having to be quiet in the classroom.

"There they are," my brother said, pointing to a court with a tall net. We ran to Ana and Carolyn who were talking with Ana Berta and two other girls. They smiled when they saw us run toward them.

"Hi, *cuatitos*. How was your class?" Ana asked. "

Okay, I guess." Armando said.

One of the girls asked, "Are these the twins?"

"Yes," Ana said with pride in her voice.

"They're so cute." The girl smiled, squatted, and asked us our names. Her blue plaid uniform skirt skimmed the surface of the blacktop.

"I'm Fernando," I said, taken aback. I pointed to my brother's chest with my thumb, "And he's Armando." I looked into her blue-eyed freckled face. Her wavy red hair was pulled tight into a ponytail like Ana's, only hers wasn't braided. I was intimidated by this strange-looking girl.

"You're cute. Are you in the first grade?" the girl asked.

"Uh-huh,"

"Which room?" I pointed to our classroom. The girl stood and turned to my sisters.

"I think that's Sister Andrea's class. She's kinda mean."

"Where's Martha?" I asked, looking to Ana.

"She's playing with the fifth-graders, *cuatito*."

"*Cuatito*? What's that mean?" Freckles asked.

"It means little twin."

"How cute."

Is everything cute to this girl?

"Can we come to your class after recess?" Armando asked.

"No," Ana said. "You have to stay in your own classroom."

35

She pointed to a corner of the playground. "Look, there are swings over there; go play on them. There are lots of kids your age. Try and meet some." I hung my head. She squatted and looked at me.

"Carolyn and I have to stay here with the big kids. We'll see you after school. Do you remember where to meet us?"

"Yeah, on the corner."

I didn't want to go but I didn't want to get in trouble with our teacher for being in the wrong part of the playground. We made our way to the swings, which were the big ones, not like those in kindergarten.

We got on adjoining swings. I pumped my legs and looked over at my brother. He pumped harder and swung higher. I pumped even harder. I felt like I was flying.

Somebody pushed me from behind. I turned my head but couldn't see who it was. On the third push, he ran under me on the upswing. He stopped and smiled at me. I didn't have time to be scared. I looked over and saw that another boy was doing the same to Armando. When the other boy ran under my brother's swing, he walked over and stood next to the boy who pushed me. They were twins. One said something to the other. They ran back around, pushed us hard, and sprinted under us again. We all laughed.

I stopped pumping my legs, dragged my feet on the ground, and came to a stop. We got off the swings. The boys stood half a head taller than us. They had black hair and eyes and their light brown skin matched ours. The four of us stood for a moment. Then one hopped on the other's back, pumped his legs, and slapped, as if riding a horse. The horse bucked. My brother and I laughed again. The more we laughed, the harder the rider slapped, and the horse bucked. The rider dismounted, "I'm Gilbert and he's Robert."

"Hi. I'm Fernando, he's Armando."

"You guys want to play with us?" Robert asked. He had a small chip in one of his front teeth.

"Yeah," we both said.

"Let's teeter-totter," Gilbert yelled. The twins raced across the playground with us, trying to keep up. Gilbert got on one end of the teeter-totter, I got on the other. Our brothers took the one next to us. Gilbert pushed hard against the ground, and I held on to the handgrip. He outweighed me and caused me to lift off my seat when he bottomed out. Robert did the same with Armando. This was a lot of fun. The bell rang and the playground silenced.

Gilbert got off the teeter-totter and came over to me and whispered, "Let's play at lunchtime."

"Okay," I said out loud and realized that I broke the silence rule. I sneaked a peek to see if Sister heard me. The boys ran back to their second-grade class. I didn't want to go back to my room but knew I had to. Dutifully, I walked back in silence, sat at my desk and looked out the windows to the playground. St. Jude was going to be fun after all. Maybe, more fun than kindergarten.

Sister Andrea began our second lesson. She stood, took a long stick with a rubber tip, and pointed to the first letter that was written on green cards in bold white letters over the chalkboard. "Children, repeat after me, A."

"A," we said.

She pointed to the next letter, "B."

"C."

I was getting antsy. Anxious to play with our new friends, I looked out again to the playground, wondering how long before recess.

When we got to M, I looked out the window once more. Sister Andrea stopped her lesson.

Sister jerked me from my daydreaming. "Fernando Garcia, stop looking out and pay attention."

"Okay," I said.

"You will address me as Sister Andrea." She stared down her nose at me.

Scared and confused, I answered, "Okay."

She pushed up her glasses and looked at me. "I just told you to address me by my name," she said raising her voice. I froze, not knowing what I was supposed to do. She continued staring for a moment, then went on with her lesson.

After the alphabet, Sister wrote the numbers one through twenty on the blackboard, calling out each number as she wrote it. When she finished writing them, she used her stick to lead us in reading them. I looked to my brother. He saw me and began saying his numbers with enthusiasm, bobbing his head up and down with each number and exaggerating his lips with the pronunciations. We had lost our baby teeth, and his front teeth were halfway in. I laughed. Sister Andrea didn't see him but saw me not paying attention and laughing.

"Fernando Garcia," she said again, "you must pay attention." Her tone was cold and direct. "How will you ever learn if you are so easily distracted?" Sister spoke louder this time. I bolted upright and looked to the front. I didn't know what *distracted* was.

Just before the lunch bell rang, Sister said, "Soon a classroom monitor will come in and sit with you while I go to the convent. You are to mind her as you would mind me. When you finish eating, put your trash in the trash can outside the door on your way to the playground."

When the bell rang, Sister walked to my desk and announced we could pick up our lunches at the back of the classroom behind the divider where our lunches sat on a shelf. As I started to get up, she put a hand on my shoulder, keeping me in my seat. My brother and the rest of the kids walked to the back. She looked down at me.

"Fernando, you will stay in your seat after you eat lunch. Do not go to the playground. I want to talk to you when I come back from the convent."

I managed to mutter, "Okay." Her look told me something was wrong.

A big girl came in with her lunch, just as Sister had said. The girl sat at the teacher's desk. Two big boys walked into our classroom carrying a wooden crate filled with small cartons of cold milk like we had in kindergarten. We lined up with our nickels to buy milk and went back to our desks. I ate my lunch slowly, trying to understand what I had done and what Sister wanted to talk to me about. I wanted to tell my brother but was too afraid to break the silence rule. The recess bell rang, and my classmates and brother left.

I sat with my empty milk carton, waxed paper wadded up, and lunch bag on my desk. The big girl looked at me and said, "It's time for recess. You can go out now."

"I can't. Sister told me to stay here," I said, trying not to cry. She shrugged and left.

I was abandoned and uncertain of what was going to happen when Sister got back. I looked to the blackboard with the numbers written in big letters. I could hear the loud chatter of a playground full of kids. I looked over at the clock over the windows. Robert and Gilbert appeared at the windows and cupped their hands over their eyes, and peered in. Robert made faces. Gilbert jumped up and down and pulled his ears out. I forgot about my dire circumstance and laughed.

Someone came in the back door, and I turned. It was my brother. When I turned back to the windows, the twins were gone. "Why didn't you come out to recess? Robert and Gilbert want to know where you are."

"I can't because Sister told me to stay in here because she wants to talk to me, and I think I might be in trouble." I started crying. My brother looked at me, then started crying, too. The tall black figure of Sister Andrea came through the door. She walked over. Her stern face seemed to soften. I made myself stop crying, afraid it would make her even madder. I wiped tears. My brother stood statue-still.

"Fernando, I need for you to pay attention in class." I nodded, looking down at my hands. "And when you address me, you need to say 'Sister' or 'Sister Andrea.' Do you understand?"

"Okay—I mean, yes, Sister."

"That's better. You may go outside and play." She walked to her desk and sat. I gathered my trash. My brother and I walked quietly to the back of the room and out the door.

Robert and Gilbert were outside. "How come you had to stay in?" Gilbert asked.

"Sister wants me to call her Sister Andrea."

Gilbert thought for a second, "Why don't you call her Sister Meanie Beanie? That's what we call her."

I laughed. "Come on, let's go," Robert yelled. The twins took off and we chased after. We ran back to the teeter-totters. Before we mounted, Robert looked at Gilbert.

"Which one do you want for a best friend?" Gilbert pointed at me and I agreed. Robert chose my brother and my brother Robert. The four of us were inseparable for the two years we attended St. Jude.

From that day on, I was careful not to look out to the playground, and to address Sister Andrea correctly.

After school, my brother and I made our way to the corner as our sisters had instructed. Robert and Gilbert came out of their classroom. "Do you guys want to play?" Gilbert said.

"We can't. We're supposed to meet our sisters and go home."

"Okay. See you tomorrow." The twins ran to the bicycle rack, mounted two old bikes, and raced out of the playground.

We got to the corner where our three sisters and cousin were waiting for us. Ana took my hand and Martha took my brother's as we crossed the street. We talked excitedly about our new friends on the walk home. I didn't mention to my sisters the trouble I had gotten into with Sister Andrea. They might have told Ma.

"Oh, *cuatitos*, that's so nice," Ana said.

Carolyn raised her eyebrows, "And they're twins, too?"

"Yeah. They're in the second grade and they're fun." Ana looked at Carolyn. "They must be Lillian Maestas's brothers. Isn't Vangie in your class, Martha?"

"Yes, she is. And then there is Marion Maestas, too. She's in the fourth grade."

"How many kids do they have?" Carolyn asked.

"Vangie says they have another little brother and sister at home," Martha said.

"Hey, that makes seven, like our family," Carolyn said.

When we got home my brother and I ran in, anxious to tell Ma, about our new friends.

Ma was delighted. "*Y como se llaman?*"

"Robert and Gilbert,"

"*Ah sí,*" she said, smiling. "*Roberto y Gilberto.*"

Afterward, despite Sister Meanie Beanie, we looked forward to going to St. Jude. It seemed the whole school liked seeing the four twins' pal around.

41

4.

1st Grade – Taking Flight
Armando

Trust me, I know what I'm doing.
Sledge Hammer

"**P**RAY EVERY NIGHT before you go to sleep," Sister Andrea said. "God loves children and you can show your love for Him by praying to Him. It's also a good time to petition God for help." I didn't know what *petition* meant. It was another one of those strange words that Sister used. I figured that it meant something like asking for something.

I thought about what Sister said when I lay on my mat that night. God, I was told, was all-knowing and all-powerful and I had a special petition for Him. Fernando and I had seen neighborhood boys riding bikes up and down Acacia Street since we moved in over the summer. Sometimes they rode alone, sometimes in groups. I was envious of them when I walked to the rec center or the corner market in our neighborhood and saw their bike parked outside. I could tell which boys were in there from their bikes.

It was mid-December, just before Christmas vacation. Sister Andrea taught us Christmas carols. Besides the ones about Jesus, we learned *Rudolph the Red Nose Reindeer* and *Santa Clause is Coming to Town*.

Later when I was playing at recess, I heard a boy tell a kid that there wasn't a Santa Clause. "Yes there is," the kid said.

"Is not. Your parents buy toys and then tell you they're him."
Then the kid said, "Yes there is," and walked off.

But the boy who said there was no Santa was so sure of himself that it shook my faith in the kindly fat man dressed in red. Could It be true? Pa and my big sisters had always told me that Santa comes late on Christmas Eve and leaves presents.

"Be good, because Santa Clause is coming and he only brings toys to good kids," I'd always heard. But come to think of it, a lot of big people smiled when they said it.

The day finally came when the school bell rang, marking the beginning of Christmas vacation. Fernando and I met our sisters outside the school.

"How was your day?" Carolyn asked.

I ignored her question. I needed an answer. "Is there a Santa Clause?" she took my hand; Ana took my brother's. We stepped off the sidewalk and to the street, with Martha and Ana Berta following.

"Of course, there's a Santa Clause, *cuatito*, why?" Carolyn said when we reached the other side.

"A boy at recess said there's no Santa Clause."

"Well, don't listen to him," Ana said.

If my big sisters said there was a Santa Clause, then there was a Santa Clause.

I lay on my mat that night, the house was dark and quiet. Next to me, Fernando breathed in a slow rhythm. Tony on the couch snored softly. I made my petition in silence. *Dear God, I really, really want a bike for Christmas.*

It felt as if Christmas morning would never get here, but it did, and standing next to the tree was a beautiful, gleaming red bicycle. So, like always, my sisters were right. That stupid boy didn't know what he was talking about. Fernando and I spent Christmas day taking turns riding up and down the sidewalk. The training wheels kept us from falling over.

One Saturday morning in early spring Tony took us to the sidewalk and said, "Time to take the training wheels off." *I wasn't convinced.* I looked at him with nervous eyes, hoping that he'd change his mind. But the look of determination said, *I'm not having it.* He used dad's wrench to remove the bracket that held the small wheels in place. Then straddled the bike and placed the rear tire between his legs. My bike was all but my best friend, always welcoming me, but today it would be the source of severe pain when I would crash. Tony rolled up my pant leg just above my ankle.

"Why did you do that?"

"So your cuff doesn't get caught up in the bike chain while you peddle." So that's why the boys do that. Our big brother was smart. Fernando standing next to us, rolled his pant leg up too.

Tony helped me onto the seat.

"What if I fall?"

"You won't." He pushed on the seat, and got me started.

"But what if I do?"

"Darn it, Armando, you won't, I'll be right here. Now pump," he said as he jogged. Fernando ran behind us. For the first time, our bike was a two-wheeler, just like the big boys in the neighborhood. The front tire twitched spasmodically as I tried to control it.

"Relax, *hermanito*, I'm right here, Tony panted. I heard his tennis shoes hitting the sidewalk as we sped up.

"You're holding the handlebars too tight," pant, pant, "just relax." The front tire stopped swiveling as we gained speed.

"Good, good," the ride became smooth. A wonderous feeling of control came over me.

"Keep pumping, you're doing great." Tony's feet hit the ground faster, his pants came in quick deep gulps. Cool morning air felt good against my face. My fear and nervousness turned to a great sense of accomplishment and confidence and then into sheer joy. I pumped faster and faster. Air whizzed past my cheeks and ears as I pumped as hard and fast as my six-year-old legs could.

"I feel like I'm flying." I yelled over my shoulder. But Tony didn't answer. "This is fun," I shouted louder. No answer. I looked back, Tony and Fernando were halfway down the block. Tony with hands on knees was stooped over breathing hard and looking laughing at me.

I'm riding alone! The front tire jerked but I took control. And even though I had stopped pumping its peddles, my two-wheeler glided down Acacia Street straight and true. If my bike had wings we would have surely flown.

5.

1st Grade – The Maestas House
Fernando

*The secret to success in business is having
good ideas and the resolve to implement them.*

TOWARD THE END of first-grade year, Robert and Gilbert
invited Armando and me to their home.

"Our mom wants to meet you and your mom," Robert said.
"Come over Saturday and we can play."

"Okay." I said with a broad grin. Until now we had merely
walked to Mikey and Genie's Gastelum's house next door to
play, or to Ronald Washington's, two doors down. This was a
formal invitation. Ma agreed to drive us over. She had said she
was curious about the Maestas after hearing about the twins
from us.

"Can we go now, Ma?" I asked for the third time. My
brother and I had got up early and wolfed down our *Breakfast
of Champions* – Wheaties. Ma made sure we had bathed the
night before and were well-groomed in the morning.

"*Si, si ya vamanos,* Ma said exasperated after applying
some make-up and brushing her hair. I noticed she put on
her nice dress and shoes. We ran to our 1948 powder-blue station wagon with the squeaky side door and hopped in. It was

a typical morning in early June. The temperature was in the mid-70's and the sky overcast.

Ma drove down Acacia Street, turned onto Boston Avenue, up the hill past St. Jude's and onto National Avenue. She found the Maestas home thee blocks down National.

"Look, Ma, they have a two-story house," Armando said. The craftsman style home looked like the one Dorothy and Toto lived in. It had beige wood paneling and steep triangular roof lines. The trim boards along the edge of the roof were dark green. Ma drove onto their large lot and parked on the concrete driveway at the back door. The property was an island in an otherwise developed neighborhood and the only two-story house.

The screen door flew open. Gilbert ran out and yelled, "the *cuatitos* are here." Robert and a smaller boy who looked like their shrunken triplet followed. A dark-haired woman, cradling a toddler, stepped out. She had the same nose, eyes and mouth as the twins. Lilian, our sister's classmate and the oldest of the Maestas children, also came out, likely wanting to see her mother's reaction to meeting Armando and me.

Mrs. Maestas was overweight, like Ma but was a couple inches shorter and appeared to be a few years younger. She had short black hair and wore a dress with a high neckline and a hem below the knees. She had a big easy smile and a small chip in her front tooth like Robert had. She walked to the car.

"*Hola, senora*," ma said as she got out of the car. Armando and I jumped out and stood next to the twins.

"*Benos dias, Senora Garcia.*"

"*Por favor, llamame Carolina.*" (Please call me Carolina.)

"*Y mi nombre es Maria.*" (And my name is Maria.) "I have wanted to meet your boys since I heard about them from my boys. Let me guess who's who." She pointed at me, "this is Armando."

"No Mrs. Maestas, I'm Fernando."

She laughed, "let me guess again," she pointed to my brother, "this is Armando," and laughed again. The shrunken triplet looked back and forth at my brother and me.

"Carolina, this is Patricia." She turned the child in her arms toward Ma. Patricia buried her face in her mother's neck. Mrs. Maestas looked to her side, "this is Ricky, and this is my oldest, Lillian." Ma seemed as delighted as Mrs. Maestas. I was antsy to play.

I introduced the twins to Ma and was tired of the small talk.

"Carolina, please come in," Mrs. said as she gestured to the house. Ma followed her in. it was unusual for our shy mother to accept an invitation with such ease.

"Come on, let's go," I said. The four of us raced to a giant fig tree in the yard. Armando and I got to the tree first. I jumped and wrapped my arms around a branch, curled a leg up and over, and began to climb. I heard leaves rustle next to me and saw Gilbert effortlessly pass me. Two mockingbirds eating fruit on the branches squawked and took flight. I stopped climbing and sat on a wide limb.

"What took you so long?" Robert asked with his chipped tooth smile as he settled in. Gilbert sat on a branch opposite his brother. The four of us balanced ourselves on the limbs, talked, and ate sweet black figs.

"You guys sure have a big yard," I said. Besides the fig, there were two full-grown apricot trees dotted yellow-gold with countless ripe apricots. Tall, wild oats covered three-quarters of the yard. A wooden tool shed with a gabled roof sat next to the garage. By the shed lay a pile of used lumber. A well-worn path cut diagonally from the house porch to the city sidewalk. The sidewalk led to the corner grocery store, a taco stand and a malt shop.

A few minutes later, we saw Ma walk out the back door with Mrs. Maestas. They were still talking, Ricky stood by his mother. We yelled good-bye to Ma, she waved. *"Portesen bien,"* (behave) she warned.

"We will Ma," Armando yelled back. The black skin from a fig covered most of one of his front teeth. Ma smiled and drove away. After we couldn't eat any more figs, we climbed down and walked to their wooden front porch. Gilbert and I sat on the steps, Robert and my brother shared the double wide bench against the house wall. We talked.

Our families had a lot in common, we were both single-income households and were Mexican-American Catholics. The twins had four sisters and one brother. Like my family they were loud and laughed easily.

While we talked two of the twin's sisters, Vangie and Marion walked the path from the far corner of the yard towards the house eating candy bars. They greeted when they got to the porch.

"Hi *cuatitos*, we heard you were coming today, Vangie said.

"Hi Vangie, hi Marion," I said. My heart fluttered. Both girls smiled broadly, showing perfectly aligned white teeth. Vangie had deep black eyes, an olive complexion and wore her jet-black hair in a bob. Marion was light skinned, light brown eyes, thick light-brown shoulder length hair with the ends curled in toward her milky-white neck. Vangie wore jeans, a dark blue t-shirt and black and white Converse tennis shoes. Marion wore a white blouse with lace at the neckline and at the end of her short sleeves. She had pink peddle-pushers on with low-cut white tennis shoes. In my eyes either of the girls could have been on the cover of teen magazines our sister Martha read.

'How's Martha," Vangie asked.

"Good, she was doing her homework so she can watch *American Bandstand* this afternoon."

"Marion and I are going to watch it too. Tell Martha to come with you next time and we can watch it together."

"Okay, I will." My mind raced as I tried to come up with something to keep the dialog going. "Where'd you get the candy?" my brother asked, horning in on my conversation.

"At the store, silly, where else?" The girls looked at each other giggled, and walked onto the porch and through the front door. My eyes followed them.

"I wish we had money to buy some candy," I lamented.

Robert put his hand to his chin, then his face lit up. "Let's make some money."

"How?" I asked.

"We'll sell apricots."

"Sell apricots?"

Robert became animated, "We'll put 'um in bags and load them on Ricky's wagon and sell them to our neighbors."

"Armando and I'll get the wagon, Gilbert you and Fernando get some bags from Ma and meet us under the trees."

We hustled into action.

Robert took my twin to the garage to fish out the wagon. I followed Gilbert through the back door, past the stark laundry room and to the kitchen. Unlike our home, there was no picture of Our Lady of Guadalupe on the wall or statues of saints. The flower-print linoleum floor in front of the sink and refrigerator was worn thin.

"Ma, we're getting some lunch bags," Gilbert yelled.

"What for?" Mrs. Maestas yelled back from somewhere in the house.

"We're going to sell apricots."

"You're selling apricots?"

"Yeah Ma, we want to make some money."

"You know where the bags are," she said with a chuckle, "don't take too many."

Gilbert grabbed out a small bunch of bags from a cabinet. We met our brothers under the bigger of the two trees. Gilbert climbed the rough trunk and to the higher branches with the ease of a chimpanzee. "Get ready," he yelled. He grabbed a limb in each hand and shook with all his might. It rained fruit. They bounced off my head and shoulders and fell to the ground. I wiped the ones with white bird poop on my t-shirt and jeans before putting them in my bag. I ate some of the ones that had burst. They tasted better than the ones Ma brought home from the store. *With apricots like these we should make a lot of money.*

A tall skinny lady in a plain long blue skirt, dark apron and black scarf covering her hair ambled out of the house. She walked next to me and began to put fruit in the pockets of her apron. A few strands of stringy gray hair fell from the scarf and landed on her thin neck. She looked at me with her black beady eyes, the corners of her thin lips edged up in a faint smile. She didn't say a word. When she filled her pockets, she wandered back to the house.

"Who was that?" I asked Robert.

"Grandma,"

"She lives with you?"

"Yeah, her bedroom is upstairs by ours."

"How come she didn't say anything?"

"Grandma doesn't talk to people. She stays in her room when someone comes over."

"Does she talk to you guys?"

"Not very much."

Gilbert climbed down and helped bag the fruit. In minutes we had the wagon filled with bulging bags, initiating the first of many business enterprises with the twins. We discussed how much we should ask per bag.

"How about twenty-five cents?" I asked.

"That sounds like a lot, how about twenty cents?" Robert suggested, we all agreed.

We pulled the wagon to the next-door neighbor's house. The lawn was green and mowed. The bushes were trimmed and the porch had a fresh coat of white paint. Gilbert knocked. A slim pretty, middle-aged white woman neatly dressed came to the door. Her face lit up.

"Ah, the twins. How are you boys?"

Before Gilbert could answer she asked. "And who is this with you?" Again she didn't let Gilbert reply. "Are you twins too?"

"Yes, ma'am," I said. I was flattered and self-conscience that this pretty woman would talk to me.

"How wonderful, what are your names?"

"I'm Fernando and this is Armando."

"I'm Robert's best friend," my brother said with a big smile. A piece of fig skin was still stuck to his tooth. "And he's Gilbert's best friend." *There he goes again.*

She stifled a giggle. "I'll bet the four of you have a lot of fun." She eyed the wagon.

"What do you boys have there?"

"Apricots," my twin said.

"We're selling them, Mrs. Stidman," Gilbert said. He reached into a bag and held out an apricot. "Wanna try one?"

"They look good and ripe." She held it but didn't bite into it. "How much are you asking?"

"Fifteen cents a bag."

She looked to the wagon, "I'll buy two bags." I handed them over.

"I'll be right back boys," she stepped away. I shifted my feet side to side. When she returned, she smiled and handed Gilbert a quarter and a nickel.

Hod dog, our first customer. Gilbert pocketed the money. "Thanks, Mrs. Stidman."

"Good luck with your sales boys?"

Robert turned the wagon, and we stepped away.

"I thought we said twenty cents a bag?" Armando said when we reached the street.

"I know but I didn't want to scare her off, I'll say twenty-five next time.

We hit three more houses along National with two rejections and one sale for the full twenty-five cents. We got to the corner house. it had a weed-infested lawn.

"This is Spooky's house," Gilbert said.

"Is he a friend of yours?"

"Kinda, he hangs around with us sometimes. He goes to public school."

"Will he be home? Should we see if he wants to play when we get done?"

"Nah, he usually hangs around with Butch and Fighter on Saturdays."

"Fighter?"

"He got into a fight once, so that's what we call him." The porch was strewn with bicycle parts, empty beer cans, and a porch swing with one end lying on the floor. We walked to the back of the house and knocked on the screen door.

A woman's voice yelled, "Who is it?"

"It's Robert and Gilbert, Mrs. Sandoval."

"Who?"

"It's Robert and Gilbert," Robert yelled.

"What do you want?"

"We're selling apricots."

"You're what?"

"We're selling apricots."

A short chubby lady wearing a frayed apron opened the door. Her unkept black hair was pulled back and held in place with a red rubber band.

"I couldn't hear you. What do you want?"

"Do want to buy some apricots?"

She eyed the wagon, turned and yelled into the house. "Hey Nacho, wanna buy some apricots?"

A man's voice hollered out, "What?"

53

"WANNA BUY SOME APRICOTS?"

"APRICOTS?"

"YEAH, THE MAESTAS BOYS ARE SELLING APRICOTS."

"WHO?"

"ROBERT AND GILBERT, damn it."

"TELL'EM TO COME IN."

The hinges complained as she pushed open the screen door. Robert grabbed a bag, and we followed her inside and to the kitchen with stacks of dirty dishes on the counters. She led us to the living room.

A fat man wearing a white tank-top undershirt with a hole in the belly and pajama bottoms sat in a beat-up recliner. A partially eaten bag of potato chips sat on his lap. A chubby, barefoot kid, Ricky's age, sat on the old couch. The kid had a butch haircut, tattered cutoff jeans and a t-shirt that rode up his stomach showing off his bellybutton. They were watching *The Attack of the Fifty-foot Woman*, on TV.

"You boys selling apricots?" he didn't wait for an answer, "How much?"

"Twenty-five cents a bag," Gilbert said.

"A little steep, no?" He reached for the bag, "Let me try one."

The kid walked over and stood next to the fat man. Robert handed one over, the kid grabbed one out of the bag and stuffed it into his mouth. He grinned. He spit the pit onto the floor.

"Pick that up, *mijo*, and put it in the trash."

The man popped one into his mouth. "Well, it's pretty good." Orange-colored saliva seeped from the corner of his mouth. "How much?" he wiped his mouth with his tank-top.

Couldn't he remember what Gilbert just said?

"Twenty-five cents a bag."

The man spit the seed into his hand. "Let me try another one." Robert handed another over. The fat kid snatched two more and wolfed them down with a dumb grin on his face.

"No boys, I don't think I'll buy any today." He turned back to the TV, not bothering to say good-bye. We walked out of the smelly house and to the sidewalk.

"That fat guy just wanted some free fruit," Gilbert said.

Robert shook his head. "And that stupid fat kid would've eaten a whole bag if we didn't get outta there.

We soldiered on. Gilbert got pretty good at sizing up customers and adjusting the prices. We sold out by mid-afternoon. We earned two dollars and seventy-five cents, which was more money than my brother and I had ever had.

"What do you want to do with the money?" I asked.

"Are you guys hungry?" Gilbert asked.

"Yeah," we hadn't eaten since the fig tree.

"Let's go to the taco shop." He said it so casually I wasn't sure how to respond. Armando and I had never bought restaurant food before.

The twins led us two blocks up National to Reyes Ricos Tacos. A short, heavy-set Mexican woman in a neat, white apron with red fringes greeted us.

"*Hola, muchachos.*"

"Hi, Mrs. Reyes," Gilbert responded. Her black-and-white hair was woven into a single tight braid.

The soles of my tennis shoes squeaked on the floor. A handful of flies appeared to be engaged in an aerial dogfight circled in front of us. I resisted the urge to swat them. Oily rivulets ran down the back wall.

Mrs. Reyes stood behind a small wooden counter. The cracked skin on her calloused hands spoke of years of hard labor.

"How are *ju*?"

"Fine Mrs. Reyes, can we get two orders of five rolled tacos?"

"*Si, si mijito, jus uno minute.*" She turned and yelled to the back of the shop. "*Oye, Viejo, hagame diez rolles.*"

55

"*De volada vieja*," (Right away old lady.) a man's voice called out from behind the partition. Pa's *ranchera* music played from the kitchen. I heard shuffling feet, the ting of metal on metal, and grease popping. I was starved, my mouth watered.

"Do you know the lady?" I whispered.

"Yeah, she and Mr. Reyes always sit in the back pew of the church on Sunday's. Negro, their oldest son, went to St. Jude school a long time ago."

The aroma of frying corn tortillas saturated the air of the bright, yellow-walled shop. The smell reminded me of Ma's kitchen.

"How *ees ju mama, mijo*?"

"She's fine."

"*Ah, que bueno.*"

The cook placed the two orders on the shoulder high pass through. Mrs. Reyes took them and set them on the counter. Steam fumes snaked between the chopped lettuce guacamole and the crumbly Mexican cheese. I grabbed the paper plates while Gilbert dug fifty-cents out of his pocket.

"Thanks, Mrs. Reyes."

"*Que Dios les bendiga.*"

We met our brothers outside. Robert handed Gilbert a grape Nehi soda. This was the tall bottle, not the twelve-ounce ones Armando and I were used to sharing. My share was half of the grape soda and two and a half tacos.

"Man, these are good," my twin said.

We talked about our windfall and strategized about the future. "Hey, maybe we can sell figs next time," Robert said with his mouth full of food. A missile of tortilla shot out of his mouth and landed on my arm. I flicked it off and reached to Gilbert for another sip. Little ice burgs of cheese floated in the soda.

"We could shine shoes for ten cents," my brother suggested.

"That's a really good idea," I said.

By the time we got to the front porch, the tacos were gone, and we continued to pass the sodas back and forth. Business plans were offered and argued. The afternoon light began to wane, and evening approached. I was as happy as I had ever been. Armando and I were disappointed when Ma pulled into the yard. Our first visit to the twin's house was great: our mothers enjoyed meeting their sons and they became instant friends. I ate all the figs and apricots I wanted, I got to talk to the twin's pretty sisters, we made money and were able to buy tacos at a taco shop. And to my amazement, we still had a dollar and a quarter left.

We said good-bye to the twins and to Mrs. Maestas and hopped in the car. I was exhausted from our eventful day. Ma pulled out of the yard and onto National Avenue, "How did it go?"

I began to tell her about the fig tree and bagging apricots, the scary grandma. Then my brother joined, soon we were talking over each other, relating all that we had seen and done.

"Can we come back next week?" I asked.

"*Vamos a ver*," Ma said with a smile.

6.

2nd Grade – First Holy Communion
Armando

"Do this in remembrance of me."
Jesus Christ

MY BROTHER FERNANDO AND I walked slowly toward the altar with our girl partners, looking like dwarf brides and grooms. We wore the pants that our parents had custom made for this most holy occasion. The Tijuana tailor took waist and length measurements and advised on style, material and color. The navy blue slacks had neat cuffs, pressed creases and baggy legs. My older brother and sisters were jealous; they never got such lavish items as tailored clothes. My father's truck-driving salary allowed for few extravagances. But we were mama's little *cuatitos,* and this important occasion warranted loosening the purse strings.

Our shirts were a brilliant Clorox white and ironed as only Ma knew how. The little girls wore lacy dresses, veils and patent leather shoes, all white. Everyone carried small prayer books draped with rosaries.

The long-awaited moment of receiving the body of Christ neared. The first few aisles on either side of the church were reserved for us new communicants. Our parents and families sat in pews behind our second grade class. The rest of the parish members sat in the pews behind them.

The first row of boys on the left side of the church stood and walked to the center aisle. Simultaneously, the girls seated on the right side stood and did the same, forming small couples. We had seen our parents and older brother and sisters receive this most blessed sacrament at every Sunday Mass we ever attended. At long last the time had come for our first Holy Communion.

I knelt at the marble Communion rail feeling light-headed, as we had fasted from solid food since the midnight before as the church dictated. The priests walked along the Communion rail with altar boys holding shiny brass patens under our chins to catch whatever minute scraps of the sacred Communion host that may fall. As the priest neared, I heard him saying the Latin prayer of the Eucharist over and over as he gave out Communion.

"Never ever touch the host," warned Sister Mary Carl, "that is only for the consecrated hands of the priest."

"If I washed my hands real, real good, could I touch the host?"

"No, you cannot. Your hands have not been consecrated."

We were told to stick out our tongues where the priest would place the host and swallow it immediately, then walk back to our pew, kneel and pray with our face buried in our hands. The nuns did a fine job preparing us for this profound moment in our religious lives.

They taught us the sacraments. Baptism cleansed our souls as infants. Adam and Eve disobeyed God and we, their children, inherited their "Original Sin." We were newborn babies and were already tainted with sin. No one's soul was allowed into heaven until this Original Sin was forgiven through Baptism and by the redeeming death of Jesus.

"But where did all of the people's souls go who died before Jesus was crucified and was able to redeem them?" I asked.

"Limbo," said Sister. "It's where the good unbaptized people go."

She told us that Limbo was kind of like heaven except you were denied to be in the presence of God.

"Yes," answered Sister Mary Carl, a little annoyed at my next question.

"Since a lot of people died between the time of Adams and Eve's sin and the redeeming death of Jesus, there was a huge crowd waiting to get in. But no, there wasn't a stampede of souls trampling heaven's gate keeper, St. Peter. The gates of heaven are not large but Christian souls are patient and good at waiting their turns," she said.

"Not everyone is allowed in, but since Christians are baptized, they are allowed entrance."

The baptismal ceremony was a ritual performed in the church by a priest. He anointed the baby's forehead with oil while reading the baptismal prayers and pouring holy water over the infant's head. Then he recited the prayer that washed away the child's Original Sin.

She told us in emergencies, though, as when a person who wasn't baptized was seriously injured in a car accident or wounded on the battlefield and knew that they would die soon, then anyone could baptize them by pouring holy water over their head and saying: "I baptize thee in the name of the Father and of the Son and of the Holy Ghost." Regular water would do if there was no holy water. I asked that if the mortally wounded had only seconds to live and the water was minutes away, could we spit on his head. My question was never answered.

I worried about my first grade neighbor Chris. He was a public school kid and probably not baptized. His family never went to church and I never saw them pray. I didn't want him missing out on being in heaven with me. I explained the seriousness of his unbaptized situation and offered to help. I sneaked an empty aspirin bottle into church and filled it with holy water from the font at the front door. I explained the sacrament to him in my dad's garage.

"Why do I need to be baptized?" he asked.

"Because you have an Original Sin on your soul."

"How did I get it?"

"Because Adam and Eve disobeyed God when they lived in the Garden of Eden and ate some forbidden fruit. So everyone born after that had the sin they committed on their soul, so we can't get into heaven unless you are baptized, like me."

"But if I had been in the Garden of Eden I wouldn't have eaten the fruit even if Eve was naked."

"But you weren't there, so you have the Original Sin."

It was so easy to understand. Why couldn't he comprehend that he was already a sinner even if he didn't do anything? At least he did understand that he didn't want to miss out on the bliss of heaven so he agreed to be baptized. Just like the missionaries that I heard about who baptized pagan babies in Africa, I performed the brief ceremony on Chris. Only seven years old and I had already saved my first soul.

After Baptism came the sacrament of Holy Eucharist or Holy Communion. This is when one receives the body of Jesus through the bread being changed into the body of Christ by a priest during Mass. On the night before He was crucified, at "The Last Supper," Jesus instructed His apostles on how to remember Him. He grabbed a loaf of bread, blessed it, broke it into pieces, then gave each a piece, saying that they should gather in His name and eat his body in the form of this consecrated bread. Then He took a cup of wine and blessed it and told them that they should drink his blood in the form of the consecrated wine. And the sacrament of the Holy Eucharist was born.

The church figured that since the Communion host was now the body of Christ, it must be considered holy. Since it was holy, then it should be treated with the utmost reverence. The Church instructed its followers to fast from food and drink from the midnight before receiving the host. I guess the church figured Jesus would not be happy to share your stomach with what you had for breakfast. We were allowed to drink only water during the fasting period.

I saw a skinny fifth grade girl faint one morning while kneeling in the pew. She had an aisle seat and fell; a splat was heard as her pale face hit the marble. A nun and one of the moms rushed to her. She was helped out of the church. I bet she was hungry.

Before receiving Communion we had to cleanse our souls from sin. They must be free of the splotches of sin, and white as a bottle of milk. We were taught about the sacrament of Penance, otherwise known as Confession; the forgiveness of sins.

A sin was breaking any of the Ten Commandments or any transgressions relating to them, so obeying God was extended to obeying the priests and nuns and parents. Thou shalt not bear false witness against thy neighbor, also meant not lying, especially to the priests, nuns, or parents. Most of the Ten Commandments were pretty straightforward and fairly easy to understand: thou shall not kill, thou shall not steal, honor thy father and thy mother, but I didn't understand what thou shalt not commit adultery or not coveting thy neighbor's wife was. I simply knew that it meant not doing or even thinking of anything nasty. Sister told us we were not to touch certain parts of our body too much, even when we bathed. If we didn't understand what she meant, then we should see her at recess time. I was curious to know more about it, but was too embarrassed to ask.

Sins of the flesh were among the worst a person could commit. Kids' sins included such staples as lying to or disobeying our parents or teachers and fighting with our siblings. Small sins were called venial sins, big ones were called mortal sins and punishable by being sent to the fires of hell forever. Kids rarely committed mortal sins, like murder. I didn't worry much about murdering, although I had a nagging desire to one day kill my three-year-old sister Carmen.

"No, Armando," Sister answered. "If you kill your little sister by accident God will not punish you, however, He knows your intentions. If you did it intentionally but tried to pretend it was an accident then God will know."

So if I killed my little sister and made it look like an accident then I'd probably be let go by the police and not get the electric chair, but God would know and punish me later. I could just see my little sister in heaven looking down at me in hell and getting the last laugh. But, if it really was an accident that looked suspicious, then I would get the chair but go to heaven. What if somehow she could be gotten rid of and it really was an accident? Then I wouldn't get it from anybody. I prayed for divine intervention.

Our first confession was Friday afternoon before the Sunday of our First Communion. We were marched from our second grade classroom to the church where Father Sheridan waited in his confessional to hear our sins. God was able to forgive your sins through your confession to His representative on earth, the ordained priest. I was very nervous. Surly he would recognize my voice and know that it was me who tried to look at one of my older sisters once when I was lying on her bed and she was changing her clothes. If I didn't tell him of this great sin then it wouldn't be forgiven, and I would receive Holy Communion with a terrible sin on my soul.

"You must tell ALL your sins to the priest, no matter what they are, so your soul will be pure enough for our Lord's presence," warned Sister.

We heard from an older kid at school once about a girl who didn't confess all her sins to the priest and when she took Communion the host burned her tongue. The image of steam bellowing from a screaming girl's mouth and nostrils, and the pain and humiliation for her was near equal to the fear I felt of confessing my grievous sin.

There were three doors in the side wall of the church. A small red signal light over the center door was lit, indicating that Father was in there. Sister lined up three children on either side of Father's confessional and sat the rest of us in pews to think about our sins and have our list ready while we waited our turns. She opened a door, pushing the first little sinner into the dark box, then did the same on the other side.

In a few minutes, Peggy came out, walked to the front of the church, knelt and said her penance prayers. Jackie took Peggy's place in the confessional. Sister signaled the next little lamb to wait its turn. The door on the other side of father's confessional opened and Phillip stepped out to join Peggy in the pew and the holy car wash began. One by one little splotched souls entered the confessional and milk-white ones exited. Their sins could not have been as grave as mine. Maybe an earthquake would happen before it was my turn, or Father would have a heart attack.

When my turn came I opened the door, entered the dark cubicle, and closed it behind me. There was a small kneeling pad and a little window like a screened panel on the wall in front of the kneeler. I knelt on the pad and folded my sweaty little hands in the prayer position. I heard mumbling; maybe that kid's sins were real, real bad and mine by comparison would not seem so big. Maybe he murdered someone. There was a brief moment of silence then the little door slid open. I could see through the screen the silhouette of the Irish priest's face. My nervousness erased months of preparation and practice for this moment. I knelt silently. Father waited a few seconds. He cleared his throat, and finally asked. "Are you here to confess?"

"Um yes, Father."

"You may start."

"Uh, I forgot how."

The kindly priest said, "Bless me, Father . . . "

"Oh yeah. Bless me, Father, for I have sinned. This is my first confession. Since I was born I've fought with my brothers and sisters a whole bunch of times." His fist went to his mouth as he coughed to hide a chuckle.

"And I disobeyed my parents a lot of times too; I wish I could tell you how many times, but, um, maybe about a thousand?" Another chuckling cough.

Quick, I'd better make some sins up so I won't have to tell him the whopper.

"And—and, Father, I threw some rocks at my neighbor's cat, but my mom told me to because it kept pooping in our garden. And once after we saw the Three Stooges, I poked my little sister in the eyes. And—and—um . . ." I was in a tug-of-war: too humiliated to tell this holy man of my lecherous sin, but if I didn't then Jesus would throw a barbeque in my mouth. There was no escaping. I felt dizzy and wanted to cry.

"And—and, Father," my voice trembled. "I committed a sin of the flesh." Tears blurred my vision.

He straightened, and drew closer to me and whispered. "Yes, son. Tell me about it."

"Well, Father, I—I tried to look at my older sister when she was changing clothes, once."

My voice broke with emotion.

"Hmm. Did you see anything?"

"No, Father. She knew I was in bed and kept looking at me. I couldn't raise the covers enough to get a real good look. I saw something that looked like my uncle Sam's bald head."

His hands came to his face and his head bobbed up and down as he went into a coughing fit. I felt terrible for making Father Sheridan feel so bad.

I was relieved when Father, after his coughing, assured me that I hadn't committed the worst of sins but that it was somewhere in a shady area between venial and mortal. He said that God was proud of me for having the courage to confess it. I felt an immediate sense of relief. He made me promise to never try that again. It was an invasion of privacy.

"Would you be embarrassed if people saw you undress?"

"Yes, Father. I will never ever do it again."

"Very good, my son. For your penance say three Hail Marys and three Our Fathers and now say the Act of Contrition."

"O my God, I am heartily sorry for having offended Thee and I detest all my sins because of Thy just punishments . . ."

As I prayed the prayer of contrition Sister Mary Carl taught us, he recited the Latin prayers of forgiveness, ending them in English.

"I absolve thee in the name of the Father, the Son and the Holy Ghost."

He made the sign of the cross toward me.

"Now, go and sin no more. You're a good boy."

"Gee, thank you, Father."

When I walked out of the confessional toward the penance pews everyone was looking at me. My soul, after saying my penance, shined as brilliantly as the sunlight that shone through the stained-glass windows in the church. It was ready for Our Lord. What a feeling. I could be killed on the way home and I would go straight to heaven. I had the urge to skip all the way to our house.

"How was your confession?" I asked my brother.

"It was real hard to tell Father Sheridan that I got angry at Pa one time and I stuck my tongue out at him when his back was turned. But I knew that if I didn't then I might go to hell, so I told him. You know I think it would be better if we never committed any sins, then we wouldn't have to worry about confessing them or going to hell."

We agreed that was a good solution. We'd have to obey our parents, no fighting, no lying and keeping our hands to ourselves. I barely stayed clean over the weekend. I flicked a booger at my little sister, but I missed so it didn't count. Keeping my soul sinless was not as easy as I thought it was going to be.

I WALK SLOWLY DOWN THE AISLE with Jane in her white lacy dress and veil as my partner. Fernando and Sandy walk slowly just ahead of us. The church was overfilled with new communicants, proud parents, grandparents, brothers, sisters, whining babies, and the unlucky parishioners who forgot that this Sunday's nine o'clock Mass was the annual First Holy Communion Sunday service which meant the rite will last a half hour longer than normal. I am anxious to get Jesus inside of me so that I can go home and play, yet at the same time I worry that my soul may not have been pure enough to receive Our Lord.

Finally I get to the communion rail and kneel ready to receive Jesus. As the priest approached and it came my turn to receive the host, I did as I was taught by Sister Mary Carl: I closed my eyes, raised my head and opened my mouth and stuck out my tongue. Father repeated the Latin communion incantation over and over as he placed the pure white communion wafers on our tongues. I closed my mouth and tried to swallow it immediately, but couldn't. It was like cardboard and stuck to the roof of my mouth. I tried to dislodge it with my tongue, but the upward pressure only seemed to make it stick even more. I managed to lower it but as I tried to swallow it, it got stuck in my throat. I tried again and nearly choked. Now I had to hock to get the host back in my mouth with my lips closed so as not to accidentally discharge the bread onto the floor. Jesus was just not cooperating. I stood and began walking to my pew, still trying to swallow. He finally softened to a mush with saliva and slid down. I got back to my pew knelt and put my hands over my face. Not sure what to do I said a Hail Mary then waited for something to happen.

Jesus was in me but I didn't feel any different. No floating sensation, no visions. I felt a little dizzy but that was probably from not eating food since last night.

Toward the end of Mass I felt something on the roof of my mouth; I put a finger to it and drew out a small glob of a curious white paste. I stared at it then realized, IT'S JESUS! I shot my finger back in my mouth and swallowed his arm or leg or whatever body part it might be. Holy smokes! Was this a sin? Do I need to confess it? Will Father be so understanding this time? My mouth isn't heating up so maybe I'm okay.

Outside the church is a crowd of excited new communicants and proud families. Pa takes our picture against the wall of the church with our neatly combed hair, our prayer books, rosaries and new tailored pants.

Upon arriving home my brother and I quickly change into our playclothes. Ma makes sure we put our new clothes, prayer books and rosaries away properly. That afternoon Ma made a big ham dinner for our family and a few of my aunts and uncles.

I can't wait to return to my next Mass and join my family and the ranks of the communicant community. I look down on little first graders and kindergarteners who are too young to receive Holy Communion with us big kids.

The nuns encouraged us school children to receive Communion on the first Friday of each month as a special devotion to the Sacred Heart of Jesus, so we second graders join the third through eighth graders and receive Communion during Mass before school. As we have fasted from food since midnight, we are allowed to either bring our own breakfast or buy a cinnamon roll and a carton of milk from the school. After begging Ma, she allowed us the fifteen cents each for the roll and milk so we were able to eat them at our desks just like our older sisters and the rest of the big kids. Boy, in the name of the Father and the Son and the Holy Ghost, this is great!

7.

2nd Grade – The Heroes
Fernando

"Real heroes don't try to be heroes, they just are."
Fernando Garcia

MY BROTHER TONY was one of my first heroes. He was intelligent, highly motivated, and disciplined. He teemed with energy and was a hard worker with an iron will.

I was seven years old when he taught me and Armando how to start a fire in the big metal barrel in the backyard to burn dried yard waste and house trash. It wasn't unusual to see him surrounded by a cloud of dust when raking or knocking down weeds. He lured my brother and me into working with him by telling us stories, sagas he undoubtedly studied in high school English Literature. Stories like Odysseus, the hero of Greek mythology, and the Old English story of the champion Beowulf who killed the monster, Grendel.

Unconscious of the hot sun or the sweat on our brows, we worked alongside him in starry-eyed wonder as Tony spun the yarns. "Odysseus led his men around the Isle of the Sirens who lured sailors by singing so beautifully that they got too close to shore and drowned when their ships wrecked on rocks just below the surface . . . Odysseus and his men lifted a tree trunk that they had sharpened and rammed it into the eye of the Cyclops, barely escaping the boulders the Cyclops heaved at them . . ."

Tony taught us to shoot his pellet rifle. He set tin cans on a tree stump in the backyard, showed us how to load the pellet and pump air into the rifle's air chamber. The pump handle was hard to cock but I was determined to show him how strong I was.

"Never, ever, point this at a person." Tony warned.

"I won't," I said.

"Fernando, you go first. Lie down here next to me. Rest your elbows on the ground and put the butt of the gun to your shoulder and hold the barrel with your left hand. Now, squeeze the trigger. Don't pull it because the barrel will move, and you won't hit your target." I felt like a soldier going into battle.

With Tony's patience, I managed to hit one of the cans. "I did it," I yelled. "Can I shoot again?"

"Okay. But just one more time, then it's Armando's turn."

Tony also taught us to stand on his shoulders and how to do flips off his knees while he lay on the grass. "Run to me and don't stop, don't be afraid, you have to tell yourself you can do it. When you get to me, put your hands on my knees and jump, I'll put my hands on your shoulders and help you flip over." We had trouble the first couple of tries but in no time, we were flipping like seasoned acrobats and amazed that we could perform such a difficult trick with ease. He took us to the rec center, at Balboa School, and showed off our tumbling. Neighborhood kids clapped. I liked the attention, especially from the bigger kids.

Tony was short for his age but a giant in my eyes. No one in the neighborhood had a big brother as cool as ours. Our seventeen-year-old brother knew just about everything there was to know in the whole world.

The only man that stood larger than Tony was Pa.

"Come on *muchachos*, let's go for a ride," Pa announced the day before Thanksgiving. He grabbed a tuft of my hair and gave it a tug. Armando and I were always happy to go with Pa, especially since Ma wouldn't be in the car. We knew he would stop at a liquor store on the way back from wherever we went, buy himself a beer and candy bars for us.

We jumped into the backseat. Pa pulled a cigarette pack from his shirt pocket and lit up. He slid into the driver's seat and rolled his window down. I liked to stand close to Pa with my arms on top of the headrest and watch while he magically pulled levers and worked foot pedals to start and drive our car. Pa turned the car's radio to *Radio Ranchito*, which broadcast from Tijuana. He listened to Mexican *corridos* as we drove to the outskirts of town with us asking him endless questions.

"Where are we going?"

"You'll see in a little while."

"Did you like school when you were little?"

"I didn't like grammar school too much, but I liked high school a lot. I especially liked playing football."

"You got to play football?"

"Sure did. We won the mid-state championship the three years I played. Our little Lindsay High beat the big teams like Bakersfield, Fresno, and Tulare."

"Wow, Pa, I didn't know that."

After a long ride we came to a steep drop in the road. At the bottom of the depression, Pa slowed and turned left. Seemingly out of nowhere a dirt road appeared. Hardy dull-green native vegetation as tall as a man framed either side of the single lane. A tall cloud of brown dust trailed the car. Our ride with Pa was turning into another adventure.

We came to a weather-beaten wooden building. A big faded white sign with red lettering on the shake shingle roof announced *Johnson's Turkeys*. A bed of crushed rock lay in front of the old house. The gravel crunched under the tires as Pa pulled onto the parking area. I saw a handful of white turkeys penned in a wire enclosure as big as a city block. The loose dusty ground inside the pen was devoid of vegetation. A pungent odor filled the car.

"Hang on, boys. I'll be right back." Pa dropped the stub of his cigarette on the ground, stepped on it, slammed the door shut, and strode into the front door. Pa and a tall, skinny man in blue overalls and wide-brimmed straw hat walked out a minute later and to the turkey pen. The man handed Pa two white cords then unraveled a wire that kept the flimsy gate shut. Puffs of dusty powder floated around their shoes when they entered the enclosure.

The man threw some pellets onto the barren ground. Turkeys ran toward them and pecked. In a cat-like swipe the man snagged a bird by its neck just under its head and hugged the body to his chest with his free arm. He said something to Pa and Pa circled one of the cords several times around the turkey, pinning its wings to its body. Pa took the other cord and tied the ankles. They walked out of the pen with the man holding the bird upside down by its feet. Pa retied the wire gate.

They came to the rear of our station wagon. Pa pulled up the window and dropped the tailgate. The man laid the bird in the cargo area. My brother and I stood on the back seat and watched, fascinated by the show. Pa closed the back of the car.

The men headed back to the building. As they walked past, I saw deep creases that ran down the man's red face, the skin on the back of his neck looked like leather. Minutes later Pa came back to the car, the man stood on his porch and leaned against the post that supported the roof. I wondered if the post would give way and the porch collapse on him.

I was scared of the turkey and happy that Pa was back in the car.

"Y'all have yourselves a real nice Thanksgivin' now," the man said. His walnut-sized Adam's apple bounced. "You, too," Pa said. He lit another cigarette and started the car.

"Wow, Pa, what are we going to do with it?" I asked.

"You'll see when we get home," he said with a smile as he backed out and drove toward the paved road.

"Are we going to keep it?"

"Yes, we're going to keep it."

"I thought turkeys were fatter and brown like the ones in our books at school."

"Those are wild turkeys. They eat brown acorns and brown bugs. This one has been raised on white corn and white bread." Pa was a really smart man.

We pulled into a liquor store. Pa got a can of Bulldog Ale and us our treats. "We got work to do when we get home," Pa said when we got back in the car. I was disappointed we were going to have to work. Pa pulled a can opener from the glove box and made two holes in the top of the can and got back on the road.

"How come the man we got the turkey from talked funny?"

"He's probably from Oklahoma. That's how they talk over there."

"Where's Oklahoma?"

"Next to Texas." I knew about Texas. That's where The Lone Ranger and Tonto were from.

"I worked with Okies in the farm fields of Northern and Central California, that's what they call people from Oklahoma. A lot of those poor people lost their farms during the Great Depression and the Dust Bowl."

"What's the Dust Bowl?" I asked, chewing on my candy bar.

"About twenty years ago a big wind blew across Oklahoma, Kansas, and parts of Texas. The wind picked up the topsoil and blew it away in giant brown clouds. The farmers couldn't plant, so they didn't have any crops to sell, and the banks took their land. The farmers drove their families to California and worked with us in the fields."

"But why did the banks get the farms?" I asked.

"The banks gave them loans, and because they didn't have money, they had to give their farms to the banks." It sounded complicated. I dropped the subject.

Meanwhile, the turkey lodged an occasional complaint to Pa's deaf ears. I looked back, wondering if it could come over the rear seat and hurt me. It looked back at me with black, beady eyes. It opened and closed its big yellow beak. No one had tied its mouth shut. Pa glanced back at me through the rearview mirror. He must have noticed me turning my head around.

"Don't worry, mijo, he can't hurt you." Pa said confidently but I wasn't so sure. I wasn't as brave as Pa, no one was, not even the Lone Ranger.

We pulled in front of our white clapboard house. Armando and I jumped out and ran to the back of the car. Pa opened the rear end, grabbed the turkey's ankles, and slid it out. He carried it upside down like the Okie did. Pa walked toward the backyard as the turkey complained. We followed three steps behind. Pa stopped halfway through the side yard, looked over his shoulder at us then grabbed the turkey by its neck and let go of its ankles. He lifted the head to his face. "Settle down or I'll have to get rough." Pa gave it a couple of soft mocking slaps to the sides of its face as if the bird could understand his threat. We laughed. He continued to the backyard with the bird's head dangling an inch from the ground.

I was antsy to see what Pa would do next. I wondered if the turkey was going to be a pet. Ma insisted on not having any animals, but maybe Pa was going to get us one despite Ma's wishes. I started to think of training it and names we could give it. Maybe we could use one of the white cords as a leash and walk it up and down the neighborhood like Mrs. Gastelum did when she walked their little dog Panchito.

When we got to the backyard, Pa knelt on the grass and laid the bird down and held it with his knee, then untied the wings.

"Fernando, when I get up, take a wing. Armando, you take the other. Hold on tight." I was afraid but didn't want to disappoint Pa. I held the huge wing with all my might. Pa helped my brother with the other wing, Pa kept his hand around the bird's neck. The powerful bird struggled to get loose. "Hold tight for just a second, *muchachos*."

I looked to my brother, a grimace of determination on his face. Little did we know that we were in a life-and-death struggle. Pa pulled his jackknife from his jeans pocket and opened it. He grabbed the turkey's neck with one hand and its head with the other. He straddled its beak between two fingers. Pa put the blade to the turkey's neck and with a quick swipe sliced the head clean off. My idea about the turkey being a pet was settled in an instant.

Blood splattered my T-shirt. The bird rocketed into the air, flapping its wings, pumping blood like a fountain. We fell on our butts. Pa laughed.

I jumped to my feet, "Pa, Pa," I yelled, "he's going to get away."

Smiling, Pa showed me the head in his hand, "He won't get too far." A droplet of blood ran down his large fingers.

We watched the turkey soar until it stopped flapping and came down landing near the bamboo stand by the back fence. The headless bird sprinted around the yard, ran into the metal trash bin, ricocheted off and continued to run. It hit the house wall, and toppled over.

Pa sauntered over, my twin and I approached cautiously. We got close, but not too close. "Look," Armando pointed to the turkey's feet, its claws slowly opened and closed, the wings jerked in short, spasmodic bursts. Pa tossed the head under the orange tree, pulled his red handkerchief from his back pocket and wiped blood off his fingers and knife blade.

"He'll stop squirming in a minute." Pa picked it up by its feet, carried it to the tree stump, and laid it on the grass, leaving a thin, red trail as he walked. This was the most exciting thing I'd ever been a part of. The corpse finally stilled. I stood nervously, wondering if the turkey could suddenly come back to life. I thought about the Disney cartoon and the headless horseman.

"I'm going into the house for a minute. You boys keep an eye on him and don't let him get away," he chuckled. I hoped Pa was kidding. We stepped back, transfixed. The blood coming out of its neck had slowed to a trickle, its talons stopped clutching.

Pa walked out the back door, struggling with a large vat of warm water, and set it on the ground next to the turkey. "We'll dunk it in the water. It'll make taking the feathers off easier."

"Ma's gonna cook it?"

"Yes, your mother is going to cook it."

"Are we going to eat it?"

"Of course we're going to eat it. Tomorrow is Thanksgiving, remember?" With all the excitement I had forgotten about the holiday.

"So we get to pull the feathers off?" Armando asked, his voice animated.

"Yes, in a couple of minutes." Pa picked up the bird by its feet, put it in the vat and pushed the turkey into the water.

"Armando, come here. I want you to hold it under." My brother stepped over and held it down in the rosy-red water. Pa went back into the house and came out with a meat cleaver and a white rag. "Armando, step back." Pa handed my brother the rag. "Do a good job wiping your hands."

My brother looked over at the blood stain on my T-shirt. "Pa, can I wipe my hands on my shirt?"

"No."

Pa pulled the bird out of the vat and set it on the tree stump. Rivulets of water sheeted off the feathers and soaked into the dry wood of the stump. Pa lifted the vat, carried it to a fruit tree and poured it into the basin. A tidal wave of pink water rushed toward the trunk.

"What are we going to do now?" I asked.

"We have to take the feet off."

"How, Pa?"

Pa set the legs in the center of the stump, picked up the cleaver and raised it, "Like this," the cleaver flashed in the sunlight and landed on the stump with a thud. This was getting more and more exciting. Pa picked up the yellow feet and turned the boney claws toward us and growled then threw them under the fruit tree next to the head.

"Save those and we can surprise your sisters with an early Christmas present." My brother and I laughed.

"Let's pull the feathers off, *muchachos*." I grabbed a handful and tugged.

"Careful, *mijo*, hold the turkey down with your other hand so when you pull you don't tear the skin." He showed us it was easier to pull off just a few at a time. The feathers came off with little effort, slowly the white skin underneath was exposed. Pa went back into the house and came out with a can of beer and joined in the feather pulling.

"So you played football at your high school?" I asked tossing a handful of feathers into the pile.

"Yeah, I was a freshman at Lindsay High School and the coach saw me run the four-forty during PE and asked me to try out for the football team the following year. I was big for my age and strong. We won the mid-state championship the three years I played."

"Really, Pa?"

"Yeah really, on Friday afternoons the whole town would close up early so they could watch the games. One year we played at Tulare under their stadium lights. It was our first and only night game. We were so good, we almost scored a hundred points." We listened in awe.

"We had one of our players get killed during a game."

"What happened?"

"He was running downfield with the ball and two of the other team's players tackled him. One of the boys made a shoe-string tackle and the other kid grabbed him by his helmet and they snapped his neck. Six of us boys on the team carried his coffin during the funeral." Dad shook his head at the memory.

"Did you ever get hurt?" I asked.

"I sure did. Got three teeth knocked out on a tackle. I was rushed to the dentist. When I sat in his chair and he started working on me, I saw the light on the ceiling turned blue I was in so much pain."

Pa had finished his beer, raised the empty can, and shook it. I got the message and hopped to it, eager to please my father. "Atta boy, cowboy," he said as I handed him the can. He pulled his knife back out of his pocket and punctured two holes in the top, took a swig, and went back to plucking feathers and to his stories. Our father's stories were as good as our older brother's epic sagas.

My father never left the rough-and-tumble lifestyle of the migrant worker camps of his youth. He had an earthiness and zest for life that kept us rooted and kept us close to our cultural roots.

We not only had the greatest brother in the neighborhood, we had the best father in the whole world.

I hoped one day to be as great as they were.

8.

2nd Grade – The Marble
Armando

"Bodily orifices were given to little children by God to probe and explore. It is undoubtedly the reason He made them mysterious, dark, inviting."
Armando Garcia

OUR NEIGHBOR GENIE GASTELUM, Fernando, and I were sitting on the sidewalk on a search-and-destroy mission killing red ants. I had been stung on my bare feet earlier in the day. We snapped at the little red devils with cut rubber bands. Larry Flores, who lived three doors up, came over with his bag of marbles and held them up.

"Wanna play?"

"Yeah." We raced home and got our bags. The four of us met in Genie's backyard. I drew a circle in the dirt the size of a bicycle tire with a stick. We each put ten marbles in the circle and took turns trying to knock them out. If a marble was knocked out in one turn, the kid not only got to keep the marble, but had another try at knocking more out until he missed. Then, the next boy got his turn. We squatted and knelt or sat on our rear-ends to get the best angle possible for a shot. I had a good game. I wound up with five new marbles. I put them in my bag and walked to our house for a grape Kool-Aid victory drink. Larry accused me of cheating. Sore loser.

I got the urge to poo and walked to the bathroom and locked the door. I took a few squares of toilet paper and put them on top of the toilet seat and took my pants off. I put my feet on the paper squares. Martha had learned about germs in school. "Germs are teeny, tiny bugs that you can't even see and they can make you really sick. They're everywhere."

I was grossed out by the concept and figured there must be an extra lot of them on toilet seats. The thought of them lying in wait for me scared me enough to insulate myself wherever I went to the bathroom.

As I squatted, I wondered what might happen if I stuck one of my marbles up my rear end. Would it hurt? Would it feel good? Maybe it wouldn't be a good thing to do, but the idea intrigued me. There was only one way to find out. I finished going to the bathroom, flushed, and took a cat's eye marble out of the bag in my pocket. I lined it up as best as I could and pushed. There was a little resistance, but it slid in easier than I could have hoped for. I put my pants back on and waited for a sensation but didn't feel any different than before. I squatted and stood, squatted and stood, shook my behind. Still no difference. A little disappointed, it was time to get it back out.

I pulled my pants down. But wait. How was I going to take it out? I bent over and poked my finger up there. My finger was a lot harder to get up than the marble. Instead of getting it out, I only pushed it up farther.

Oh crap! What was I going to do?

"Hey, I have to use the bathroom. Hurry up," Martha said from behind the door.

"Be right out," I said in an easy, steady tone. In a panic, I tried putting my finger up again, hoping I could curl it around the marble. But I could only feel its smooth surface push up even farther. Darn, what should I do?

"Hey, what are you doing in there?"

81

"Almost done," *double darn*, "be right out," *better wait till later*. I grabbed some toilet paper, wiped my finger, flushed, pulled my jeans up and washed my hands. I walked out nonchalantly.

"About time," Martha murmured on her way in. "You're not the only one that has to use the bathroom, you know. What the heck were you doing in there?"

"I'm sorry. It was just hard to get it out this time."

"Boy, does it stink in here," she said as she lifted her hand to her nose.

I walked into my bedroom at a loss as to what I should do. Should I tell Ma? No, she'd only get mad. If I told any of my sisters, they would scold me for being such a tonto and probably tell Ma. My older brother might have been sympathetic, but he wasn't around. I looked for my twin and found him back on the sidewalk snapping his rubber band at ants.

"Hey, *cuatito* I need to talk to you for a minute."

"What about?"

"Come on, I need for us to go to the bedroom." He followed me to our room. When I explained my problem in hushed tones he started laughing.

"It's not funny."

"Sorry, how'd it get up there?"

"How do you think it got up there? I pushed it up with my finger." He laughed again.

"Stop it. I'm really scared."

"Why did you put it up there?"

"I just wanted to know how it would feel."

"So how does it feel?"

"Like nothing's up there." I told him the details of the experiment and my failed attempts at getting it out.

"Is it a jumbo?"

"No."

"A steely?"

"No, it was a cat's eye I won off of Larry today."

"He thought you cheated. Did you?"

"No."

"Too bad it wasn't a steely"

"Why?"

"Because then we could have used Tony's big magnet."

"Aw man, that would've been good." I told him that I hadn't thought about how I was going to get it out, that after I tried with my finger the marble only went up farther and it left a mess on my finger. He laughed again.

"It's not funny," I said again in a loud, hoarse whisper. I took a swing at him. He turned and my blow hit him on the back.

"I'm sorry, I'm sorry."

Maybe I should have kept this to myself.

We discussed options: use a Popsicle stick to get behind it and tease it out? Or a teaspoon like a scoop? He told me there was no way he was going to use any of his fingers. Frustrated, I decided to leave it for the time being. Maybe a better idea would come. I went about the rest of the day with the weight of the deep dark secret on my shoulders.

At dinner, Pa asked everyone how their day went. Martha said that her friend Monica's mom had taken them to the beach. Ana and Carolyn said they helped Ma with house chores and got their uniforms laundered. Armando said that we played marbles with our neighborhood friends and that I had won some cat's eyes. He looked down at his plate, hiding a smile. I looked down, dejected.

Fernando told me later that he was worried about my problem and was tempted to tell everyone at the table to see if someone could come up with an idea. But we had a code of silence that would not be broken, no matter the consequences. Besides, there's little doubt had it gotten to Ma, she would've gotten mad and scolded me. She would have said that she would die of embarrassment if word got out and what would the neighbors think? We had been through similar situations with her before. Saturday after dinner meant Armando and I would to take our weekly bath and be spotless for Mass the next morning.

We sat in the tub two-thirds full of warm water.

"Hey, look up there and see if you can see anything."

"Okay."

I stood, turned, bent over, and mooned him. "See anything?" "Nah, I just see your hole and it's closed."

I put my hands on my cheeks and pulled them apart. "See anything now?" I was desperate. This might be my last chance for a way out.

"No, it's still closed. Pull harder."

I pulled harder but no matter how hard I tried, it wasn't enough.

After dinner the family gathered around the TV for the weekly Saturday night serials. Ma, as usual, didn't join us but chose to spend her time on her sewing machine in my parents' bedroom. We were engrossed in *Have Gun Will Travel* with Paladin and his gun-for-hire adventures. It was good to be distracted for a while.

My brother and I lay in our bed that night and talked in low, conspiratorial tones before Martha came in.

"What are we going to do?" my brother asked.

"I don't know. I just hope Ma won't have to take me to the doctor if she finds out."

"Ma wouldn't take you to the doctor. She'll make Pa do it. Ma would never be able to talk to the doctor about what you did."

"I guess you're right. I hope Pa won't be too mad at me. I wonder if the cat's eye will plug up my hole and I'll never be able to go poo-poo again." I heard a muffled giggle. "It's not funny."

"I'm sorry."

Martha walked in after she showered, settled in and started to tell us about her annoying friend, Betty. For once I was happy to hear her prattle.

It was hard getting to sleep and when it did come, it came in short, fitful stages. I dreamed dad was plunging a toilet, he called the toilet all manner of Spanish profanities, but the toilet would not unclog. In a semiconscious state I worried I might explode by the end of the next week. The only solution I could come up with was to never eat again.

The next day after Sunday's eleven o'clock Mass, everyone slid into their Sunday routines. Pa sat at the kitchen table and drank his coffee while he read the Sunday paper, waiting for a football game to come on a little later. Ma began to prepare a chicken mole dinner. My sisters cleaned their rooms while listening to KCBQ, the rock-and-roll station.

My brother gestured for me to me to go to the backyard. "Did you get any ideas last night?" he asked while he took a Popsicle stick and teaspoon from his back pocket. He also had Ma's Mentholatum jar and a couple of paper napkins. "Do you want to go into the bathroom?" he whispered.

"No thanks, this morning after church when I went to the bathroom I heard a 'clink' hit the bottom of the toilet."

We were giddy with relief.

9.

3rd Grade – Double Trouble
Fernando

"It was our poor sister Martha's ill fate to have her pesky twin brothers born on her fourth birthday. Years of therapy and antidepressants have helped her cope."
A remorseful brother

Factoid - The odds of having to share your birthday with two siblings are a hundred and thirty-three thousand to one.

P A HAD A GREAT SENSE OF HUMOR and laughed easily. This gift was passed down to his children. Dinnertimes were lively and full of laughter. When friends joined us, I don't know what they enjoyed more, Ma's Mexican dishes or our loud animated conversations.

Our first caper with Martha, even though it was unintentional, was on her seventh birthday. Martha had begged Ma for a party. Ma put her off since my twin and I were in diapers and in constant need of care. The idea of hosting a party was too much. When Armando and I were three Ma relented.

Ma cleaned and decorated our rented house, baked a birthday cake, and bought candles for the big event. Martha invited several of her second-grade friends. The party was going well until Becky, one of the girls, needed to use the bathroom.

Martha led her to the bathroom with the rest of the girls following. When she opened the door, the six girls screamed and laughed. Armando and I had stripped off our clothes and were standing in the toilet, flushing it, and giggled as the water tickled our feet. We joined them in their laughter, although we weren't sure what they were laughing and screaming about. Mortified, Martha yelled, "Mama! Mama! The twins are standing naked in the toilet."

Ma came to the rescue, scolded us as she pulled us out and dried our feet. On Monday when Martha came home from school, she told Ma that the only thing her friends talked about was her naked twin brothers with their feet in the toilet.

Four years later, when my brother and I were seven, we moved from our two-bedroom house on Acacia Street to a three-bedroom house on Euclid Avenue. Tony had started his vocational training and lived at the seminary, so during the school year the family was down to eight.

With the extra room, our cousin, Socorro, from Hermosillo, came to stay for a semester of high school. Armando, Martha, and I transferred from St. Jude Academy to St. Rita's Grammar School at the beginning of the following school year.

Armando and I shared a bedroom with Martha. Ana, Carolyn, and Socorro slept in a freestanding room constructed of concrete blocks a few paces off the back porch. Three-year-old Carmen slept in the third bedroom with Ma and Pa.

Martha was smart, sensitive, and finicky. She could out smell a bloodhound. She would react to a mild odor at the end of the block as if it were under her nose. She made a perfect target for our tricks.

One afternoon my brother and I were across the street visiting our neighbor, Hector. His dad had come down from Los Angeles on one of his rare visits to see his son and five-year-old daughter. Mr. Torelli invited us to go him and Hector for a drive in his older-model Chrysler sedan. While the car was in need of body and upholstery work, Mr. Torelli was always fashionably dressed. His shirts were starched, his pants ironed, and shoes polished to a sheen. Not a hair on his head stood out of place.

He drove us to a joke shop. "You can get one thing each," he said.

"Don't get anything t-t-too expensive," whispered Hector. "My da-da-dad's a little tight right now." Hector had a stutter, especially if he was excited or nervous. I opted for a rubber pencil.

It looked real but when you tried to write, the tip bent. Armando got a cool-looking ring with a bright red stone mounted on its face. The needle size hole in the middle of the stone was hardly perceptible. The ring had a thin tube connected to a small rubber bladder that you filled with water. One would snake the tube between his fingers and hold the bladder in his palm. Hector got a small pile of fake dog shit.

Unlike Pa, Mr. Torelli didn't laugh much. "Nice seeing you boys," he said, when he dropped us off and picked up Hector's pain-in-the-neck little sister.

"What did you do?" Ma asked when we walked into the kitchen.

"Mr. Torelli drove us to a swimming pool but it was closed so he took us downtown and we went into a joke shop, then we went to Balboa Park and played football. But Hector got hurt when I tackled him so he brought us home."

"*Les gusto?*"

"Nah, it was pretty boring. Mostly we just drove around."

"Gringos are strange.," Ma said with a shrug.

Armando and I walked into the living room where Martha was lying on the couch with a copy of *The Saturday Evening Post* magazine. My brother walked to the kitchen. I heard water run in the sink.

"Hi, Martha. Look what Hector's dad bought me."

She lowered her magazine and turned her head. "It's just a pencil."

"No. Watch." I dragged the tip of my pencil along the magazine to demonstrate the fascinating rubber tip.

"Why did you get that?" she asked, disturbed and unimpressed.

"Hector told us to get something cheap because his father didn't have much money."

"Well, it looks cheap," she said, turning back to her magazine. My brother walked in with his new ring on.

"Hey, Martha, look what I got for you." She dropped her magazine again and looked at the pretty ring inches from her nose.

"Oooh," she said, and sat up. My brother squeezed. A jet of water hit her between the eyes. In less than a second her surprised joy turned to rage. He bolted out the front door. I roared with laughter. Martha shot up and bolted after him with water dripping off her face. She chased him several laps around Ma's guava tree screaming, "Get over here, get over here."

Terror-stricken Armando yelled, "No, no." Realizing she was not going to catch him, she stormed into the house and looked at me.

"What's so funny?" She seethed. She snatched the fake pencil from my hand, broke it in half, and handed it back. I sat staring at my new broken fake pencil. I didn't have to ask why she did it.

THREE WEEKS LATER THE THREE OF US talked quietly from our beds with the lights off, the incident with the ring forgotten. Tomorrow would be another routine weekday with an early rising and the three of us walking to school. Martha was gossiping about her school friend Monica Ferris and her weird family. "Monica's mother constantly nags at her dad. Maybe it's his fault because he takes it. Pa would never take nagging like that, and her mother blames everyone else if Monica's little brat brother misbehaves. You'd think he was a prince or something." We lay quietly listening to her prattle on. I looked over, Armando lay staring at the ceiling.

"I got to go to the bathroom," she said, and slid out of her bed. "I'll be right back."

"Good thing she told us she was coming back," my brother whispered. "I thought maybe she was going to Disneyland." I giggled.

I wondered what would happen if I sneaked into her bed. "Hay, *cuate*," I whispered, "what do you think if I snuck into Martha's bed?"

"Heck yeah. Do it." I hurried over and wedged myself between the edge of the bed and the wall. I snuggled below the blanket line, fluffed them and lay in wait. Martha returned, got back into bed, and happily continued her monologue.

"And Monica told me that her mother made her dad get a night job at the Fedco gas station because she wanted more money," Monica said, blah, blah, blah. I could hear my brother quietly wheezing with laughter with a pillow over his mouth.

I lay in my hiding spot, waiting for the right moment to let her know I was there but she wouldn't stop talking. I smiled at how hard she would laugh when I let her in on the gag. Blah, blah, blah. I was starting to get nervous. The longer she talked, the more worried I got, and it was getting hot. I realized I hadn't thought of an exit plan, and it was becoming apparent that I was in a serious no-win situation. How was I going to let her know without scaring her and getting the crap beat out of me? Not to mention, if things didn't work out well, what Pa might do if she got mad enough and told him.

"It was so embarrassing when Pa and I pulled into the gas station and Mr. Farris asked us how much gas we wanted. The poor guy even had to wash the windshield."

I broke into a sweat. *Maybe if I wait until she falls asleep I can sneak out, but how can I without crawling over her? Maybe I can slide out at the end of the bed. But the way she's talking, I might be here till midnight. Got to think of something else. What if I introduce myself in a quiet enough voice? She won't be startled, and we could all laugh and I can get back to my bed. Yeah, that should work.*

I cleared my throat so quietly I could hardly hear it myself. "Hi," I said in a tiny voice. But with her talking, she didn't hear me. What I did hear was my brother's muffled gasping.

"Her little brother snuck into his parents' cabinet and played with their expensive camera even though they were told to never touch the camera and her brother lied and said he didn't so you know what Monica's mother said?" *Of course I don't know.* "When Mr. Ferris asked him again, her mother cut him off and said that someone must have broken into their house and gotten in there.' Can you believe that?"

Man, can Martha talk.

"Hi," I said a little louder, but she still didn't hear me. *Sweet Jesus, what have I gotten myself into?* I wished I hadn't listened to my stupid brother's encouragement. He was safe, I was about to get beat to death.

"Monica is always bragging about how her stuff is better than mine."

Then, it came to me. Why not just lightly tap her on the leg? *Should have thought of that before.* "Your family's car is nice but ours has power steering."

I timidly reached over to tap her thigh but I was pensive. As my hand neared, I flexed my finger to tap but wound up scratching her with the tip of my fingernail. A horror movie screech filled the room. She sprang from her bed. I was stunned at how fast she could move. My heart jumped into my throat. There was a second's confusion when she stood away and looked to the bed. I leaped out and catapulted into our bed, landing on my brother. He roared. I wiggled off and snapped the covers over myself.

When she realized who it was and what had happened, she sprung on me like a cat on a three-legged mouse. I grabbed the pillow and covered myself. The blows came fast and furious. My brother's laughing added to her fury. Martha gave him a few blows to his unprotected head, then turned back to me. I was glad he hadn't covered himself.

"I'm sorry, I'm sorry, I'm sorry," I pleaded. But my appeal for mercy was futile. After hits to my head and shoulders she got back into her bed, heaving, but attacked again when she heard our wheezing.

Martha was no longer interested in telling us about stupid Monica and her stupid mother and her stupid father and her stupid little brother. An eternity passed before sleep came.

She didn't talk to us in the morning or on the way to or back from school. I was afraid I was really going to be in for it that night.

Pa rolled out of bed to have dinner before going back to bed for another few hours to get rested for his graveyard shift. "Time to eat," Ma called out. My sisters and twin happily joined

I stayed in my room, hoping against hope no one would notice my absence.

"Fernando, it's time to eat." This time it was Pa's voice and he only had to call out once. I went to the table. Ma was serving little Carmen her plate, Ana and Carolyn were talking about the big volleyball game they were going to play against Our Lady of Peace Academy on Friday. Pa was talking to my brother about Pa's glory days at Lindsay High School, and Martha was sitting quietly across the table.

"I'm hungry, let's pray," said Carolyn. She started us off and we joined in. "Bless us O Lord and these Thy gifts which we are about to receive . . ." There was always a moment of silence after we finished with our prayer. Dad grabbed a tortilla, tore it in half, placed it over his *carne molida*, scooped, and pushed the huge portion into his mouth.

"Tony, don't take such big bites," Ma reprimanded yet again. I picked up my fork and started to eat. Martha looked over at me.

In an even, emotionless tone she said, "Fernando, please tell Pa what you did last night."

I put my fork down, gulped, and described what I had done. Pa didn't realize he was supposed to be angry. He cocked his head back and laughed, coughing up his food and nearly choking. Martha stared deadly darts across the table at me. My dumb brother laughed with Pa.

10.

3rd Grade – Euclid Avenue Warriors
Fernando

"Blood is what makes a man a man."
Author unknown

IT WAS THE END OF THE FIRST MONTH of summer vacation from third grade. Armando and I were bored, bored with TV, bored with trips to the refrigerator hoping to find a hidden treat we didn't find on the last trip, bored with each other. We would've been happy to go up to the Mayfair Market to buy candy, but we had no money or soda bottles to return for deposit. Ma was on the verge of kicking us out of the house when a big delivery truck with So-Cal Freight Lines written on its side backed into the driveway. It was Pa in a company truck.

We ran out the door as the engine revved. The late morning air was humid and warm; it was going to be a hot day. Pa parked and climbed down the two-step metal ladder attached to the side of the cab.

"Hi, Pa."

"Hi, boys."

"What're you doing home?"

"Got something for you two." He went to the back of the truck, pulled on the lock lever, and opened the double doors. A four-foot-tall metal platform stood on edge. Pa pulled on a handle and the platform slowly unfolded until it was level with the cargo bed. Sitting on the bed was a rough-sawn wooden crate. The box was tall enough for a big man to stand in with room to spare and wide enough for him to stretch his arms out without touching the sides. "Thought you boys might like this."

"Wow, Pa, is it for us?"

"Yup, I delivered a commercial freezer packed in this box—it was my last drop and the customer asked me get rid of it. I was on my way back to the yard and figured you boys would like it."

I stood in awe. Pa smiled and hoisted us onto the hydraulic platform then climbed up and joined us. "You boys push on the corners so I can get my dolly under it."

We jumped to it. Pa got down and pushed on the lift lever. The hydraulic motor squealed as the platform descended. Our bodies jolted and the crate rocked when the platform hit the driveway with a loud "clank."

Pa maneuvered the box onto the driveway. "Go ahead, *muchachos*, and clear the way." We guided him through the back gate and the patio. We moved bicycles, broken patio furniture, and two worn car tires. He hauled the crate to the concrete steps that led to the lower yard. I ran down, my brother stayed behind with Pa. He lowered the box one cautious step at a time until he got to the dirt. The three of us pushed and tugged until we got the box in place.

Rivulets of sweat rolled down the side of Pa's head and disappeared under his collar. He pulled a red and white paisley handkerchief from his back pocket and wiped his shining forehead.

"Okay, boys. I'll see you after work," he and carried the dolly back up the slope.

"Bye, Pa, and thanks a lot." I stood admiring the crate; it was absolutely beautiful. "Hey, let's get Chad and Chris," I said.

"Okay. I'll go tell Dave, Chucky, and Robert."

We ran to the neighbors' houses. Within minutes seven animated boys looked at the crate in wonderment. "This is cool," Chucky said.

Chad smiled, "It's boss, man."

"Hey, let's make a club," Dave said. Heads nodded.

"How do we get in?" Chucky asked. Chad walked a lap around the crate.

"We'll have to cut out a door."

I drew a rectangle with my finger. "We should make it this big."

"No, that's too small," Dave said and outlined a larger door.

"No, that's too big." Chucky said, "maybe we should put it on the back side, like a secret door."

Chad made the best suggestion. "If we cut a door on the roof, then we'll be safe from enemies." Everyone agreed.

"Fernando, you and Chucky work on a ladder, the rest of us will cut the hole." Armando ran up to the garage and came back with dad's two handsaws. One had a bent blade and the other a broken handle. Both were dull. "Does your dad have a bucket we can use?" Chad asked.

"Yeah, why?"

"We'll need it to get on the roof."

Armando ran back up and returned with the bucket. Chad stood on it and hoisted himself up then helped the others onto the roof.

While Chucky and I worked on the ladder. Chad and his crew worked on the access hole. Chucky and I grabbed some bone-dry and twisted two-by-fours out of a heap by the stairs.

With priority given to the rooftop door, I had to use the saw with the broken handle. Our two crew's steeled determination overcame our lack of resources. Chucky and I took turns cutting through the two-by-fours while Chris, Chad's six-year-old brother, looked on. The roof crew took turns on their saw, counting twenty-five strokes each so no one worker would hog the saw.

I counted my strokes, then turned the saw over to Chucky. "Take some extra strokes and I'll get us some nails." I ran to Pa's junky garage and moved a bunch of useless items Pa refused to get rid of and got to the workbench. I found a coffee can half full of rusty nails and a hammer with a broken claw. Chucky was tired by the time I got back and handed over the saw. I attacked the steel-hardened wood with hard strokes. I held the saw in one hand and the lumber in place with the other. In my enthusiasm I pulled too hard on the back stroke. The saw jumped the cut and snagged my thumb. A hunk of my thumbnail pulled up, a small part of nail remained attached like a hinge. Chucky's eyes opened wide. Chris stepped back and looked away. I pushed the nail back in place and held my thumb to stop the blood before it started to flow.

I handed Chucky the saw. "Keep cutting, I'm gonna get a Band-Aid." I sneaked into the bathroom, found the Band-Aids, and tip-toed out. If Ma found out, she would have scrubbed the wound and wiped it with alcohol. Besides the pain, it would take time away from our project. I got back, put on the Band-Aid, and took another turn on the saw. Cherry-red blood seeped through the bandage and my thumb throbbed, but I was undeterred: I was on a mission.

"You're bleeding," Chris said.

"It'll stop in a minute." I had to put up a good front. It sounded like the crew on top were making progress. I heard arguing over getting another chance with the saw.

By the time we finished cutting the fourth rung Chucky and I were soaked in sweat. I laid the two-by-four rails on the ground, set the first rung, and started nailing. Every third or fourth nail bent with the hammer blows. I had to stop and pull the stubborn nails out before trying the next one. I had trouble getting the last nail into the top rung. After I bent two nails in the same hole, I set a third nail and gave it a mighty whack. The cut end of the two-by-four split but the tip of the nail finally penetrated the runner. The rest of the nail bent to the side. I gave it three more whacks for good measure and stood, satisfied that the last nail was finally embedded. I put the ladder against the wall of the crate. It leaned to one side.

"One leg is longer than the other." Chris said.

I took some dirt and packed it under the short leg. "There, that should do it."

When I put my weight on the first rung, the ladder tilted a little before it settled. When I got on the roof I called to Chucky and Chris, "Come on." They climbed up.

"Cool ladder," Robert said. He climbed down and back up. The roof crew finished cutting the entrance.

"I want to be the first one in," I said, sat on the edge and peered into the deep, dark chasm. I hesitated, "Come on, hurry up," Chad coaxed. I closed my eyes, scooted off the roof and landed with a jolt.

I looked around, "Oh man, this is great."

"Let me go next, let me go next," Chris said. Chad grabbed his little brother by the arms and lowered him to me. Dave followed with the rest of the boys behind him. Chad was the last man in. He handed down a bag of Oreo cookies he had filched from his mother's kitchen while waiting one of his turns at cutting. He sat on the edge and jumped in. We stood in wonder at the clubhouse.

We agreed that Chad, at the double-digit age of eleven, should be our president. He opened the bag of cookies, took out two, and passed the bag around. When the bag got to me I took the last three, crumpled it, and threw it into a corner.

The small gaps between boards of the crate and the opening on the top gave just enough light to conduct business.

"Okay, men," Chad began, "we'll sit cross-legged Indian style in a circle." I sat and got a splinter in my butt but didn't say anything. I didn't want to disrupt our first meeting. I lifted my cheek, felt for the splinter, pinched and pulled it out.

"We need a club name," said our president. There was a moment's pause. I hadn't thought about needing a name, but his suggestion made sense. Chucky raised his hand.

"How about The Bird's Eye Club?" There was momentary silence.

"How about The Popeye Club?" Chris volunteered.

"How about the He-Man Club?" Armando said.

"The Batman Club," someone yelled.

Chad clasped his hands behind his back in thought then came up with a winner. "Men, how about, The Euclid Avenue Warriors?"

"Yeah," someone said.

"Cool," someone else said. Smiles formed on our excited faces.

"Next, we need to have some rules." It hadn't occurred to me that we should have club rules either. It became apparent that we chose the right man for president.

"Rule number one, no girls allowed." Unanimous approval.

"Rule number two, no talking to girls." Another good rule. "If a club member is caught talking to a girl, he'll be thrown out of the club." "

Can I talk to Mommy?" Chris asked with a worried look.

Chad took a moment before announcing his decision. "Yeah, okay, everyone can talk to their moms." Chris relaxed.

These were good rules, but it didn't occur to us that besides my four sisters, who weren't the least bit interested in our activities, there was not one single girl in the entire neighborhood. There were no girls to talk to even if we wanted to. I didn't mention that I intended to talk to my sisters. Hopefully, no one would notice.

"Rule number three, bring three cents or an empty soda bottle as dues to each meeting." The three-cent rule shouldn't be too hard to keep as Armando and I were good at collecting empties carelessly discarded by rich people. With seven members, we should have a lot of money in the club in no time.

After laying down the rules with no objections, Chad brought up another issue none of us had considered. "What if our club grows so big that we wouldn't be able to recognize another member when we're outside the club?" Chad was ready with the solution. "We are going to have a secret signal." He formed circles with his pointer fingers and thumbs, inverted them, and placed them over his eyes like a pair of glasses. We all made the sign and looked at one another. The club was getting better by the minute.

Afternoon sun beat on the clubhouse and seven bodies upped the temperature but we ignored it. Having our own personal space was well worth the sacrifice. Besides, we were out of sight from enemies and prying parents.

"Now, we should have a club handshake. Everybody stand up." We stood. I reached over to Chucky standing next to me and Chucky extended his hand. Chad looked at us, "No, wait." I pulled my hand back. "Spit in your hands first." I heard simultaneous hocking as I spit into the palm of my right hand.

"Now, shake hands with the guy next to you." I reached back to Chucky, and we shook. While I spat an average amount of saliva into my hand, Chucky laid a big one in his. I resolved to match his with the next handshake. A deep feeling of kinship toward my club members washed over me. "Okay, everybody sit down."

An idea came to me that would bind the club members for life. I raised my hand. Chad recognized me and gave me permission to speak.

"I saw this movie on TV about a pioneer who saved an Indian's life. He grabbed the Indian who had fallen off his horse in a buffalo hunt and pulled the Indian onto his own horse. The chief was really happy because the Indian the pioneer saved was his son. The pioneer and Indian he saved became blood brothers. That was the best movie I ever saw. I think we should all become blood brothers."

"What's a blood brother?" Chris asked.

Chad explained. "The cowboy and the Indian brave cut their wrists and put them together and exchanged their blood, and that's how you become a blood brother."

"They did it at night in front of a big bonfire with the whole Indian village there. And they were best friends forever," I said. Excited murmurs filled the clubhouse.

"Okay, who wants to be first?" Heads turned looking for volunteers.

"How about you, Chris?" I said. Everyone looked at Chris. He looked around at the excited faces. Flattered with the attention he said, "Okay."

"Who'll be his blood brother?"

"How about Robert?" I said. Everyone looked at Robert.

"Who me?" he said, then his eyes lit up.

"How about you, Fernando? It was your idea." All eyes turned to me. I tried to think of an argument. Chad called for a vote. All hands shot into the air.

"We'll need a knife," Chad said.

"I'll get it," Armando said, and jumped to his feet. He looked at the entrance high overhead. "How do I get out?"

"We should've brought the ladder in with us," Chucky said. Silence filled the clubhouse.

"I have to be home before dark," Dave said.

"Mommy will want me home for dinner," Chris whimpered.

Our president, faced with his first crisis, took control. "Fernando, you get on all fours. Armando, stand on his back and Robert and I will boost you up the rest of the way." I rolled into a crouch, knees and palms on the floor. Tennis shoes dug into my back. Chad and Robert straddled me. I heard grunts as they lifted my brother. Footsteps scurried off the roof and

101

down the ladder. Armando was back in seconds. He lay on his stomach and handed down one of Ma's carving knives to Chad. It looked like a machete. He dropped back in and stood with the rest of the club, ready to see blood flow. *I needed to think of something fast.*

"Hey, there could be germs on the knife and Chris and me could get really sick. Maybe we should wait until Ma washes it." *Who could argue with that?*

"I'll go get some matches," my brother said, and was back on the roof and down the ladder in no time. I was running out of ideas and starting to really dislike my brother.

He came back with two stick matches that Ma had in the kitchen to light the stove burners. Chad held the ends of the matches, struck them on a wall, and held the flame to the blade as he turned it side to side. He blew on the matches and tossed them over his shoulder.

"Okay. Chris and Fernando, sit down." Everyone circled us. Bloodlust hung heavy in the air.

"What are you going to do?" Chris asked, looking nervous. Chad drew in a breath and spoke in a low, reassuring tone.

"We're going to make an itsy-bitsy cut on your wrist that you'll hardly even feel at all so you can become a cool blood brother with Fernando just like in the movie." It took a moment for Chris to understand what he volunteered for. He started crying.

I smelled smoke and heard crackling. "Fire!" Robert yelled. The matches Chad had nonchalantly thrown over his shoulder had not gone completely out and landed on the cookie package.

"Oh crap!" Chad yelled. "Put it out!" Four sets of black tennis shoes ran to the corner, stomped on the floor, each other, and the small flame. Some of the guys coughed from the unsettled dust and smoke as the fire was crushed. Chris cried again.

I stood, my mind in a blur for a plan to get myself out of the situation. I nervously rubbed the Band-Aid on my wounded thumb. A trickle of blood oozed out. I scanned Chris's arms and legs. He had a beauty of a scab on his left knee.

"Chris, pick that scab on your knee."

He looked at me through tears. "What?"

"Quick, Chris, pick the scab." I pointed to it. I ripped the Band-Aid off my thumbnail. "Ow!"

The guys turned back from the fire, ready to continue with the blood ceremony. I leaned over and put my thumb to Chris's knee.

"We did it. Chris and I are blood brothers," I said with a victorious smile.

"That's not fair," my brother said.

"You are now blood brothers," Chad announced. He must have figured Chris would have told their mother that we cut Chris and Chad would have been in a lot of trouble. Chris wiped tears and snot from his face.

Cheated out of butchery, the members grumbled.

"Okay," I said. "Who's next?" Guys vociferously volunteered other guys. I yelled over everyone. "How about my brother?" Everyone looked at him.

"Shut up, you're not the president," he said angrily.

"You shut up."

"No, you shut up."

Seeing the situation getting out of hand, Chad took control, "Meeting's over. Let's all go outside." The guys grumbled.

I got back on my hands and knees as each member stepped on my back and dug in their feet. Chad boosted one after another. Chad got on all fours, and it was finally my turn to step on someone. Greatly relieved, a little dizzy and anxious to get out of the sweatbox, I accidentally stepped on Chad's neck and pushed down.

"Ouch, get off my head," Chad screamed.

"Oops, sorry." I repositioned my foot between his shoulders, stood, and reached out to the waiting hands of Chucky and

Dave. They pulled me out far enough that I was able to curl my knee on the roof and boost myself up. The eighty-five-degree afternoon air felt cool on my face after the humid sauna-like clubhouse.

Chad was a good ten pounds heavier and three inches taller than the rest of us. "Hand down the bucket," he said. Dave climbed down the ladder and retrieved the bucket and handed it down to Chad. He stood on the bucket and reached up. Dave and I grabbed his hands and pulled with all our might. My brother saw us struggling, hustled over, and grabbed a handful of hair and pulled.

"Ow, Not by my hair," he screamed. We all let go and he fell back onto the bucket, lost his balance, and fell to the floor.

"God darn it."

"You shouldn't take the Lord's name in vain," I called down.

"Too bad," came out of the darkness.

Chad got back on the bucket and reached again. Dave and I pulled. Chad's head started to come out of the hole. My brother reached down and wrapped his hands around Chad's chin and pulled hard, causing the back of Chad's head to hit the side of the roof. "Hey," he yelled.

"Sorry, I'm just trying to help." My brother let go of his head and grabbed the back of Chad's T-shirt, pulled up, and tore the collar free from the shirt.

"Look, Armando, just stop helping," Chad hollered. Robert and Chucky stepped up, grabbed an elbow each, and helped. My arms were about to give out when we finally got him out. Relieved to have been spared Ma's butcher knife, I was anxious to end the day and get to my bedroom.

I walked to the ladder, turned, and lowered my foot onto the top rung and heard a creak. Before I could react, the rung with the bent nail gave way. I grabbed for the corner of the box but it was too late. I flailed my arms and tried to rebalance myself. I fell and landed on my back with a thud, the ladder fell next to me. My wind was knocked out, puffs of dust exploded out from under me. I lay dazed with my eyes closed. *I should have done a better job of driving the last nail.* The guys looked over the edge.

"He's dead," someone said. I heard Chris start to cry again.

"Are you alive?" someone else called down. I opened my eyes. "Yeah, he's alive."

I rolled over onto my knees and slowly got up. I looked at my thumb smeared with blood as it started to ooze and throb again. I could smell smoke on my filthy T-shirt and felt a headache coming on.

"Fix the ladder and bring it back," Chad said. I didn't bother to answer. I turned and made my way up the hill toward the house. The club members would have to figure out how to get down on their own.

"When's the next meeting?" called Chris behind me. Unbeknownst to us, this would be the first and last meeting of The Euclid Avenue Warriors.

11.

3rd Grade – Playground Commanders
Armando

"Truly, truly I say unto thee unless you become like little children you shall not enter the kingdom of heaven."
Jesus Christ

SISTER MARIE LUCILLE, THE FOURTH-GRADE TEACHER, sitting at her desk, heard shuffling in the hallway. Her students were at their desks immersed in essay writing. She walked quietly to the door and peered out. Eye-squinting morning sunlight shone brilliantly through the large window at the end of the hall. Sunrays reflected on the polished linoleum floor were obscured by the imposing and unquestionable figure of Sister Mary Constance, mother superior of the convent. The school principal's arms were extended out on either side. She walked, pinching an ear of Armando and Fernando, the third-grade twins. They were short and had to cock their heads up and walk on tiptoes to lessen the pull and pain inflicted by the walrus-like principal. They dragged a shoe occasionally letting out a soft "ow," "ouch," and "ow."

"Oh, my," whispered Sister Lucille. "What have they done now?"

Sister Constance was not able to walk in a normal fashion. Her bulk, habit, and even her black soft-soled shoes made her walk like a duck in slow motion. Her mass swung to one side, then to the other. The long black skirt of her habit swept the floor as she waddled in the direction of her office.

The boys kept their neatly combed heads as high as possible. "Ow, ouch, ow."

Sister Lucille was looking forward to having them in her class next year, but alas, it wouldn't be next year. They were destined to fail the third grade and grace the aging Mrs. Alexander's classroom for another school term. She couldn't help but notice them on the playground during recess. Their high energy and playground antics were well-known by the playground mothers who were in charge of monitoring the children at play.

The boys, unbeknownst to them, were a constant source of entertainment and laughter for the nuns who lived within the stifling confines of the convent and were subject to the moody whims of the Mother Superior.

For the first few months in the school, most of the boys played the regular games of four square, dodge ball, and tether ball. But when these two entered the third grade, they became bored with the prescribed games, which were too confining for their free spirits. The games they decided to play had a pattern.

Their classmates gathered around them, then each twin picked a boy, taking turns, until two sides of equal number and talent were chosen. The twins were always unanimously chosen by the boys in their class to lead them in exciting games.

After the armies were determined, they were led into battle. The tactic was crude but exciting and always involved a lot of running at full speed, battle screams, repeated frontal attacks with lots of hand-to-hand combat. A dozen or more boys on either side raced toward each other with their general's arm in the air leading the charge. Mock fights broke out when sides collided and tried to gain advantage over the other. After intense combat the generals raised an arm and led their soldiers from the battlefield with his men at his heels.

"Follow me," a general yelled, his troops close behind. After a brief strategy meeting a general announced another attack.

"Attack! Get those chicken-livered cowards." A dozen horse-mounted soldiers charged toward their mortal enemies, unintentionally disrupting the games of jump rope, hopscotch, or four square. On one occasion, a panicked playground mother who served as a monitor had to grab her toddler out of harm's way. The threat posed to little ones added to the authenticity of the battle and excitement of the campaign.

When a television show called *The Americans*, a series about brothers on opposite sides of the Civil War, was aired, the game was called "The Americans." Each twin-general led a band of screaming Yankees or whooping Rebels. Seldom did tempers flare or real fights break out. When Harold, the Rebel, and John, the Yankee, wound up wrestling over a disputed cheap-shot by Harold, the leaders called a truce, mediated, and came to terms on appropriate action. In most cases the boys and their armies agreed to the verdict and the battle resumed. Playground monitors couldn't help but to take notice of the twins' skills in conflict resolution.

What were the bookends in trouble for this time? wondered Sister Marie Lucille. "They aren't bad boys," she confided to Sister Elvira Marie, the first-grade teacher. "They don't fight or push around the younger kids or damage anything and are respectful of authority."

"They sure have a lot of fun, though," said Sister Elvira, laughing.

Sisters Lucille and Elvira Marie felt the need to be discreet in their admiration of the twins, lest the mother superior find out. They often shared a laugh describing the antics of the twins.

The generals were fearless and possessed powerful magnetic personalities that drew boys toward them. Typical casualties were sprained wrists, stubbed fingers, ripped shirts, torn pant knees, and lots of missing shirt buttons. An occasional bloody nose would stain a white uniform shirt.

"You're the roughest boys in this school," scolded Sister Constance to the dwarf generals Fernando Robert E. Lee and Armando Ulysses S. Grant Garcia.

Her round, pale face was red with anger. "I will not have you leading boys in your gang war games. Do you understand?"

Two blank faces looked at one another. Of course, they didn't understand. They had no idea what she was talking about. In their little minds, recess was a time for having fun. They and their classmates were having fun, a lot of fun, unlike the indoctrinated who played games defined by white lines, balls attached to poles, and boxes painted on asphalt. The games the twins played had no restrictions and made use of the entire playground. The only requirements for their style of play were an unencumbered spirit, a well-developed imagination, and boundless energy.

The boys, adhering to their cultural protocol, were too respectful to make eye contact with an authority figure as they stood at Sister Constance's large wooden desk. They stared red-faced at the floor, confused as to what the rotund principal's scolding was about, and embarrassed that students were hearing her admonition echoing through the hall.

She stood up. "I will not allow you two to lead your own games. And look at me when I talk to you!"

They obeyed the woman dressed in white and black. Her swollen cheeks were flush, her fists set on her wide hips. The nun took up most of their field of vision. Her eyes, opened wide, were magnified by her bifocals.

"What have you got to say for yourselves?" The twins were not sure what she wanted. "Well, what have you got to say?"

"I'm sorry?"

"What? Speak up? What did you say?"

"Uh, we're sorry."

"I am keeping an eye on the both of you. If you continue in this behavior I am going to . . ." Blah, blah, blah. Their attention spans had reached their limit.

It was impossible for them to concentrate on any one topic for more than a couple of minutes. Nothing in their little world remained still for very long, even the words on the pages of the books that they were to study each night.

In future years, people who study such behaviors would identify and label these inabilities to concentrate or read because letters on pages moved or imaginations replaced reality. It wasn't that the boys weren't intelligent. They were just more interested in leading armies and devising war plans or entertaining the other students than they were in studying. Some teachers treated such conditions with pointer sticks whacked to the butt or admonitions and stints in the corners of a classroom. Others, like Sister Lucille, took the time to try and understand the child's condition, work with the parents, and take appropriate action.

Sister Constance felt her authority threatened by the two free spirits standing before her. She was determined to make them bend to her will. The principal's hollering eased as her diatribe wound down, luring the boys attention back to the present.

"Do you understand me?" Silence. "Boys, do you understand?"

"Yes, Sister."

"If you continue with this behavior, I will be looking for your mother and father on parent night."

Ah yes, parent night. The one night of the year when parents were able to talk one-on-one with teachers and get first-hand reports as to how their children were doing. Graded students' assignments and tests with scores sat on their desks. The classroom walls were adorned with students' best essays, graded test papers, and artwork for the parents to admire. That is, for some of the parents. There were few, if any, papers the twins submitted to their teacher's worthy of posting. The scholastic deck of cards was stacked against them.

There was much consternation in the Garcia household in the days leading up to parent night. It was a given that the twins would have poor grades and there would be embarrassment for Ma and Pa in front of the teacher. It seemed unfair to the twins that they were cursed with four older siblings who excelled in schoolwork and behavior. It would be a given that Martha would be strapped with the miserable and nearly impossible task of tutoring her little brothers who had the collective intellect and attention span of a burro.

Martha felt cheated by the fates for having been selected to be born closest in age to her brothers. It was a routine that played out several times during their school years. The boys would come home with their report cards. After reviewing them, their father, who never scolded them for the poor marks, would come up with an edict that Martha would tutor them.

Accepting the responsibility placed on her by Pa, she would set up a classroom complete with blackboard and makeshift desks in the garage and attempt to make the best of a near impossible situation.

Her older sisters never had to deal with Mama's spoiled brats. Teaching the unteachable was Martha's cursed duty. In adulthood, she would become a loving and successful bilingual teacher in an elementary school that administered to the underserved. She would be loved by her students and respected by their parents. The twins thought that maybe they should ask her for compensation since it was their basic training that was responsible, they were certain, for her success as a teacher.

Parent night was never going to be good for the boys, but to add misbehavior to the equation could be grounds for serious punishment. The aftermath of parent night focused their determination to improve their behavior on the playground and apply themselves in the classroom. But these good intentions lasted only until the ring of the next recess bell. The dreaded season culminating with parent night was antithetical to the joyous season of Christmas. There was the festive season of gifts and joy and the season of dread and anxiety. The most awful was the eve of parent night. The twins would go to bed fearing the worst.

"Now, back to your classroom, and no more of your hooligan behavior!" The boys sheepishly walked down the hallway.

"What's a hooligan?" asked General Lee.

"Who knows?" answered General Grant.

Sister Lucille shook her head in dismay. Sister Lucille was tall, wore glasses with thick lenses and had a stern-looking face. The twins felt intimidated by her appearance when they passed her fourth-grade classroom. They were matched by a large set of lips and a look of ill temper. She secretly loved the boys. It seemed that nothing surprised her anymore when it came to these two and their antics.

Sister Lucille backed away from the hallway, her class still engrossed in writing their essays. Two little shiny combed heads passed her class unaware of her presence. They were in quiet conversation about the scolding that they had just received, trying to understand just exactly what the principal's point was.

"Do you think we're not supposed to have battles anymore?" asked Armando, astonished at the thought. "Do you think that's what she meant?"

"Maybe she didn't like the gauntlet we set up like the one we saw in the Indian movie," Fernando answered.

"Do you mean when we made two lines and made one guy run through it while the rest of us pounded him? Maybe that's what she meant."

They opened the double doors, Sister saw them race each other down the flight of stairs, a broken rule, and back to their third-grade classroom. She put a hand to her mouth, constraining laughter.

For the next two recess periods, the twins joined the other kids in the sanctioned games. The problem was that there was no free-spirited running, little if any strategy, and not a battle cry to be heard. The children that played the confined games were overly concerned with trivial rules and regulations. A misstep over a white line, an incidental dribble, mistakenly grabbing a rope of the tether ball. The only students who cared about these minutiae were the same ones who never drew outside the lines, didn't talk in class, had little if any sense of adventure, and lived in constant fear of breaking rules. Imaginations were to be expressed, not suppressed. It was recess time, and they were supposed to be having fun. None of this made sense.

The following week, at a lunchtime recess, Sister Lucille noticed Sister Constance in a full-waddle battle march heading down the hall toward the playground. The principal's eyes said it all. "Someone is going to die for this."

Sister Lucille slid into her classroom and walked to the window, looking out onto the playground. She noticed that the boys of the third grade had gathered in the middle of the playground. Half of their number had aligned themselves with one leader and the other half with the other. Two little arms shot into the air and two bands of soldiers raced in opposite directions. One group ran through the four-square section, the other trampled through the hopscotchers.

Sister faintly heard one little leader encouraging his men. "Come on. Let's get those back-stabbing Roman chickens."

Sister Lucille called the twins' sister Martha over.

"Yes, Sister?" Martha nervously answered. Was this going to be about her brothers getting into some kind of trouble again?

"Have your brothers been to the movies lately?"

"Yes, Sister. We saw *Hannibal* on Saturday. It's a movie about General Hannibal and his army and elephants fighting the Romans."

"I see," said Sister Lucille.

"Hannibal and the Romans."

"Okay. Thank you, Martha." Relieved, Martha left.

Sister Lucille walked to her empty classroom, closed the door, and laughed out loud.

12.

3rd Grade – Reforming Burros
Armando

*"Withhold not correction from the child: for if you
beat him with the rod, he shall not die."*
Biblical Proverb

IT WAS MARTHA'S ILL FATE to have to teach Fernando and me when we got our quarterly report cards. Pa would hold court at the kitchen table and go over our reports.

He always coached the same. "Armando, if you could get this D up to a C in math and this C minus to a C in geography, that would be good. Now, in religion if you could . . ."

He never got angry or scolded us because of poor grades. He told us he also flunked the third grade due to a language barrier, or so he said. He came to the US when he was ten and was thrown into public school.

When Pa saw our report cards he decreed that Martha, four years older and a good student, was to tutor us. She dreamed of becoming a teacher one day. Martha set up a classroom in Pa's musty garage. She took down the old chalkboard from the wall in the kitchen and hung it on a garage wall. She swept the part of the floor that would be her classroom. Two empty metal paint buckets served as our chairs and a wide board set on wooden boxes became our desk.

115

Our lessons were held on Saturday mornings. It didn't take long before we got bored and started messing around, making each other laugh. Martha got mad and wanted to quit but Pa's word was law.

During our first English lesson, Martha was trying to teach us how to diagram a sentence. she kept trying to explain but we didn't get it. "It's so easy," she exclaimed. "I can't believe you don't get it. Look, this word is the verb, an action word, and this one is the noun, which names a person, place, or thing." All she got from us were blank stares.

"Okay. Let's leave that alone for now and try math. We'll do some division." She wrote a problem on the blackboard. My mind and eyes wandered. I noticed that Pa hadn't fixed my bike tire sitting in a back corner and the punching bag was still flat, even though he promised to fix it weeks ago.

"Armando, pay attention."

"Wha—oh, okay."

Martha pointed to the divisor and said, "Tell me what this is."

"Is it the verb?"

"That was in English. We're in math now."

Before she could explain I smiled and said with confidence, "Oh, yeah. That's the noun, right?"

She threw her hands into the air. "Jeez, you guys are really dumb." That was our cue.

"Hey," I said, "maybe we're dumb as donkeys. hee-haw, hee-haw."

My brother laughed. He got on his hands and knees and kicked up his back feet. We laughed and laughed. The more exasperated Martha got, the more we liked it.

"If you two don't stop and pay attention I'm going to tell Pa." We behaved for the next ten minutes.

Occasionally our cousin Marilyn came to spend Saturday with Martha. It was fun when she came. Marilyn was lively and pretty, she always had her sandy-blonde hair coifed, stylish clothes, and perfectly aligned white teeth. My brother and I were good at entertaining her. Marilyn's mom had a good-paying job as a translator at the county courthouse, so Marilyn always showed up with spending money.

Martha and Marilyn would walk up Euclid Avenue to the Thrifty Drugstore and buy ice cream cones and bubble gum and a *Mad* magazine. Marilyn usually had enough to give Fernando and me a little money and we'd go with them.

The girl cousins would spend the afternoon lying on Martha's bed, reading to each other and laughing. On this Saturday, Marilyn sat in on our tutoring lesson. She watched Fernando and me having a great time getting under Martha's skin.

As Martha neared her breaking point, Marilyn said, "May I interrupt?" A little surprised, Martha said yes. "I need to talk to you for a minute." She motioned Martha to follow her outside. "We'll be right back." She closed the door behind them. We heard whispered conversation and sat in silence, not sure what to do. Fernando decided to take the chalk and eraser from Martha's desk and hide them behind Pa's broken floor freezer.

"Hey, look" he said, and pulled out a half-full bottle of wine. We had suspected that Pa had a stash somewhere, now we knew it. Fernando scampered back to his seat and folded his hands on top of the desk-board. We couldn't wait for Martha to get back. The girls walked in and stood. Marilyn looked serious while Martha spoke. "I heard Ma and Pa talking about you guys not learning and they're thinking of sending you to reform school." We stared at Martha trying not laugh, she hadn't noticed the missing chalk and erasure, "Have you guys ever heard of reform school?"

"Kinda," Fernando answered.

I looked for an opening to say something funny, but before I could Marilyn started in. "There's a reform school in El Cajon. Do you know where El Cajon is?"

"Yeah," I said, "that's where Freddie lives. It's hot there in the summer."

"Yeah," Marilyn said seriously. "It's *really* hot out there. That's where the reform school is. It's where they send boys who fool around and don't want to learn in regular schools. It's a place where there are real mean teachers who look for any reason to whack you with a stick. The stick has lots of stickers that get stuck under your skin, and they sting and make red welts that hurt, and when the boys misbehave, they hit them on their legs and arms and backs."

We sat silently as our sister and cousin spun their shocking tale of life for misbehaving boys.

Our cousin spoke in an ominous monotone. I studied her face to see if she was kidding, but she didn't smile even once. She looked to Martha. She wasn't smiling either. Martha took over.

"And the boys have to sleep on beds made of wooden planks with no mattresses or pillows. The planks have sharp spikes that poke through, and the spikes are in the exact shape of each boy's body, so if they try to move around at night the spikes poke their skin and make them bleed."

"Aw," I said, not wanting to believe that there were such places, "they don't treat boys like that."

Marilyn gave us a hard look. "My mother sees judges send boys to reform schools all the time. She even went to a reform school once. She told me she saw the boys eating really gross food. They use the same soup day after day, and sometimes it starts to smell bad, especially when flies fall in and get mixed up in it, and the boys teeth get brown stains. But the cooks and the teachers don't care because it's cheaper to serve it like that so they can pocket the money they were supposed to spend on good food. They put bread outside all day long in the hot sun so it gets stale and hard and then they make you eat it and watch you to make sure that you chew and swallow it. And there's no escape from reform school because there are tall fences with barbed wire and mean guards with wooden clubs. People think the fences are to keep bad people out, but really they are there to keep the boys in."

"I'll write mom and dad a letter and tell them how bad it is in there," Fernando said.

Martha took over without a moment's hesitation.

"They let you write letters all right, but the director, who used to be a prison warden, opens and reads them before they go out in the mail and if the boys say anything bad about them, they punish you by making you drink water out of the toilet."

I looked to Fernando. He was staring eyes wide, and his mouth open.

"One boy got a package from his mother and they opened it and found cookies. They ate some, then spit on the rest and made him eat them."

When my sister stopped talking, she looked to Marilyn. Marilyn walked to the door, opened it, looked side to side, closed it, and leaned her back against the door. She spoke in a low voice to keep anyone outside from hearing her.

"I heard my mom talking to your mother on the phone yesterday. She said that your parents are thinking of sending you guys to a reform school because you get such bad grades and don't listen to Martha."

We sat stunned. Who could ever even think of sending us to such a place? But maybe we're not behaving like we should sometimes. I don't like doing homework or studying for tests, so I don't get good grades. Maybe Ma and Pa don't know what else to do with us. And worst of all, Martha would get the last laugh. I wonder if she would write to us when we were being tortured in reform school with stinging red welts on our arms and legs and eating stale bread with our brown teeth. She would probably write about what a great time she and Marilyn were having reading *Mad* magazines, eating candy, and chewing bubble gum. I wonder if we could escape somehow and come home and behave so they'd never send us back there again?

Having Martha as a teacher in the dirty, cold garage, and sitting on hard paint bucket seats didn't seem so bad anymore. Martha took her position in front of the chalk board. "Hey, where's the chalk?"

Fernando jumped to his feet and replaced the chalk and erasure. We listened to Martha for the rest of the session. Martha was even able to teach us how to do simple division.

A little while later Martha dismissed us, satisfied that she had finally taught her "dumb as burros" brothers something.

Later that afternoon I heard them laughing hysterically through the bedroom door. *They must be reading one of their dumb magazines.*

In our bed that night we talked about what the girls had said. Our confused minds reeled. Since Fernando had the bottom bunk, it was up to him to flick off the light switch by the door, the bare light bulb flashed off. I heard the bunk's springs when he got into bed.

"Do you think Ma would really send us to a reform school?" I asked.

"I don't know about her, but Pa might." The despair in his voice was palpable. We said nothing more. Spike-riddled beds, putrid food, and barbed wire fences loomed large.

We had recently seen an old movie about some boys that got sent to a reform school and one of the boys was put in a cold room all by himself for misbehaving. In the morning they found him dead. In this movie, the boys in the school revolted and chased the director and beat him up and the police came and arrested him. In the reform school my sister and Marilyn were talking about, there would be no chance for rebellion.

We behaved for Martha the next Saturday. I learned the difference between a noun and a verb. Time, however, was on our side. After Pa saw our report cards and made Martha tutor us, he would forget about it and slowly things got back to normal. He would laugh at Fernando's and my antics around the house. Martha, not enthusiastic about tying up her Saturday mornings, would invent a holiday to give us the day off.

"This last week had St. Francis Xavier's Day, your patron saint, so we won't have class." It got no argument from us. The following Saturday was her patron saint's day. We didn't know if there was a St. Martha but we took her word for it. The lessons came to a quiet end without comment. Then, one of us would do something like sneak into Martha's bed and scare the hell out of her and make her mad, which made us laugh. And so, on it went until we got our next report cards.

13.

3rd Grade – Feliz Navidad
Fernando

"It's not what's under the tree that matters;
it's who's gathered around it."
Truth Follower

"Nah, it's pretty much about the presents."
Armando Garcia

I WILL NEVER FORGET THE CHRISTMAS OF 1957. Armando and I were in the first year of our two-year stint in Mrs. Alexander's third grade. Despite Martha's best efforts in her jerry-rigged garage-classroom, we flunked. Being held back, however, may have not been a bad thing. Several of the boys in that class became career criminals. Two were killed as young men in drug deals gone bad.

Pa loved Christmas, the colored lights in house windows, the music, his children's excitement. The fact that he rarely got gifts didn't bother him. For me, the only day of the year that equaled the last day of school before Christmas was the last day of school before summer vacation. Christmastime also meant that our parents and older sisters would spend a day in the kitchen making tamales.

Ma shopped early in the week before tamale-making day. She put her order in at *El Indio* Market in Old Town San Diego for the cornmeal *masa*. She gathered special ingredients and cooked a large pot of *carne-con-chile*. A few days before Christmas Eve, Ma organized an assembly line on the kitchen table.

Ana and Pa held freshly washed corn husks in one hand and a spoon or butter knife in the other. They scooped the grainy, pink mortar-like *masa* from the clay bowl and wiped a thick coat on the husks. Ma was particular about the correct amount and position of the *masa* on the husks and made them redo any that didn't meet her standards. Too much or too close to the edge and it would seep from the husk while cooking, causing waste and extra cleanup. They handed the smeared husks to Carolyn, who spread a heaping tablespoon of the *carne-con-chile* onto the *masa*. The ratio had to be just right. Then, Carolyn handed the tamale to Martha, who added a few raisins and a black olive then handed them to Ma. Ma folded them as if she were diapering a baby. She placed them in rectangular metal pans like soldiers in formation. Ma and Martha kept the ingredient bowls filled to keep a smooth production going. When enough tamales for a batch were ready, Ma placed them in her pressure cooker, turned the burner on, and began to work on the next batch. This holiday culinary tradition took place in millions of Mexican homes throughout the United States and Mexico.

By the end of the day they had enough tamales to have after midnight Mass, send to Chad and Chris's family, the Tanners, next door, Hector's family, the Torelli's, across the street, and for New Year's Eve when a handful of relatives came over. Mrs. Tanner told Ma that she and her husband fought for the last of the tamales and refried beans.

Pa bought a large-screen TV-and-stereo combo and Bing Crosby's *White Christmas* album with his Christmas bonus. The album had traditional songs and hymns, as well as a lively Irish Christmas jig. After Bing finished crooning, Pa played Alfredo Jimenez and Javier Solis albums while the tamales were assembled. He was as content as he ever was surrounded by his family, a beer within reach, and listening to "Paseo de Guanajuato" or any other of his hundreds of favorite Mexican folk songs. Our home had the wonderful aroma blend of Ma's Mexican food and the sweet scent from our decorated Christmas tree.

Pa begged, borrowed, stole, and worked overtime shifts to give us memorable Christmases. We always got our Christmas tree two weeks before the big day. Every year Pa would spend an hour trying to get a square cut on the tree trunk to make a suitable tree stand. The process involved dull saws, bent nails, and lots of Mexican cuss words. Once the tree was ready, the three of us carried it to the living room. I'd stand back and let Pa know which leg of the stand to shim to make the tree straight. Our sisters did a fine job decorating, as well as Scotch-taping Christmas cards we received through the mail to the living room walls.

"*Andale, vamonos antes que llegamos tarde,*" Ma prodded us. She never in all my years at home allowed us to be late for any Mass, much less the Christmas Eve midnight Mass. We left for church at 11:30.

Three-quarter scale statues of Baby Jesus lying in the straw-lined crib with Mary, Joseph, the Magi, and barn animals looking on stood to one side of the church's entrance. The Star of Bethlehem hovered above. A soft light hidden on the manger ceiling gave the scene a calm, peaceful aura.

We walked in fifteen minutes early; the adult choir was singing religious Christmas songs. Even though we were early, we still had to sit near the back. By the time Mass started, the ushers shoehorned in as many parishioners as possible into the pews then set up folding chairs in the aisles for late arrivals. Those unlucky souls would have to kneel on the marble floor during the consecration and Communion. I was glad Ma got us there early.

Armando and I, unable to stop fidgeting, sat between Ma and Pa. My empty stomach growled, and my mind was on presents. Ma gave me an occasional stare, reminding me that I was to behave. Four-year-old Carmen sat on Ma's lap. Ana, Martha, and Carolyn sat on the other side of Ma. Tony, home from the seminary, sat at the end of the pew.

Once Mass started, the choir sang Latin hymns in earnest, they were way too loud. Four of the most experienced altar boys led monsignor and his two assistant priests from the sacristy to the altar to celebrate the High Mass. The priests wore special advent vestments.

Christmas and Easter services called in the seasonal Catholics, who only attended Mass twice a year. They were easy to spot. They were the people who hesitated before standing, kneeling, or sitting during the service. I saw them take clues from the regulars and follow their lead. These semi-pagans seemed unaware of the sanctity of receiving Communion.

They knelt with the rest of us after receiving the host, oblivious that they were supposed to look pious. They didn't cover their faces with their hands or meditate like me. Although it was hard for me to meditate on Jesus and not think about my present under the tree.

The collection baskets overflowed with cash and the special Christmas envelopes that the parish mailed out the previous week. Did the twice-a-year Catholics hope they could buy their way out of their sin of missing Sunday Masses?

The gospel reading describing the birth of Jesus was too long. A morsel of relief came by Father Vidra, who gave the homily. I was spared the pastor's indecipherable croaking Irish brogue. Thankfully, Father Vidra kept it short, he must have made the choice not to scold the wayward Catholics. An admonishing sermon tonight might affect the Easter collection.

Communion lines were long and slow. Fortunately, all three priests distributed the hosts. Even Pa took Communion on this holy night. I wondered on my way back to our pew if Pa went to the church's mandatory once-a-year confession before receiving. I couldn't imagine him in a confessional. He would either have to lie or spend the afternoon saying his penance.

The High Mass finally ended, the procession of priests and altar boys walked off the altar and back into the sacristy. We made our way out of the pew. The choir screamed *Adeste Fideles*, their voices overwhelming the big organ. I had to take baby steps in the aisle to keep from stepping on someone's heels. I heard unsanctioned conversations as we filed out, undoubtedly from the twice-a-year Catholics, who didn't know they were supposed to be quiet and reverent until out of the church. Holy water ran down the side of the marble font and onto the floor at the door from careless fingers. These seasonal Catholics were getting on my nerves.

The cold December air on my face gave me a rush of new life as I stepped out of the stuffy vestibule. My brother and I raced to the parking lot.

As was his way, Pa lit a cigarette before getting into the driver's seat and Ma nagged him about it, as was her way. After waiting for what seemed like an hour to exit the parking lot, we headed home. It had sprinkled and raindrops on the windows reflected the taillights of the cars ahead, giving the lights a kaleidoscope red star-like quality.

Armando and I sat in the rear cargo area of our station wagon. Spontaneous conversations erupted. "I wonder what those presents from Abe, Conrad, and Gil are?" I said.

"Don't know, but we're going to have to wait till tomorrow morning to find out," Armando said.

"I'm so tired I could fall asleep right now," Carolyn said.

"What do you think you got for Christmas, Carmen?" Tony asked.

"Those cigarettes are going to kill you, Antonio." As usual, Pa ignored the comment from Ma as a wisp of blue-white smoke curled its way toward the back of the car.

We pulled into the driveway and were greeted by the colored lights on our Christmas tree at the window. This was the only time of the year Ma allowed us to waste electricity. As soon as we got into the house, Pa popped open a beer and fired up the stereo. I chose not to tell him that Sister Marie Carl told us that we were supposed to drink water when we got home after receiving communion. I figured that either Jesus was gone by then or He would have to have a beer with Pa. Ma heated and served the tamales to her starving family.

Shortly before going to bed, I took one last look at the tree and wondered what the two long, rectangular boxes with my and Armando's names had in them. Besides our presents, there were three flat, square gifts for our sisters and one small box for Carmen all given to us by our three older boy cousins, Abe, Gil, and Conrad. They had never given us gifts before. Was it because of what my parents had done for them a few years earlier?

My Uncle Sam left his sons in a Catholic orphanage when he got home after WWII. He had divorced and was given custody of his sons, but wasn't able to take care of them. Abe, the oldest of the boys, told me he cried, grabbed his father's leg, and begged him not to leave them. But Sam did. A few months later, Pa and Ma drove to the orphanage and negotiated with the nuns for their release. They brought them to San Diego and got them temporary housing with an aunt. As soon as they were old enough, they each joined a branch of the military. They adored my parents and never forgot what they did for them.

Armando and I idolized our cousins. I had dreams of one day joining the military like they had and valiantly fighting America's enemies. I looked forward to the day I could learn to shoot a real weapon and don a neatly pressed military uniform. My dream was to become a combat hero with medals on my chest. Who knows? I might be wounded and even get more medals. Exhausted and with a full stomach, I walked to our bedroom and crawled into our twin-size bed. My twin slept at the foot, I at the head. I fell into the sleep of the dead.

"It's Christmas." Carmen announced from the door of our bedroom. There was a moment of disorientation as my mind cast out the shadowy webs of my dream. Her words sunk in, it's Christmas! My brother and I rushed to the living room in our T-shirts and pajama bottoms. Martha had already sneaked out of our room and joined Ana and Carolyn who were instructed by Ma to talk softly. Tony was in the bathroom getting ready for the day. Our parents were in the kitchen talking over cups of Nescafé.

I stopped on my way to the kitchen and did a quick check to make sure my gift was still under the tree. "Come on, Pa," I said. He laughed, rose, carried his cup into the living room, and sat on his recliner, Ma on the couch.

Martha knelt near the tree and played Santa Claus, reading the labels and handing out presents. I begged her for mine. She took my present and read the tag. "To Fernando from Abe, Gil, and Conrad." She did the same for my twin. I ripped off the ribbons, gift wrap, and opened the top of the long, cardboard box and turned it upside down. A super cool bolt-action military-style rifle with a dark wood-stained stock, black rubber bayonet, and leather shoulder strap slipped out.

"Oh, man. Wait till the guys see these." It was the best Christmas gift I had ever gotten. I slid my hand down the barrel, over the black bolt, and onto the stock I could hardly wait to get down to the canyon with the neighborhood boys and fight the Japs and Krauts.

Our three sisters freaked when they opened their presents. They each got a record album from our cousins. *The Fabulous*

Fabian for Ana; Carolyn got the new Latin American sensation, Richie Vallens; and Martha the teenage heartthrob, Frankie Avalon. Martha patted her feet on the floor, unable to control her excitement while Ana and Carolyn held their albums against their chests, starry-eyed. Carmen got a glossy colored *Snow-White* book along with a porcelain statue of the fairy tale girl. Tony scored a Super 8 Kodak home movie camera with a projector and screen from Pa. He put batteries in and began filming.

I scoffed at my siblings' presents. Their's paled compared to mine. My brother and I went into action. We grabbed our weapons and stealthily crept in and out of rooms, behind doors, and under tables shooting any family member that posed a threat. I preferred a quick death by bullet as opposed to stabbing them with the bayonet. That seemed too cruel.

"Would you stop that?" Martha scolded after I shot her a second time from behind the recliner. She pushed away the barrel tip of my rifle. Next time I'll use the bayonet.

After opening gifts, Pa put his *Ranchera* album on and Ma made *huevos rancheros y firjoles* with corn tortillas for breakfast. Pa saturated his meal in hot salsa. My brother and I checked our rifles behind the kitchen door, wolfed down our food, ran to our bedroom, and changed into play clothes. We slung our gun straps around our shoulders and raced next door to Chris and Chad's.

The neighbor boys looked at our guns with envious eyes. The four of us were soon in the lower yard engaged in intense combat. Christmas day was a typical mid-sixties San Diego morning, perfect for warfare. My brother and I took turns with our friends using the rifles. The Americans got the cool rifles. The Japanese, attempting to overrun the American defensives, used sticks as theirs. I shot Chris and he had to fall dead and count to five before reemerging as an attacking enemy. Armando and Chris were next to use the rifles. Chad and I attacked. I scaled the fence with my rifle stick in my right hand. I was at the top of the split rail fence when I was hit. I fell forward, mortally wounded, and landed awkwardly on my left hand. I screamed and turned onto my back clutching my wrist.

Chad ran to me. "Are you okay?"

"No," I gasped. I leaned over, wracked in pain, holding my hand to my chest as I began to hobble home.

"Can I still use your rifle?"

"I don't care."

"He must really be hurt.," Armando said.

I made my way to the kitchen. Pa was having another coffee. "Pa, I'm hurt." He reached for my hand, gently stretched and turned my arm.

"It doesn't look too bad. Try opening and closing your fist." I tried but it hurt too much. "Maybe you just need to rest it a little."

"But, Pa, it hurts a lot." Ma came over to take a look. She went to her bedroom and came out with her *Mentolato* and an elastic cloth bandage. It hurt when she daubed my wrist. She asked Tony to wrap it.

"I'll be really careful, *cuate*. Just tell me if I'm wrapping it too tight," he said. After two tries he managed to put it on just tight enough to give me support without too much pain. I went to my room and lay on my bed. I heard my sisters in the living room taking turns with the stereo turntable. I wanted to sleep but the pain wouldn't allow it. I took another look at my arm. My hand had turned purple. I went back into the kitchen, cradling it, and showed Pa.

"It doesn't look good, Carolina."

Ma sighed. *"Llevalo al doctor."*

Pa drove me to the emergency room; I had never been in a hospital. The X-ray showed a fractured bone in my wrist. Two hours later we walked out of the hospital. A plaster cast covered my forearm and wrist and wrapped around the base of my thumb. The ER doc who set my cast gave me pills for the pain.

My sisters and brothers looked curiously at my cast. No one in the family had ever had one before. They were relieved that my arm had been taken care of and signed my cast with a felt-tip pen. My twin didn't sign; I think he was envious. The year before he had contracted pneumonia and got to spend a week at the hospital and got lots of attention from everybody.

Ma had us kneel and pray in front of the statue of St. Jude for his recovery. I prayed for him even though I was jealous. The attention I got from my cast evened the score.

Ma prepared a ham, given to Pa by his company, for dinner. My brother and I sat at the table with our rifles slung over the backs of our chairs. We fell into bed early that evening. I was exhausted from lack of sleep the previous night, my roller-coaster day, and the intense combat.

Armando and I laid our rifles under the bed and the bayonets under our pillows in the event of a surprise enemy attack. I had to lie in an awkward position to accommodate my cast.

The pain slowly returned as the second dose of medication began to wear off. I complained to Ma, she gave me another pill and told me to go back to bed. As the medication began to do its magic I relaxed. I had second thoughts about becoming a wounded combat soldier as I waited for sleep. The medals and glory were not as seductive as they had been before. I drifted off to sleep with Bing Crosby singing "Christmas in Killarney" on the new stereo.

14.

4th Grade – The Roaring Roadmaster
Fernando

"There will always be cars and a need for good mechanics."
Antonio Mendoza Garcia

ARMANDO WALKED UP THE DRIVEWAY weighed down with shopping bags filled with empty soda bottles. We had been collecting them for two weeks and hit a bonanza from our sisters' party the night before. The three-cent deposit per bottle meant that we had enough buying power to get a serious amount of candy: Look candy bars, Abba-Zabas, Big Hunks, a mother lode. The fact that it was Saturday made our upbeat tempo even happier. No school, no church, and there was a full day separating us from another five-day school week.

"What's up, *muchachos*?" Pa asked, lifting the long, heavy, steel hood of the family's white 1953 Buick Roadmaster. The car had big, wide whitewall tires with shiny hubcaps. The vertical gleaming chrome bars of the grille resembled the teeth of a predatory dinosaur. One of the bars was gone when Pa bought the car, giving it the appearance of a missing tooth. Its horn was as big and loud as Texas. In a choir, Japanese and European cars would have been altos; the Buick's horn was a deep, deafening baritone.

"Hold on a minute, let me show you something." My shoulders drooped. I was anxious to get to our shopping spree.

"It'll just take a minute." But Pa's lessons never took *just a minute*. I dreaded we were in for one of his moments to teach us something that I couldn't care less about. "What do you boys want to be when you grow up?"

"Oh, a soldier, I guess," I answered, trying to keep the exchange short.

"And you, *Chato*? What do you think you want to do?"

"A football player," he answered half-heartedly.

"Can we go now?"

"Just hang on a minute, did I ever tell you about the time that I loaned my car to a friend in Mexico?"

The bottles made a sorrowful clink as we set them down.

Our bags of gold looked at me yearning to be spent. And had we ever heard the story about the time that he loaned his car to his friend Juan, who forgot to put enough oil in the engine even though Pa had reminded him to do it and how the motor was ruined and then Juan fixed it so it ran like a clock? Only about a thousand times, the car always ran like a stupid clock when Juan got done.

Pa started his story as he poked his head in and out from under the hood.

"I told my friend Juan to be sure to check the oil before using the car. He didn't and wound up burning the motor. He felt terrible about it, so you know what he did?" *Yeah, I know what he did.* "He fixed it himself." *Yeah, he pushed it under a tree.* "He pushed the car under a tree, threw a chain over a big sturdy branch, hooked it up to the engine, and pulled it out with a pulley," blah, blah, blah. "The car ran like a clock after he was done."

We acted interested and oohed and aahed as he came to the climax of the story. As I listened, I imagined the big branch giving way and pictured it, along with the engine, fall on top of Juan, squashing him like a *cucaracha*. Now, that would have been a story worth listening to again.

"Wow, Pa, that was great," Armando said bending over and reaching for the bags.

Pa eyed him. "Hang on. Look, Armando, Fernando—" he used our full names when he wanted to make an important point, hoping that we'd pay better attention. But our diminutive attention spans were exhausted by the time Pa mentioned Juan's name. I want you two to think about the three of us opening a car repair shop when you get older. As long as there are cars, there'll always be a need for mechanics."

"Great idea, Pa," Armando said. "Can we go now?" Pa either didn't hear my brother's plea or chose to ignore it. We were in for career counseling whether we wanted it or not.

"Look here, boys, I'll show you how to put oil in the car. I'll be back in just a minute." My twin and I looked at each other with an, *aw crap*, look.

Pa walked into his garage. An out-of-commission commercial-size floor freezer took up part of one section of the back wall. It was given to him in trade years earlier from a store owner friend who owed Pa money. The shop keeper said, "It's a good freezer, it just doesn't work." Claiming another portion of the floor was a three-speed bicycle without wheels, Ma's Kirby vacuum cleaner that Pa insisted on repairing and our Aunt Sara's chamber pot that she used when she came to visit and caused me to gag every time I saw it. There was an ancient mechanical key cash register, inherited from Pa's older sister Maria, undoubtedly, from one of her and her husband Al's failed businesses. Perhaps Pa thought the register would come in handy when Garcia & Sons Auto Repair opened.

Pa entered the garage and hit the on/off light switch, careful not to touch the metal casing. The casing had a short that shocked fingers. My twin and I learned that lesson, once each. Pa disappeared into the maze and came out with a quart of motor oil, a can opener, and a dirty shop rag. He stopped at the front of the car, tapped the front bumper, and said, "Jump up here, boys."

We put a foot on the bumper, a hand on the grimy radiator, and pulled ourselves up. I stood on one side of Pa, Armando on the other.

Pa rolled up the sleeves of the frayed woolen plaid shirt that he wore on Saturdays. He ducked his head under the hood and reached for a small metal handle. He pulled out a flat, thin metal rod as long as my arm from a tube that disappeared into the mysterious workings of the engine. "This is the dipstick." He took the rag, wrapped it around the stick, and wiped off the slimy black oil. "We're going to check the oil level." He slid the stick back into the tube and pulled it out.

"How do you know if the motor needs oil," I asked.

Pa held the stick for us to see. "When the oil mark is below this line it means your engine is a quart low. Never let the oil get below this line. That's what happened when I lent Juan my car." I stared at the end of the stick, intrigued. It was plain to see the relation between the mark left by the oil and the mark on the dipstick. I had just learned how to check the oil level. Pretty cool. I looked to my brother, he was picking his nose and staring down at the bags of soda bottles.

Pa grabbed a grimy black cap from the top of the engine and unscrewed it. I looked over at my brother again. He rolled his eyes, put a hand over his mouth miming a yawn. I turned away and hid my laughter. He climbed off the bumper, walked to the car door, and slid into the driver's seat.

"He's never going to learn," Pa muttered. "Now, pay attention." He held up the cap. "This is the oil filler-tube cap." He set it on top of a round metal disc the size of a platter and about four inches tall. I stared and wondered what it was. Pa noticed, reached over and tapped it, "This is the air filter housing."

While Pa was opening the top of the can of oil I sneaked a look at my brother through the small opening between the hood and the body of the car. He had reached under the seat and grabbed one of Pa's empty beer cans that were stashed to hide from Ma. My brother held the can in one hand and a cigarette butt from the ashtray in the other, pretending to drive. He looked at me, brought the can to his lips, and pantomimed a deep drink, then wiped his lips with his forearm. It was hard not to burst out laughing.

"This is the spout where you pour the oil in," Pa said. I was impressed. I didn't know Pa knew so much about auto mechanics. Maybe Pa was on to something with his repair shop idea.

The steering wheel shaft under the hood moved side to side. I took another peek. My brother was turning the steering wheel. The beer can was gone, but he was wearing Pa's wire-rimmed sunglasses and had the cigarette butt hanging loosely from his lips.

Pa, engrossed in his activity, didn't notice. He slowly and carefully put the rim of the oil can to the mouth of the oil filler tube and tilted the can. The oil oozed out. "When you pour the oil into the filler tube, be very careful not to get it on the engine. If oil gets onto the hot exhaust manifold, it'll burn and make a lot of smoke."

"BLAAAAAA" went the Roadmaster's mighty horn. I reeled. Pa jumped, banging his head on the underside of the hood. His hand jerked. A stream of oil covered part of the engine.

"*Ay cabron!*" he yelled. He pulled back the can of oil and hollered, "Get out of the car!" I tried to think of something sad . . . real sad. The car door slowly opened and closed. My brother shuffled around wearing a "I'm sorry" look.

"You're hopeless," Pa said sharply and waved his hand dismissively. "Go on, get out of here."

I jumped off the bumper. We grabbed the bags of bottles and slinked out of the driveway. Once on the sidewalk, we started walking as fast as the heavy bags allowed. We broke out laughing as soon as we were out of Pa's earshot.

"You don't know when not to fool around," I stammered.

"I didn't mean to scare him. I just leaned on the metal ring inside the steering wheel. I didn't know it was part of the horn." Two blocks later my brother pointed. "Look!" Pa passed us in the Roadmaster trailing clouds of smoke.

15.

4th Grade – First Day
Fernando

"Blessed are the merciful for they shall obtain mercy."
Jesus Christ

"SEE YOU AFTER SCHOOL, MA," I YELLED.

"*Adios, mijos, tienen quidado,*" Ma shouted from the kitchen. "And don't be so hard on your shoes this year, try to make them last."

Armando and I walked out the front door to begin the trek to St. Rita's for our first day of fourth grade. Our pace was brisk. We walked with mixed emotions, excited to see our friends and looked forward to recess periods, but dreading the long hours in the classroom, homework assignments, and tests that we never seemed to be prepared for. For the first time since kindergarten, we walked without any of our siblings. Martha, who had graduated from grammar school, joined our older sisters at Regina Celi, the all-girls Catholic high school. We went along Euclid Avenue toward Market Street, toting our new three-ring binders. Inside the binder was a three-ring plastic bag with pens, number two pencils, and an eraser.

The mid-September morning was cloudless, the air heavy and warm, foretelling the ninety-degree temperatures we would have to deal with on our walk home. We wore short-sleeved uniform shirts and heavy brown corduroy pants. We wouldn't need our uniform cardigan sweaters for another two months. Ma insisted that we wear a t-shirt underneath our shirts. *"Solamente los frescos no se ponen una camisa sin camiseta."* (Only sissies wear a shirt without a t-shirt.) I was glad that Ma was so wise about the ways of the world.

"I'm sure happy we finally got out of Mrs. Alexander's class," Armando said stepping out of the driveway and onto the unpaved shoulder of the street.

"Me, too. I hope this year isn't too hard. I wonder what Sister Lucille is going to be like?"

"I don't know, but I don't think I want to get in trouble with her."

"Me either."

Sister Marie Lucille appeared to be in her mid-twenties. Her tall form was magnified by her flowing black-and-white habit. She had a pale, stern look and a deceptive look of ill temper. Her deep blue eyes looked small, piercing, offset by her large lips. I felt intimidated when I saw her around school during our two years in third grade.

My brother picked up the baseball-sized rock he had hidden in the weeds on the last day of third grade. He dropped it and gave it a hard kick, continuing the competition we started last year. The challenge was to keep the rock in front of us so as not to have to veer off our path. If your kick kept the rock directly in front, you got another try. If it veered too far to either side, it was your opponent's turn. The one with the most straight kicks won. It was only the first day of school and the toes of our new brown leather shoes were already scuffed.

At the bottom of the hill, we looked up at the large billboard sign. A beautiful suggestively dressed woman held a lit cigarette between bright red-nailed fingers. An oversized red-and- white pack of cigarettes floated next to her hand. "Lucky Strike Means Fine Tobacco," read the caption.

I'm never going to smoke or let my kids or wife smoke when I get older," I said.

"Me, too."

"Pa says he wishes he never started." I looked up and down the road, no cars were in sight. I walked over to the huge sign, picked up a dirt clod, threw it at the woman, and scored a hit to her forehead.

"Good one," Armando said, admiring the dirty mark.

We turned left into a neighborhood of lower middle-class homes. Most of the houses were in need of paint and repair.

"Hey, look." I pointed to two dogs behind a rickety four-foot- tall chain-link fence. They seemed to be attached. One dog had mounted the other from behind and panted as he moved his hips in short, quick, rhythmic thrusts.

"What are they doing?" my brother asked.

I thought for a moment. "I think maybe the back dog has fleas. He must be scratching." We stood watching the unusual behavior for a few seconds, shrugged our shoulders, and continued our rock kicking toward the unknown school year. I felt a pang of pity for the afflicted animal and petitioned St. Francis, the patron saint of animals, to help him with his fleas.

We got near school and my brother hid the rock under a juniper bush. We crossed Imperial Avenue, walked past the Shell gas station and to the front of the parish church. We entered through the large wooden double doors and left the bright sun, traffic noise, and morning heat behind and into the dim cool vestibule. We dipped our fingers in the marble holy water font and made the sign of the cross on ourselves and made our way into the high-ceiling sanctuary of the church. The children's 8:15 Mass was half-over. My brother leaned into my ear.

"We'll leave the house ten minutes later tomorrow."

The school children were arranged by class. The eighth, sixth, fourth, and second grades on the right side of the church and the odd number grades on the left. The older grades sat toward the back and the younger to the front.

I saw the unmistakable towering figure of Sister Marie Lucille sitting behind her fourth-grade students. We walked down the side aisle and made our way to her section and sidled into one of the pews. I stole a quick glance at our new teacher. I thought I detected a hint of a smile as we made eye contact.

The Guamanian fraternal twins Joe and Louie Sablan were in the pew. Joe was shorter and heavier than his lanky brother; about the only things the twins had in common were their coloring, slanted eyes, and age. They smiled when they saw us. Their white teeth contrasted starkly with their dark complexions. I smiled back. It was good to see them.

Ginny Maher knelt in the pew in front of me. She wore a kelly-green sleeveless jumpsuit with a white uniform blouse underneath like every other girl in the school. Her matching green military overseas cap sat neatly on her head. Ginny was pretty and fun to talk to. I had fantasized over the summer what it would be like to kiss her but kept that secret to myself.

I wanted to express my affections to her last year but was too shy. I threw a dodge ball at her during recess, a common ploy used by the younger boys in the school to get a girl's attention. I was careful not to throw the ball too hard and aimed for her legs. The ball grazed her uniform skirt causing it to flit above her knee. She seemed flattered and smiled at me. I panicked and ran back to the dodge ball court with my heart aflutter. I saw James Riley talking to her on the playground a day later. During the dodgeball game I threw the ball at him with all my might and aimed for his head.

Father McGinn, the short, red-haired Irish priest, was saying Mass. He faced the altar in his green-and-gold vestments. He was dwarfed by the huge magnificent, crucified Christ above him. Jesus's hands and feet were stained with blood, his eyes shut. Blood ran from his crown of thorns and the stab wound in His side. Since this was a daily Mass, we wouldn't have to sit through one of Father McGinn's boring sermons.

The Mass ended and the students filed out, one pew at a time, forming long unbroken lines. Every student dipped his fingers into the holy water as he exited the side door blessing themselves again. Teachers followed their classes. We marched over the black asphalt playground in silence and formed neat military-style squares, each grade level standing with his classmates. We faced the flagpole put our hands over our hearts and recited the Pledge of Allegiance.

Due to overcrowding, the fourth and fifth grades were in makeshift classrooms in the cool basement of the church. The main school building was across the playground the length of a football field away.

Sister Lucille led us to her classroom and stood at the front as we filed in. She had neatly printed our names on slips of colored construction paper and folded them into name plates and set them on the desks. "Please find your seats." I was disappointed that Armando and I were seated at opposite ends of the room. To my left sat fidgety John Paulson, a royal pain in the neck and a snitch. To my astonishment, Ginny was seated to my right, a mere arm's length away. She looked over at me and smiled. I smiled back, nearly melting onto the floor. I wondered what I could do to impress her.

"Welcome, everyone. I am Sister Marie Lucille." Her name was perfectly printed at the top of the chalkboard behind her. "I have been looking forward to having you in my class this year. Now, stand and we'll say the Morning Offering."

We stood, made the sign of the cross and folded our hands. "O Jesus, through the Immaculate Heart of Mary, I offer to You my prayers, works, joys, and sufferings of this day . . ."

After praying, Sister told us to sit and started our first lesson. "Please take out your religion books." Our textbooks were neatly stacked on the shelf under our desk seats in the order we would be using them.

Another school year began. As I reached for my book, I said my own prayer. *Dear Jesus, Mary, and Joseph, I have already fought the devil on my way to school, been to Mass and offered this day up to You. Maybe this year I can get a B in something . . . anything.*

Sister Lucille was not shy about disciplining as I soon found out.

I sat behind big Kenny Wright, ducked, and whispered across the aisle. "Hey, Ginny." She looked over. "Do you think John Paulson's face hurts?" She shrugged. "Because it's killing me." She dropped her head, a muffled chuckle escaped. Bingo! Fourth grade was off to a great start.

Sister looked over and walked straight to me. All eyes followed her. She stopped in the aisle and locked her eyes on me through her thick lenses. She held my gaze for an eternity. I swallowed. She spoke quietly and calmly, "Fernando, would you like to share with the principal what was so important that it could not wait until recess?" Her words came in a slow, unsettling cadence.

"No, Sister," I said weakly. She stood expressionless for a moment then walked back to the front of the room and began the lesson. The rest of the day in the classroom flowed smoothly.

The tone was set for the rest of the year.

I heard a soft giggle and looked over. It was John Paulson; he was giddy that I had gotten in trouble.

The first day of fourth grade came to an end and we started our walk home. He got the rock out from under the bush. We talked about what happened in class that morning. "That would have been really bad if Sister had sent you to the principal, especially on the first day. Sister Constance would have let you have it but good."

"Yeah, I was really scared. That jerk John Paulson liked it that I got in trouble. He laughed at me."

"He's not right in the head," Armando said.

I began to strategize of a way I could get back at him without getting in trouble. John was a straight-A student in the classroom and an outcast on the playground. "If you knew that John was in purgatory, would you pray for his soul?" I asked.

"Probably not."

Then as an afterthought I added, "I sure as heck wouldn't pray for Sister Constance either."

MY LAST KICK VEERED OFF THE SIDE, it was my twin's turn, I was two strokes behind. An intriguing thought came to me. "Sister Lucille is kind of scary but there is something I like about her but I'm not sure what it is."

Fortunately, my brother's first kick veered onto the shoulder of the road. I smiled and walked over to take my turn.

"Hey, look at this," I said. On the dirt shoulder of the road lay a flattened lizard in perfect condition. I picked it up and blew the loose grit and dust from its gray, stiff body.

"I bet the poor little guy never saw the car coming."

Except for its eyes, the wafer-thin lizard was complete, head to tail. Even its toothpick-like fingers were still attached. The smell of rotting flesh was long gone.

"That's how I want to go," I said.

"You want to get run over by a car?"

"No, stupid, I want to die so fast that I won't feel anything when it happens." I slipped the lizard into my shirt pocket.

"Do you think lizards go to heaven or hell?" my brother said. "I don't think so. Heaven and hell are probably only for people." We walked in silence for a few minutes. I grappled with why animals wouldn't be allowed into heaven. That didn't seem fair somehow. "Maybe if it was a really good animal like some of St. Francis's pets, maybe they get to go to heaven." I pulled the lizard out of my pocket, held it up and looked into its face.

"Were you a good boy?" My brother laughed. I slipped it back into my shirt pocket; its tail peeked over the top.

"What are you going to do with your lizard?" I detected envy in his voice.

"Don't know."

His eyes lit up. "Hey, we can scare Martha with it."

"Maybe."

"We should give it a name. How about Chopper?" Armando said.

"That's pretty good." I thought for a few seconds. "What do you think of Slimy?"

"He's not really very slimy. How about Dusty?"

"That's a good one, too." We were making progress. I took the lizard back out of my pocket and gave him another look.

"Slim" I said.

"Yeah, Slim." The matter was settled. I put Slim in the three-ring plastic bag of my binder along with my extra pens and pencils. I would have to keep Slim a secret since Ma wouldn't allow us to have animals.

My fourth-grade year was off to a good start. I made Ginny laugh, I could have gotten into serious trouble but didn't, and I finally had a pet.

Sister Lucille encouraged her students to read and allowed class time to go to the school library and check out books. Over the summer, Tony, always the educator, marched us to the city library's bookmobile parked in front of our church and helped us pick out a book each. More recently he had suggested *Tom Sawyer* to me. Not wanting to miss an opportunity to get out of class, I raised my hand to get permission to go to the library. I walked across campus to the main school building.

One girl from each grade was chosen to be the check-out person. The fourth grade had Thursday afternoons. Sister Lucille chose Ginny as our library girl. We were allowed to break the silence rule and ask questions while in the library.

I stepped into the room. Book-laden shelves covered three of the four walls. Ginny sat at the check-out table; her head was bowed over a book.

"Hi, Ginny."

She looked surprised. "Oh, hi, Fernando."

"Do you know if you have *Tom Sawyer* in here?"

"I think we do. Just look over there in the novel section. The books are in alphabetical order according to author, so look in the T section for Mark Twain." She smiled as she talked. I saw her lips form the words, the same lips I had dreamed about over the summer.

I went over and ran my fingers across the book titles. I slowly, deliberately perused the books, I removed some and read the titles as if interested in them.

I stole glances at Ginny. Not able to justify procrastinating any longer, I pulled *Tom Sawyer* from the shelf and made my way to the check-out table. I tried to think of something clever to say.

"Well, I found it."

She smiled again when I handed her the book. She took the check-out card from the sleeve on the inside cover, stamped the due date, slipped it back in, and handed me the book. My hand grazed hers as we made the exchange—a jolt ran up my arm. "See you back in class," I said.

"Okay," she said.

I floated back to class.

When I got to my desk, I discreetly took Slim out of the plastic bag in my binder and put him behind the first page of my library book. I had to be careful John didn't see me, no doubt he would have snitched. Slim made a perfect bookmark.

I opened *Tom Sawyer* that night in bed and read the first few pages. Two weeks later the check-out period expired, and I had to return the book without knowing what happened after page five. I would have to wait until the next check-out day to see how the story turned out.

I didn't realize that Sister Lucille secretly loved my brother and me. We learned years later that we made her laugh often. One afternoon we were busy writing an assignment while Sister sat at her desk grading papers. John Paulson saw me whisper to Ginny. He raised a hand and pointed a finger within an inch of my nose. John sucked in air loudly to draw Sister's attention.

Just as she looked up, I snapped my teeth, biting John's finger. He let out a squeal. All heads turned, I froze with his finger in my mouth. I let go and realized that Sister saw what had happened. Ginny buried her face in her hands. Someone gasped.

Sister, John and I were locked in a three-way stare. Our eyes shifted, Sister to John, John to me, me to Sister, John to Sister, me to John.

Sister's beady eyes widened.

Oh, crap! Here it comes.

She dropped her head, it began to bob up and down.

John sat with a confused look on his dumb backstabbing face.

Sister sprang from her chair, turned to the blackboard, grabbed a piece of chalk, and wrote the spelling words for our homework assignment. Her penmanship was not as neat as it normally was. After writing the words she sat back down and did not look up from her desktop. I sighed with relief and copied the spelling words.

"And you didn't get in trouble?" my brother asked on the way home.

"No, and it looked like Sister was laughing." He thought for a minute. "I like Sister Lucille."

"Me, too."

Sister Mary Constance organized a surprise school play to honor our pastor, Monsignor Gallagher, for the twenty-fifth

anniversary of his ordination. The principal was always looking for ways to curry favor with him. She seemed nervous
around him and laughed extra hard when he tried to be funny.
I never saw her suck up to anyone but him.

The fourth grade was tasked with providing five Indian
dancers for the play, complete with costumes and headbands
with two feathers. The rest of the fourth grade was to back up
the Indians with song.

I was one of the honored five chosen by Sister Lucille. She
sent a costume pattern home for the mothers to follow. Ma
did a fine job making my brown outfit. She attached matching
brown fringes down the long shirt sleeves and along the side
of the pant legs. I went to the hobby store and bought a leather
moccasin kit and meticulously assembled it. I was proud of
my outfit.

Our dance rehearsals were held during class time in a
small storage room two doors down from our classroom. Sister
patiently taught us the song and moves that involved hopping
from foot to foot while dancing in a circle as we chopped the
air with wooden tomahawks.

Donald Sims, a scrawny black kid with a big head and large
pearly white teeth, was one of the dancers. Louie Sablan was
the chief. The other two dancers, Tommy Cohen and Tubby
Rice, had snow-white complexions. Tubby was as chubby as
Donald was skinny.

Sister held our Indian dance practices on Thursday afternoons. On one of our practice days, Ginny, as usual, was
checking books in and out of the library. Ginny walked into
our rehearsal unannounced carrying a book that looked
strangely familiar to me. She looked ashy-white throw-up sick.
She opened Tom Sawyer to page five, tilted the book and Slim
slithered onto the floor.

Before I could think, I blurted out, "My bookmark." I froze.

Sister looked down at Slim, then up at me, then back to slim. "May I have that?"

"Yeah—I mean, yeah sure—I mean yes, Sister."

Sister calmly got up from her chair, reached for a book, picked Slim off the floor, placed him in the book, and walked back to the front of the room. She excused Ginny to go back to the library. Ginny, without uttering a word, turned and exited. Sister continued our rehearsal.

"Boys, sing along with me and do your dance one more time, 'With tom-tom and tomahawk . . .'"

Sister never mentioned the incident to me again. Ginny never smiled at me again.

I described the Slim incident to my brother on the way home. "And then Sister asked me if she could have him."

"Did you give him to her?" "Of course I did, stupid."

He looked at me incredulously. "And she didn't get mad?"

"No. She just picked him up and put him in her book."

He shook his head, "Wow."

We agreed that we *really, really* liked Sister Lucille. The possibility that Sister might like us never crossed our minds.

We figured that she had a well-hidden sense of humor and that she might use the lizard to scare the hell out of Sister Alvira Marie, the short, feisty first-grade teacher, and her best friend. We kept an eye out the rest of the walk home, hoping to find another bookmark.

Our school production was held in the small, stuffy parish hall. It was a rousing success. Each of the eight grades had a short act to perform. The school and parish staffs attended, as well as parents who had a child in the production. I didn't understand why American Natives were included in the show. I wondered if one of Monsignor's assignments had been at an Indian reservation church.

I did the dance but had to lip sync when we finished dancing and the Indians and supporting fourth-grade chorale broke out into a rousing chorus of "When Irish Eyes Are Smiling." Sister Lucille told me during a rehearsal that I was throwing off too many of the singers around me.

The pastor cocked his head back and laughed. I saw his gold-crowned molars. Guamanian Louie, front and center with his arms crossed, dark hair and complexion, slanted eyes and full Indian chief feathered headdress nearly pulled off looking like an Indian. Donald, with his big, gleaming smile and horn-rimmed glasses, looked like a brainy, skinny black kid swimming in an Indian costume. He had trouble keeping his moccasins from slipping off and had to drag his feet. Only his headband stayed in place. Tubby's belly wobbled through his costume as he danced.

The three boys drew the crowd's attention and undoubtedly were why the fourth grade got loud applause and beaming smiles. Sister Lucille's face went from worry to elation as she heard the crowd's reaction. This production would be my first and only live performance on a stage. It was good to go out on top.

It was during fourth grade that my brother and I became altar boys. I was excited at the prospect of donning the altar server's black cassock and white surplice and serving Mass in front of the school. Sister must have been proud of her twin students when we finally served daily Mass. Little doubt Sister Constance scoffed at the idea that these two playground delinquents were able to achieve this coveted, holy rank. It must have irked her when she knelt at the Communion rail and I held the brass paten under her double chin. I accidentally poked her Adam's apple with the paten and her eyes fluttered.

Sister Lucille graded Armando and my work with a kind pencil. She wrote helpful notes in the margins and took extra time with us when we struggled. I earned a steady diet of C's and C pluses. I nearly got a B in English and managed to only get one D, in math, on my first report card and was able to bring that up to a C minus on my second. The Holy Family sort of answered the prayer I had made at the beginning of the year. I got a B in behavior.

Sister Lucille's love and confidence of her twin students more than made up for Constance's distrust and admonishments.

When Pa went over our report cards at the end of fourth grade, he didn't say a word about Martha having to tutor us in the garage that summer.

16.

4th Grade – Sister Marie Lucille
Armando

PRIEST: "*Intoibo ad altare Dei.*" I will go in unto the altar of God.
ALTAR BOY: "*Ad De' um qui lae ti fi cat ju vent u tem me' am.*" To God, Who giveth joy to my youth.
Opening prayers in the liturgy of the Mass

I WAS AFRAID OF SISTER MARIE LUCILLE. She was tall, wore wire-rim glasses with really thick lenses that made her eyes look way too small for her face. She had fat, blimp-like lips, and a menacing stare that made kids tremble. I had seen her use it on my friend Donny in the hallway last year when he was acting up. He told me later that he dreamed about it that night. Summer had come to an end and the new school year had started with Sister Lucille as my new fourth-grade teacher.

She assigned everyone their seat on the first day of school, gave a short welcome, and started right in on teaching. Sister had us take the religion books from the shelves under our desks. The religion book was on top of the math, geography, and English books. When time came for the morning recess Sister told the boys to remain in the classroom. Did we all already mess up? Or maybe she was going to tell us what would happen to us if we *did*.

Boys," Sister said as soon as the girls left, "you are old enough now to become altar boys. It's a great honor bestowed on you by the Church." I was intrigued. I'd seen the older boys of the school serve Mass and I thought that they looked cool wearing cassocks and surplices (cassock—a long, black dress-like garment; and a surplice: a collarless, loose-fitting shirt worn over the cassock.) "In order to be eligible you must memorize the Latin responses to the prayers that the priest says during Mass. You must also learn proper sanctuary deportment, like how to enter the sanctuary." (The sacred place in church where the altar and tabernacle are located. The tabernacle is a locked box, usually made of polished brass, where consecrated hosts that are Jesus are kept.)

"You must learn deportment in the sacristy." (Where altar boys and priests put on garments for celebrating Mass.) "A boy must learn at what time during the service to take the prayer missal that Father reads from one side of the altar to the other, when to take the cruets containing water and wine, the wash bowl, and a drying towel to Father so he can wash his hands and bless the wine; a boy must know when to ring bells when Father consecrates the host into Christ's body."

My head was spinning, thinking of all that I would have to learn to become a part of this honored group. If I could, then I'd get to wear a cassock and surplice like the big boys, plus my friends and family would see me on the altar doing all of that really cool holy stuff.

Sister handed out cards. Written on them were the Latin prayers and responses. What Father said was in black ink, and the altar boy responses were in red. There was a lot of red. The task that lay ahead of me was daunting. I mean, it was hard enough for me to try and memorize catechism questions that were in English, let alone Latin. Things didn't seem to stick in my head as easily as it did for other kids, as my report cards would attest. But I had to give it a shot.

"You have until the beginning of January to learn what it will take for you to become an altar boy and serve Mass," Sister said, then excused us. I put the card with the responses in my religion book and went out to play.

Fernando and I talked on our walk home from school and decided that we'd be altar boys. We tried reading the Latin written on the card when we got home but soon realized that we couldn't pronounce the words, let alone memorize them, and our after-school playtime with our neighborhood friends took precedence over most anything else in our lives. But I wanted to be an altar boy bad enough to keep trying to read and memorize the Latin by myself. After a few days I gave up, figuring that I had all the way to January to do so.

The autumn months passed one after another. December brought Christmas vacation and Christmas dreams, what presents I might get, dreams that replaced those of becoming an altar boy.

Another wonderful part of Christmas was that my older brother, whom I looked up to, would be home for his Christmas vacation from the seminary. It was toward the end of our big brother's time home that Fernando got the idea to ask Tony to help him learn the Latin responses. Tony knew a lot of Latin from his studies, and he had also been an altar boy as a kid. Fernando was able get them memorized. I asked Tony to help me when he was done with my twin, but his vacation time ended before he had a chance to work with me.

Fernando approached Father Vidra, the assistant pastor in charge of the altar boys, as soon as we returned to school in January and asked him if he would get one of the bigger altar boys to train him with all that a guy had to do during Mass. Soon after, Fernando served his first Mass. Now I really, really wanted to be an altar boy and join him in being a part of this elite group and serve alongside him, but I felt defeated. I asked Fernando to help me but he'd get frustrated because it was taking me so long to learn the first lines and he wanted to go out and play.

Sister Lucille approached me at a noon recess. "I spoke with your sister Martha. She tells me that you're having trouble memorizing the Latin responses. Is this true?"

"Yes, Sister. I tried but they just don't want to stick in my head."

"And that's why I haven't seen you serving Mass with Fernando?"

I hung my head, "Yes, Sister." But she, being my teacher, had to know that I had a hard time learning.

"Would you like my help?"

I looked up at her little eyes through her lenses. "Yeah! I mean, yes, Sister, I'd like that a lot."

"If you can stay after school we can begin tomorrow. And bring the card with the Latin prayers with you." "Cool, Sister!"

Sister had me walk with her around the playground after classes. She read a line in Latin and had me repeat it. We must have made an odd-looking pair, the tall Caucasian woman impeccably dressed in an immaculately ironed black-and-white habit, and me, a scruffy short Mexican-American kid in his school uniform bearing the signs of hard play: shirt missing buttons and well-worn corduroy pants with patches on the knees.

Sister read Father's opening prayer then the altar boy's response. "*Ad deum qui lae ti fi cat ju ven tu tem me um.*" I repeated it. She read it again adding another line. When we got through the response, she had me try and recite it in its entirety. I was embarrassed not remembering what I had just recited to her. She never showed signs of annoyance or frustration but calmly repeated the line as many times as necessary. Sister worked patiently with me for an hour each day. Over and over, I recited the responses. Then came the Confiteor, a long, hard prayer to memorize. It took over of a week to get the Confiteor firmly imprinted in my brain. Father Vidra was surprised when I told him that I had the Latin memorized. He drilled me on a couple of the responses then hit me with the Confiteor. I nailed it. A surprised smile spread across his face. He assigned Gil Titano, who was a grade ahead of me, to do the altar training.

Gil had me meet him in the church during lunch recess. He was the opposite of Sister Lucille.

Gil raced through the Mass procedures. I think he was more interested in going to play basketball with than having to teach. Father Vidra assigned me to serve my first Mass the next Saturday, at 6:30 in the morning, then continue to serve the early Masses from Monday to Friday. Father skipped having me serve Sunday Masses because they were longer, and he needed boys with experience.

The early morning service was good training ground for rookie altar boys to get their feet wet since there were only the school's nuns and a handful of devotees that attended them.

I was in a near panic the night before my first Mass. Except for knowing the Latin, I was nowhere near ready to serve. To not show up, was not an option. I asked Fernando that night to coach me. He tried but there wasn't time enough. He said that he'd go to the church with me the next morning for moral support.

Our Ma gave us a holler at 5:30 but she didn't have to. When I saw the grey before dawn, I couldn't get back to sleep. I thought of stories I'd heard about priests who openly scolded altar boys during the service when they made mistakes. I was likely to be humiliated in front of those attending Mass. Word would surely get around school and the parish about what a lousy job I did. Ma wished me good luck as we walked out of the house. We didn't mention how ill prepared I was. We started the walk to the church. Fernando tried to ease my anxiety, he said that I'd do okay, but I feared the worst. When we got to the church,

Fernando walked in the front doors. I made my way around to the rear side entrance and into the sacristy. I hung my head and walked in. David Lehr, a fifth-grader who had served a lot of Masses, would be the second altar boy. There were always two servers. I confided in him that I had no idea what to do while we put on our cassocks and surplices.

"You've seen a lot of Masses, right?"

"Yeah."

"So you've seen how at the start of Mass the altar boys follow Father to the altar and then kneel on either side of him, then do all the things that they have to do, right?"

"Yeah."

"So it isn't so hard. You already know a lot just from seeing it so many times. Don't worry. When you're not sure what to do, just look at me and I'll signal you."

I wanted to kiss him. David nodded toward a counter. "Your first job before Mass starts, is to take out the cruets, wash bowl and little towel that Father uses to dry his hands, and put them on the small table that's on the side of the altar." Of course, I'd seen altar boys do that before Masses. David took a box of stick matches from a drawer in the altar boys' dressing area, grabbed the taper, a long shiny brass rod with a wick at the end, lit it, and made for the altar. He lit the tall candles on the altar as I picked up the cruets and walked through the passage to the bigger room of the sacristy where a priest that I didn't recognize was putting on his vestments—alb, amice, chasuble. He was short, chubby, and bald except for a ribbon of thin white-and-red hair that ran across the lower part of his head. His small round face was pinkish-red. I'd heard that our parish was growing faster than the pastor and his assistant could keep up with and the pastor had to bring in auxiliary priests until the bishop could provide a permanent one. I caught his eye. He looked at me and nodded, half asleep. I tried sizing him up. Could he be one of those priests who yelled at altar boys when they made mistakes? He didn't look nice or mean, just serious and sleepy.

I walked through the archway of the sacristy, to the altar and glanced at my audience. The church was dimly lit. All of the school's nuns were sitting in the first pew, from the short, feisty, dark-skinned first-grade teacher Sister Alvera Marie, to the fat, moody Sister Mary Constance. There looked to be fewer than a dozen people scattered behind the nuns. At least if I got yelled at, there wouldn't be a church full of people to see it. I made eye contact with Sister Lucille. She didn't smile but gave a slight nod. Her glasses reflected the soft first rays of sunlight piercing the stained-glass windows high on the side wall. Even if nervous, I felt great pride in wearing the cassock and the white surplice, it made me feel like one of the big kids.

I genuflected in front of the tabernacle, walked to the small table covered with a white linen, set down the cruets, wash bowl and small towel, then returned to the sacristy.

The priest took his place in the sacristy ready to enter the sanctuary. David and I took our places standing shoulder to shoulder and a step behind the priest. He looked at his watch and proceeded to the altar. My first Mass as an altar boy had begun and I felt like going pee.

The priest stopped in front of the tabernacle. David continued and stopped to stand on his left side. I stood at his right in front of a small kneeling pad that sat on the first step of three steps that led to the marble altar table. We all genuflected. So far, so good.

The priest scaled the steps and started in on the prayers, he paused in between for David and me to give the responses. I gave the responses perfectly despite my nervousness. Sister did a magical job of drilling them into my head.

David cleared his throat, getting my attention and pointed stealthily to the small table, indicating that it was time for us to make for the cruets where we would pour the water and wine for the priest. Even though I'd seen the procedure enough times to know what to do, it was a great comfort to have David watch over me. I tried to stand at the same time as David, but the bottom of my cassock was caught between the heels of my shoes and the floor. I jerked backward and nearly lost my balance but managed to stay upright. I blushed, wondering if Sister Lucille had noticed. I shot a look toward David; he was hiding laughter. I pulled the cassock from under my feet and walked toward David. We met at the center of the altar in front of the tabernacle, genuflected, and made for the small table.

I took the water cruet and wash bowl, David took the wine cruet and the linen for drying hands. The priest walked down the altar steps toward us, mumbling prayers. No responses were needed for this part. The priest took the bottom step to the floor and held out his stubby, little pig-like fingers for me to pour water over them. I uncapped the cruet and held the small bowl under the priest's hands. I tipped the cruet, but nothing came out. He stopped his muffled praying, looked at me and said in a low voice. "Ya don't say."

David leaned and looked my way to see that something wasn't right, then looked at his cruet and saw that it too was empty. He reached over the priest's hands, grabbed my cruet, and made a hasty retreat into the sacristy. I broke out in a sweat. The priest shook his head and continued mumbling. I don't know if he was praying or killing time while we waited for David to return. David walked back at a brisk pace and the Mass continued. I assisted the priest in the washing of the hands. David tipped the cruet and poured a spot of wine into his chalice. The priest gave the chalice a little shake, indicating that he wanted more wine. David poured a bit more. The priest kept the chalice in position and whispered, "Come on, lad." David emptied the cruet into the chalice. We returned to our kneeling pads. The priest climbed the steps of the altar, where he blessed the wine and Communion hosts, praying softly, beseeching God the Father to send his Son to us in the form of the wine as His blood and the hosts of unleavened bread as His body. The priest put the chalice to his lips and leaned back and gulped down the blood of Jesus. David rang the bells as the sacred transference took place. I wished that I could ring the bells.

The hosts now being Christ's body meant that it was time to give out Communion. The priest unlocked the tabernacle and took out a chalice containing consecrated hosts. David cleared his throat and signaled me to go up the steps to the side of the altar where a shiny brass paten lay. Altar boys placed the paten under communicants' chins to catch whatever tiny pieces of the host that could fall to the floor. I went for the paten and knelt to receive Communion. A perk of being a server was that we were first to get Communion. I swallowed Jesus, then followed the priest down to the Communion rail where the people who would receive had walked forward and knelt.

All of the nuns approached the Communion rail and knelt in a row. I felt a strange sense of power standing in front of them—they knelt before me. We approached. Sister Constance was first. She stuck her cow-like tongue out. It had a creepy white creamy-like substance over it; I had to turn my head away. Chunky Sister Mary Jane, who taught seventh grade, was next. I placed the paten under her chin. She raised her head, closed her eyes, opened her mouth and stuck out her tongue. The priest said, "*Corpus Christi*" and placed a host on her tongue.

Sister Jane reminded me of a movie I'd seen where a lady had just gotten her head chopped off and her tongue hung out. Skinny, sickly Sister Catherine stuck out her tongue and looked like she'd just bitten a lemon. Sister Theresa opened her mouth wide and her long tongue curled out, nearly touching her chin in the grossest way. Sister Lucille received Communion gracefully. We finished Communion by giving it to the lay people and returned to the altar.

The priest said a few final prayers after Communion and descended the altar. David and I rose from our knee pads, stood a step behind him. We all genuflected and filed out.

"And just how is it that there was no water or wine in the cruets, lad?" The priest said to me as soon as we entered the sacristy. His cheeks and nose were covered with a mosaic of tiny red broken blood vessels.

"I—ah, that is Father—"

David cut in. "It's his first Mass, Father."

"Well, lad, when I said my first Mass many years ago, I was so nervous that I fouled up the consecration prayer and for all I know the congregation got empty hosts instead of Christ's body." Father laughed and I laughed with him, but more out of relief than thinking his story all that funny.

"Why didn't you fill the cruets?" David said in the backroom. "Because no one told me to," I said, pulling off my surplice. He rolled his eyes. "From now on fill them before taking them out. Jeez! You're lucky that Father didn't get mad at you."

I hung my head and mumbled, "How was I supposed to know if you didn't say anything?" I served Mass with David the following Monday through Friday and only made a few minor mistakes that no one seemed to notice.

It was a proud day the following month when Fernando and I got to serve 6:30 a.m. Mass together. We both felt nervous when the day came when we were to serve our first Sunday Mass. The church was filled with community, school friends, and our family. John Maloney, a classmate and close friend of ours, said that the women of the altar society had told Father Vidra that he should assign "the cute twins" to serve Sunday Mass, and he did.

We had no trouble getting out of bed that Sunday. We had shined our shoes the night before. Ma worked hair grease into our scalps, making it shine, and made perfect parts. She must have felt that the Catholic school system had done its magic in teaching her overactive twin boys, who had such a hard go of it when it came to studying but managed to learn Latin and the duties of the altar.

Sister Lucille told me at school on Monday that it was "lovely" seeing Fernando and me serving Mass "like perfect bookends," she said. I heard from Martha that from that time on the nuns referred to us as "The Bookends."

THE SECOND PROUDEST DAY OF MA'S LIFE was the day that my brother, Tony, was ordained a Catholic priest. But the proudest had to be the Sunday, in a full church, that her eldest son celebrated Mass with her two bookend twin boys on either side of him. And all made possible by Sister Marie Lucille who didn't at all look mean anymore.

17.

4th Grade – Hoodlums
Fernando

*"But if you do wrong, be afraid, for rulers do not bear the
sword for no reason. They are God's servants, agents
of the wrath to bring punishment on the wrongdoer."*
Romans 13:14

"NEVER FORGET, CHILDREN, God watches over all things
and over all you do. Even if you commit a sin in hiding
or if you have sinful thoughts, God knows," said Sister Marie
Lucille, "sinners and criminals always get caught." Guilt was
my constant companion; it was a heavy burden to carry. It was
a hot and humid September evening. San Diego, known for
its temperate climate, has unbearable weather in this month.
Armando and I were picking guavas from Ma's tree. The shade
from the drooping branches was a welcome respite from the
oppressive heat.

Hector saw us and yelled from across the street, "Hey, you
guys, le—le—let's go to Thrifty's and get some i—i—ice cream."
The invitation was irresistible. Hector was two years older than
us, we looked up to him.

"Okay, I yelled back, we'll be right over." My brother and
I grabbed two of the big soda bottles from our stash in Pa's
garage. Large bottles were worth a five-cent deposit, and a sin-
gle-scoop ice cream cone cost a nickel. We were in business.

"Ma, we're gonna get ice creams with Hector," I yelled. We hustled past the front porch.

"*Está bien, mijo,* be careful."

Hector always had big stories about what went on at his junior high school. He wouldn't lie to us; that would be a sin. Hector attended St. Rita's a few years, but the morals the nuns tried to instill in their students didn't seem to stick with him. We rarely saw his family go to church and never saw them pray before eating meals the few times we were invited.

"There's this big guy at my school who's so tough that he beat up three kids at the same time." I listened in wonder as he described how formidable this boy was. I was lucky to know Hector who knew that kid. I was envious of a kid that tough and wondered if I might be able to do the same one day. I had never seen a real fight at our school. Fights at St. Rita's usually involved some halfhearted shoving and a lot of daring. "Come on," one kid would dare another with a shove, followed by "come on" by the other kid and a counter shove. They would stare at each other, afraid to throw the first punch. They lost the little nerve they had when kids gathered hoping to see fists fly.

The closest thing to a fight that I was involved in was last year. John Rodden, a grade above me, didn't like that I hit him with a ball during recess, even though it was an accident. He raised his fists and hit me on the jaw. I reflexively punched back, aiming for his mouth, but missed and hit his neck. Students began to form a ring around us. When he saw the resolve on my face and no real appetite for a brawl, he backed off. He picked up a dodge ball and threw it at me to prove that he wasn't scared and walked away. I was relieved. According to Hector's sensational accounts, real blood splattering, snot slinging, haymaker fights happened all the time at his school.

Our walk to the store took us across the Highway 94 overpass. Cars sped under the bridge. Two wide lanes headed east and two west. Along with the extensive center divider of the highway, the bridge spanned an entire city block. Hector stopped and rested his arms on the metal railing and looked down at the highway traffic. Armando and I stood on either side of him. Hector then checked traffic on Euclid Avenue, hocked up phlegm, held it in his mouth for a few seconds, concentrating on the cars passing below, then spat. His timing was perfect. He hit a car's windshield and laughed, apparently unaware that God had seen him. It was impressive and scary at the same time; impressive that he had the nerve and such good timing and scary that the driver might come back for us.

"What if he comes back?"

"He ain't coming back," Hector said. He continued with tales of Gompers Junior High School. His stories made the long walk to Thrifty's shorter.

The automatic doors of the store swung open. The blast of cool air on my face felt good. I wiped my forehead with my T-shirt and made my way to the front counter. I handed the lady our soda bottles and got the deposit money. We went to the ice cream counter. I ordered a scoop of chocolate and gave the lady my nickel. My brother got a scoop of rocky road. Hector got pistachio with a scoop of strawberry on top. He was lucky, he had a dime.

We exited the store. "Hey, Hector, my man, what's shakin'?" said a skinny kid in baggy pants and a sagging T-shirt. He was about Hector's age.

"Hey, Rodney. What're you up to?"

"Came up to see about doin' a little discount shoppin' if you know what I mean," Rodney said with a wry smile. Hector and Rodney talked past my brother and me.

"Yeah, like what?" Hector asked.

"I like that new aftershave, I think they call it British Sterlin' or supin' like that."

"Yeah, that's what it's called. They charge a buck fifty a bottle for it." Hector paused. "If you can get me a bottle, I'll give you seventy-five cents."

"Shit yeah," said Rodney. "You dudes stay here, I'll be right back."

"Is he going to steal it?" I asked in disbelief. "Put it this way, he's going to get me a discount." "How do you know Rodney?"

"He's in my Spanish class at school."

I stood, hardly believing what we were talking about. I worried that if Rodney and Hector got caught, I might get in trouble for being with them. My brother had a look of intrigue on his face as he licked his cone. A few minutes later Rodney walked out.

"Come on, man. Let's get away from the front of the store." I was relieved to get away from the crime scene. We walked half way across the parking lot and stood behind a pickup truck. Rodney reached into the front of his pants and took out a cool-looking bottle with shiny calligraphy writing on the label and an oversized silver cap. "Here you go, man." He handed the bottle to Hector.

"Hold my ice cream," Hector said, handing it to me. He pulled change out of his pocket and gave it to Rodney. I sneaked a lick of Hector's pistachio. It tasted as good as my chocolate.

"A pleasure doin' business with you, Hector." He took the money. "Hasta la vista, dude, as Mrs. Sanchez would say." He chuckled and walked back to the store.

"Later, Rodney."

"Hector, why did you do that?"

"It's Roy's birthday in a couple of days and I needed to get him something," he said matter-of-factly. He slipped the bottle into his back pocket and took his ice cream back.

Roy was Hector's stepfather. While Roy and Hector's mother, loved my brother and me, they barely tolerated Hector. I had heard his mother threaten to send him to Los Angeles to live with his father. Hector knew not to cross Roy. Roy threatened to "beat your ass bloody" once when Hector was caught stealing money from his mother's purse.

Hector hated living with his mother, his pain-in-the-neck little sister and Roy. An uneasy peace loomed heavy in their home. He got the cologne to stay on Roy's good side, he feared him as much as he disliked him.

Hector chuckled at our reaction to Rodney's discount shopping. We made for home and he resumed with his stories. "My grandfather, my dad's father, fought in World War I and killed twelve German soldiers all by himself. He had to kill the last three with his bayonet when he ran out of ammo."

"Wow," was all I could say.

By the time we neared the 94 bridge, our ice creams were gone. Brown, sticky traces of ice cream coated my fingers. I rubbed my hands on my jeans. Hector walked to the side of the road and picked up a fist-sized rock.

"What're you going to do with that?"

"Y—you'll see." We were three-quarters of the way across the bridge. The sun had just set. Some drivers had turned their headlights on. Hector stopped and looked over the bridge. I was waiting for him to hock again. He looked up and down the street again and waited until there were no cars in sight. He cocked his arm. Before I could say anything, he heaved. BANG.

I panicked. We ran full speed for the last two blocks home. We shot under the guava tree. Breathlessly, I asked the same question, "Why in the heck did you do that?"

He shrugged, "Just felt like it," he waited a minute, and crossed the street.

"Man, that was scary," my brother said. We waited another five minutes before going into our house.

"Sometimes Hector does really stupid things," Armando said in our bedroom that night.

"Do you think he's going to hell?" I asked.

"I don't know. I've been thinking about what Sister Lucille said criminals and sinners always getting caught. Hector does bad things all the time and hardly ever gets caught. When he does, he can usually lie his way out of it. If God knows what he's doing, why doesn't God let him get caught by the police, or Roy?" My brother's reasoning made sense. It was a lot to think about. I fell asleep thinking of the unfairness of the world.

"I stole a candy bar from Thrifty's," my brother confided in me a few days later.

"You did?"

"If Hector can buy a stolen bottle of aftershave and not get caught, then why can't I take a five-cent candy? It's not nearly as bad. Besides, I can just go to confession." His reasoning was hard to argue against. It was strangely enticing to hear that my brother had stolen and gotten away with it.

Chad, my brother, and I built a tree fort in the eucalyptus tree that abutted the sidewalk next to their house. Chris looked on. "When's it going to be done?" he asked several times as we cut, hammered, and nailed.

"Soon," was our constant reply. I cut one-by-four hand grips and was careful to drive the nails deep into the trunk. A few hours later the crude structure was complete. We took turns climbing up the trunk and onto the platform. Chad went up a couple of times, lost interest, and left.

"Let's eat lunch up here," Armando suggested. "Go get yours and we'll meet you back here." Chris scurried to his house.

We ran home, bagged our food, and met up in the fort. "Boy, this is a lot better than the foxhole," I said. My brother and I had dug a foxhole in our back yard and put a sheet of plywood over the top. It was a great hiding place and ideal for surprise attacks.

We shared secrets as we ate. "There's this really pretty girl in our class. Her name is Angela and I want to kiss her," I volunteered.

"You want to kiss a girl?" Chris asked.

"Only once in a while."

"When I'm in my bed at night, sometimes I pick my nose and flick the boogers onto the wall," Chris confessed. Armando and I laughed; Chris looked flattered.

"Chucky showed me naked ladies in a magazine," my brother said as he chewed his peanut butter and jelly sandwich.

"Where did Chucky get a magazine with naked ladies?" I asked.

"He told me his father had it hidden under his mattress." Chris and I laughed at that one, too. I was too ashamed to admit I wanted to see the pictures.

Along with our lunches, we took weapons to shoot unsuspecting German soldiers below. Our arsenal included an array of rocks and a big bolt as hand grenades. After eating we got busy fighting enemies. It didn't long before we got bored with our play. My brother grabbed a grenade, raised and lowered it several times seemingly checking its weight. He looked at the traffic on Euclid, there wasn't much. A lone car headed our way. "Here comes a German tank," he whispered, got on his knees, put the grenade to his mouth, pulled the pin, cocked his arm, and let it fly. BANG. He scored a direct hit to the car's back door. Chris laughed out loud. We were seasoned soldiers and well hidden in our lookout.

"Okay. It's your guys' turn."

Chris looked intrigued, picked up a rock, and looked to the street. "Wait, Chris, that grenade's too big. You'll never be able to throw it far enough," Armando said. He looked over our inventory and selected a smaller one. "Here, try this one."

We waited for the next tank. Just as Chris was ready to heave it, I grabbed his arm. "That's a Chevy like Pa drives. Let's not hit any Chevys."

Chris agreed so long as we didn't hit any Dodges either since his family owned one. An Oldsmobile headed down the street. Chris readied himself. Just as the front of the car was even with the fort, Armando said, "Now!" We heard a ting as he nicked the rear bumper. Chris laughed again. This was a lot better than killing make-believe soldiers. My brother threw the next one but missed; the rock skipped harmlessly across the street.

"Darn it," he said and picked up another rock.

"No," I said, "let me try one." I grabbed the bolt. "This'll be a heck of a grenade." The bolt stuck out from the top and bottom of my fist. I was going to really kill the next one. An unsuspecting enemy tank in the form of a new DeSoto coupe came rolling down the street. I waited until the last second and threw the grenade with all my might. We heard an extra loud crack. I scored a direct hit. The three of us whooped, then saw the car slow and pull to the sidewalk in front of Chris's house.

"Uh-oh." I heard a car door open, slam, and loud undecipherable language. We scampered down the tree and bolted for home.

As my brother and I sped past the back of Chris's house, we saw him go through the door. We ran into the foxhole and crawled through the access hole and gasped in the dank, dusty air. We sat quietly looking at each other. Nothing seemed to be happening, maybe we were safe. Then we heard Ma's voice.

"Armando, Fernando, *dónde están?*"

"We're down here playing, Ma."

"Come up to the house right now."

"Okay," I yelled in the most innocent voice I could muster. "Tell her Chris did it," my brother whispered.

"No. I'll say we don't know who did it."

"No. Tell her we saw kids hiding in bushes by the eucalyptus tree do it."

"There aren't any bushes by the eucalyptus tree, stupid." We stopped scheming when we got to the back door. Pa was in the living room.

"Why were you throwing rocks at cars?" he asked before we said anything. Even though I figured it was futile, I attempted a story.

"We didn't do it."

Pa ignored my denial and looked at us. He spoke in an even tone. "A very angry man went to the Tanners' door and talked to Mrs. Tanner. We heard him from here. She told him that she asked Chris what happened. Chris said you two were throwing rocks at cars. The man came here and said he had a big dent in his car door. He wanted to know who did it and that whoever did was going to be severely punished. After he stopped yelling, I said I'd take care of it."

My brother and I looked to the floor. Any further denials would only make things worse. "You boys know better," Pa said, disappointment in his voice and pain on his face. I stole a glance at Ma's picture of Our Lady of Guadalupe on the wall. Her face looked sad, eyes downcast. I petitioned her for deliverance.

I lied again. "We were just watching Chris do it." Pa didn't buy that either. My petition to the Virgin went unanswered. Pa grabbed me by the arm, turned me, and gave me three good ones on my butt and did the same to Armando. Ma fretted as Pa meted our punishment. We ran to our bedroom crying. I lay on our bed, my brother on Martha's.

We knew not to come out of our room too soon. It might take an hour or more before we could venture out. "Stupid Chris told on us," my brother lamented. We heard our parents animated talking in the living room.

We heard Pa say, "Thank god the man isn't going to call the police or even make us pay to fix his car."

I lay on the bed ashamed, regretful and angry at myself for having caused my parents pain. I even felt sorry for the owner of the tank.

171

A few minutes later I heard the floorboards in the hall creak as footsteps neared our room. We turned quickly and lay face down on the pillows. The door opened. Someone came in and closed the door. The room filled with dread.

I dared not look up. Were we in for another spanking? Pa stood for a moment. I could feel his eyes on me. The box spring squeaked as his weight settled on the foot of the bed. The mattress depressed. I lay dead still.

He began to speak in a low voice, his tempo slow. "Sit up, boys." I sat up but averted my eyes. He took a deep breath.

"Your grandmother Antonia brought your Aunt Mary, Uncle Sam, and me to the United States from Mexico to get us away from the Mexican Revolution. We settled in Phoenix, Arizona."

I wasn't sure what or why he was talking about our long dead grandmother.

"I was ten years old and Sammy was twelve. With very little resources your grandmother managed to start a restaurant and boarding house. She was a hard worker and in three years had a successful business. With her long hours she couldn't keep an eye on me and your uncle. We started to hang around with some tough street boys."

I felt relief as Pa spoke. I was pretty sure we weren't in for another licking. I stole a look at him. He was looking at the wall.

"The boys we hung around with started with petty crimes, like stealing candy from the corner drugstore. Before long they were stealing cigarettes and teaching us to smoke. Your uncle and I were careful to get back home before your grandmother. Blackie, the ringleader, was two years older than Sammy. One day he told us to meet him in the alley behind the downtown movie house. He knew that the people in the theater wouldn't come out for another hour. Blackie had stolen a half-pint bottle of whiskey. He brought it out and made us take drinks. I gagged and coughed up the whiskey out of my mouth and nose. Blackie laughed at me. By now I was thirteen and Sammy fifteen. I was the youngest of the boys, but I was big for my age, even bigger than my older brother so people always thought I was older. After we passed the bottle around, Blackie took a wire out of his pocket and a pair of pliers. He got under the hood of a car and started it. He told us to get in. Blackie drove, with Mitch, one of the boys, in the front seat and two other boys in the back with Sammy and me. He drove us to the top of a big hill and parked near the edge of a cliff. He told us to get out and help him push the car over." Pa paused he seemed to be gathering his thoughts.

"What happened?" I asked.

"The car broke into thousands of pieces as it hit rocks and boulders bouncing to the bottom of the canyon."

"Did you get caught?"

"No, we didn't, at least not by the police. Somehow your grandmother found out what we did. She told us to kneel on the living-room floor and lashed our backs with a belt. She cried and scolded while she whipped us. She said she knew about the cigarettes and was going to tell us not to smoke but wanted to wait for the right time to talk to us about it. After the whipping she told us to come directly home from school from then on. A month later she sold her business and took us, along with our sister, to work in the farm fields of Central and Northern California. Your Uncle Sam and I learned to work hard, very hard. Without the income from the restaurant, it wasn't long before we lived hand-to-mouth. "

Wow, Pa and Uncle Sam were juvenile delinquents.

"Your grandmother contracted with a cotton farmer. We had to thin the cotton plants with hoes. I stood in the field and looked down the row. It was so long I couldn't see the end. At the end of my first day my hands were so blistered that my mother punctured the blisters, put salve on them, and wrapped them in cloth so I could keep working the next day. We learned that either you worked, or you starved. I resented having to labor so hard in the hot sun, but we had no choice. I made up my mind to never steal again."

Pa paused again; his hands clasped with elbows resting on his knees. His voice had softened, his tone conciliatory.

"Years later I went back to Phoenix on some business. I saw a bum in the street. He looked familiar. It was Mitch."

"The one who got in the front seat with Blackie?" I asked.

"Yes, the one in the front seat with Blackie. I asked Mitch what happened to the other boys we had palled around with. He said that Blackie was hanged by the state for robbing a store where a man was shot and killed, and the other two boys were serving long sentences in a state penitentiary for other crimes. Mitch said he was lucky because he never got caught."

"So Mitch got away?" I asked.

"Mitch didn't get caught by the police for whatever things he did, but when I saw him his clothes were ragged, he needed a haircut and a shave, and he smelled. I felt sorry for him. Before I left, he asked me if he could borrow five dollars. I gave him the five and went back home." Pa seemed sad. "Had we stayed in Arizona, there is no telling where your uncle and I might have wound up. We may have been in prison or executed like Blackie. Your grandmother was a wise woman to get us away from there and to teach us how to work hard, how to work honestly."

Pa had regained his composure. He took a deep breath and looked at us. "I don't want you two to wind up like our friends in Phoenix. I know that you boys know that what you did was wrong, but what you did could have caused a serious accident. Someone could have been seriously hurt, or worse." Pa looked at me, then to my brother. "You boys stay out of trouble, do you understand?"

"Yeah, Pa, we do," I answered. He looked drained, gave us a look and told we could go back outside and left the room.

We quietly walked to the backyard. We found out that Chris hadn't gotten in trouble. We considered administering some frontier justice but decided against it, probably better to leave well enough alone. In bed that night we talked about our day. "I guess God saw what we did and made it so Ma and Pa caught us," I said.

"But why didn't God make it so Hector got caught having had someone steal for him or throwing the rock at the car?" my brother said.

I lay quiet for a moment. "Maybe God loves us more. Maybe Hector will wind up in the electric chair someday." I was surprised and pleased with the wisdom of my answer.

"Yeah, you're right," my brother said. "Maybe Sister Lucille was right after all."

By the time we got back from church on Sunday, Pa seemed to have put the incident behind him. By Monday he was his old self, happy to be alive and teasing with us and our sisters. My brother and I were never tempted to throw rocks at cars again and my brother resolved to try and not steal any more candy bars.

18.

4th Grade – Spooky, Newspapers & Twin Treats
Fernando

"Never let them see you sweat."
Gillette Company deodorant commercial

THE KITCHEN WAS SATURATED with the sweet smell of pinto beans simmering on the stove. The night before Ma and I sorted out the small rocks and little dirt clods from the beans she bought in Tijuana. Afterward she put the beans in a strainer and washed them before putting them into a pot of cold water to soak overnight.

I looked at Ma standing at the counter, rolling pin in hand. She took a small ball of *masa* out of her brown clay bowl, gave it a few quick pats, and set it on her cutting board dusted with flour. She flattened the *masa* with her rolling pin into a neat round circle, then placed it in one of two iron skillets. Ma flipped hot tortillas with nimble fingers as she rolled out the next wad of *masa*. The stack of cooked tortillas rose as she worked, each tortilla not deviating a fraction of an inch in size or thickness. No motion in her process was wasted. She worked with the fluid ease of a master.

"Ma, can we go to the Maestases' house tomorrow?" I tapped the well-worn erasure end of the number two pencil on my math homework paper. I was struggling with multiplication problems. Gilbert had invited us over for a weekend sleepover.

"Did the *señora* say it was okay?"

"Yeah, they said she likes it when we come over because we say 'yes' and we call her Mrs. Maestas' and 'please' and because we put our dishes in the sink when we're done eating. Gilbert said we can spend Friday and Saturday night with them."

"Okay, but I don't want any bad reports."

"We'll be good."

"Be sure to put your play clothes in the laundry tonight. How are you doing with your homework?"

"Good," My notebook paper was rife with erasure smudges from corrections. In two places I had erased and rewritten one answer so many times the paper had worn through. Math was tedious work, but I was optimistic as I had finally figured out that seven times seven was forty-eight.

I fidgeted through Sister Lucille's lessons, anxious for this Friday to be over. I got a sixty-five percent grade on my multiplication problems from the previous night. Seventy percent was a passing grade. It was discouraging, but at least I beat the sixty percent I got the previous day. I was on the right trajectory. Sister gave the class the last half-hour of the day to do homework, as a reward for a week of good behavior.

The end-of-the-school-day bell rang just as we finished our parting prayer. The room filled with the sound of shuffling papers, binders opening and closing, students murmuring, and fifty pairs of shoes scuffling. I had my books closed and sitting on my desktop. I speed-walked to the front door.

"Be careful on your walk home," Sister said from her desk.

"Good bye, Sister, if I'm lucky I'll find another bookmark." Sister covered her mouth, hiding a smile.

I walked down the hallway into bright afternoon sunshine. Normally Armando and I would have lingered on the playground to visit with our friends before starting home, but not today.

"How did you do on the math homework?" my brother asked as we jogged on the sidewalk.

"Got a sixty-five. How about you?"

"I got a sixty-nine. Just one more problem right and I would've passed. Darn it."

"Don't tell Ma. She might change her mind about letting us go to Robert and Gilbert's," I said.

"I wouldn't tell her even if we weren't going."

The twins had told us they were making money selling newspapers and I was anxious to see what that was all about. We rushed through the front door, to our bedroom, and changed into our play clothes.

"Can we go now, Ma?"

"No. You have to do your homework first."

"We just had a little bit and Sister gave us a half-hour during class to do it."

"Okay, But I don't want to see either of you crying on Sunday night because you forgot something."

"We won't. Can we just go now, please?"

"Both of you go into the bathroom and comb your hair." We combed our hair and went back to the kitchen fidgeting.

Ma sighed, handed us a bean burrito and a napkin each, got her purse, and walked with us to the car. Our ironed clothes smelled like fresh laundry detergent. Our tennis shoes had joined our jeans that morning in the washing machine. Minutes later she pulled into the twins' driveway. Mrs. Maestas came out the back door, pleased to see us, and greeted Ma. Armando and I jumped out of the car.

"Bye, Ma."

"*Portansen bien.*"

"Hi, Mrs. Maestas," we blurted out and ran to the house.

"Hello, boys."

178

"*Hola, Carolina,*" I heard Mrs. Maestas say.

We scampered through the laundry room, kitchen and dining room and up the stairs to the boys' room. They had just changed out of their uniforms. "Hey, it's the *cuates,*" Gilbert said.

Robert looked over at us with a happy smile. "You guys want to sell newspapers with us?"

"Heck yeah. What do we have to do?" "Come on, we'll show you."

We followed them back down the stairs, out the front door, and across their yard as Robert explained the procedure.

"A manager from the newspaper company shows up in his truck behind old man Cheney's grocery store with a bunch of papers. We buy them for seven cents each and sell them on the corner for ten. So we make three cents for every one we sell. You just have to tell the manager how many papers you want."

"You mean all we have to do is stand at the corner and people buy 'em?"

"That's all you have to do."

"But we don't have money."

"That's okay. Gilbert can lend you the money and I'll lend Armando his and you guys can pay us back when we're done selling."

The Evening Tribune was San Diego's afternoon newspaper. The paper had two print runs, the home delivery edition that went out earlier in the day and the Green Sheet that was printed later and had that day's closing New York Stock Exchange quotes. The cover sheet of the late edition paper was green.

It was early June and the days had gotten progressively longer since January. The skies were crystal clear, the afternoon sun felt warm on my back.

The twins' friends, Augie, Spooky, and Porky, were behind Cheney's Market in the parking lot waiting for the newspaper manager to show up. Their bicycles lay on the sidewalk. The five of them talked as my brother and I looked on.

Augie and Porky were the twins' age. Augie shared our olive coloring but Porky had skin as white as Ma's tortilla *masa* and was chubby. He hid his unkempt sandy-blonde hair under a navy blue sweat-stained baseball cap. His tennis shoes, like his jeans, were tattered. While Augie and Spooky spoke on the same mental plane as Robert and Gilbert, God had not been so generous with Porky. His speech was slow, and he possessed the innocence and happiness of the delayed. He was able to function apparently unaware of his condition. His faithful mutts, Archie and Tonto, followed him everywhere. His dogs were jealous of any dog that approached Porky and growled at anyone who threatened him. Porky talked to his dogs with the love and patience of a parent. The twins didn't know where Porky and his dogs lived or if he even went to school.

Spooky was my age and size. He had the dark complexion of the Mexican Indios with high cheek bones and jet-black hair. He wore his long-sleeved shirt buttoned all the way up to his neck, untucked, and a pair of neatly ironed tan khaki pants. Spooky used a lot of pomade to slick his thick hair straight back with a small waterfall down his forehead like the *pachucos* did in the *barrio*. He was cocky, talked and acted tough.

Spooky looked at Gilbert. "Hey, Gilbert," did you see how scared Juanito was when I pushed him?"

"Yeah, I saw it Spooky, but he's smaller than you."

"Aw, man, he's a little chickenshit," he said with a smile.

Robert, Augie, and Porky had their own conversation. Porky was struggling to make a point. Spooky looked back at Gilbert, put his finger to his temple and made small circles. Gilbert ignored the gesture.

The lean, middle-age Green Sheet manager showed up in the parking lot just like Robert said he would. The truck brakes squealed as he came to a stop. He got out of his exhausted dark blue pickup and slammed the door. He had a full head of oily brown hair. He wore dark blue jeans and a long-sleeved light blue shirt with the sleeves rolled up to the elbow. A blurred blue-and-red Marine Corp emblem was tattooed on his left forearm. A lit cigarette hung between his lips.

Without acknowledging us, he walked to the back of the truck, stepped on the back bumper, and hoisted himself up.

The leaf springs moaned as he climbed aboard.

The bed of the truck was loaded with bundles of newspapers tied with strands of copper wire. He pulled a pair of wire cutters from his back pocket and snipped the wires from three bundles. I was surprised at the sheer volume of newspapers. *He must make a lot of money. If he gets seven cents for each paper and there are a thousand papers . . .* My mind reeled. *I guess multiplication tables are a good thing to know.*

"You boys should sell a lot of papers today, we might be in for another damn war," he said in his gravelly voice. "I would take extras if I were you."

I was nervous and excited. I watched as the manager asked each boy how many newspapers he wanted. "I want twenty-five," Augie said.

"Me too," Porky said.

The manager counted out Augie and Porky's and got their money.

"How many do you want, Robert?" The cigarette bounced on his lips and he squinted as white smoke curled into his eyes. "Twenty-five—no, make it thirty." My brother followed Robert's lead and asked for thirty. Robert handed the manager the money.

"How about you, Gilbert? You want the same?"

"Yes." He handed them over. He looked to me, "How many?"

"Thirty, sir." As I reached for my newspapers Spooky cut in front of me and grabbed them from the manager's outstretched hand. Spooky handed the manager his money and walked to his bike. Angry blood rushed to my face.

"You should've shoved him out of the way," Gilbert said. "Next time I will," I said weakly.

The manager counted out thirty more and handed them to me. Gilbert reached into his pocket and pulled out three wadded dollar bills and a handful of coins. He counted the money and handed it over. I was stunned at how much money the twins had at their disposal. Selling newspapers was obviously a highly profitable business. The manager pocketed the money, hopped off the truck, took the smoldering cigarette butt from his lips, and flicked it to the sidewalk where it rolled into the gutter. "See you boys tomorrow." He hopped in his truck and drove off. Black smoke shot out of his dual exhaust pipes.

Augie and Spooky tied the papers onto their bike racks mounted over the back tires and rode up the boulevard toward the new supermarket. The threadbare tires on Porky's bike bulged when he mounted. He rode off in the opposite direction with his dogs happily jogging on either side of him.

"All you have to do is hold the Green Sheet up so drivers can read the headline and if they want to buy one, they'll honk or yell at you," Gilbert said to Armando and me. "Then you gotta run and give them the paper and get the dime. Make sure you got fifteen cents in your hand because some people will give you a quarter, that way you don't have to count change and you can get out of traffic fast. Always take two papers at a time."

"Why?" Armando asked.

"Sometimes, if you're real lucky, two cars at the same red light will buy 'em. You won't have enough time to sell the one, then run to get the other paper and back out before the light changes." There was a lot more to selling papers than I realized. Gilbert went to the corner of the parking lot, came back with two rocks and handed me one.

"What's this for?"

"Put it on top of your papers so they don't blow away when you run back and forth."

The four of us took a corner each at the busy intersection. Robert and Gilbert flipped a coin to see who got the gas station corner; Robert won. They told us that with cars stopping for gas, he could expect to make two to three easy sales. My corner was in front of the grocery store. Gilbert took the corner that abutted an empty lot. My brother got the used-car lot corner.

A sign over the single-story wood frame office read, "DON'S DEALS, HOME OF THE HAPPY CUSTOMER."

I watched as they took their corners. My brother went behind the car lot and came out with a softball-sized rock, set his stack of papers on the sidewalk, and put the rock on top. He took two papers and started to walk to the curb. No sooner had my brother gotten to his corner than a man in a dark blue blazer, tan slacks, and brown wingtip shoes walked out of the office of the car lot and bought a newspaper. They exchanged a few words. They laughed about something, and the man went back into the small office scanning the cover of the paper. I looked over to Robert; he was handing a copy to a man who was filling his gas tank. I felt envious of them, not sure whether I would make any sales or not.

I stood at my corner, took a paper from my stack and turned it over. The headline read, "Ike Sends Military to Vietnam." I shrugged and turned to the traffic and held up the paper. I shouted out "Paper!" like I had seen newspaper boys do in the movies. Gilbert looked at me and laughed. Within seconds I got my first sale.

"Hey, kid," a man yelled from his sedan. I dashed over to the driver's side window, handed him a paper, and got the dime. I heard a honk from behind my first sale. A lady was motioning to me with a coin in her hand. I had forgotten to take the extra paper. I ran back to my pile and grabbed another, but before I got back to the curb the light turned and I lost the sale. I muttered to myself and looked over at Gilbert. He shrugged in an I-told-you-so gesture. That was the only sale I missed the rest of the afternoon.

I had to stay alert and be quick to make change. Unlike selling apricots, this was fast-paced business, nickels, dimes and quarters were coming in quickly. The music of coins jingling in my pocket kept me vigilant, anxious for my next sale. I relaxed a little when the traffic light was green and readied myself when it turned yellow. I noticed people sitting in passenger seats looking to me, scanning the headline. Anxious to make sales, I ran along the sidewalk keeping up with the cars to entice buyers, causing some to laugh.

The wide boulevard had double lanes going in both directions with lots of traffic. Some of the cars had the passenger window rolled down and the swap was easy. On other sales, like my first one, I had to run to the driver's side to make the deal. One sale took longer than normal as the driver didn't have his dime ready and I had to wait for him to fish it out of his pocket. By the time we made the exchange, the light had turned and the driver sped off. I was caught in the center of the boulevard, cars whizzed within a foot on either side of me, their wakes fluttering my T-shirt sleeves. A small hole in the string of traffic opened up. I sprinted to the corner. A driver honked, I jumped and saw the man laugh. I was tempted to throw my paperweight rock at him. I looked across to Gilbert. He was laughing, too.

I remembered to run out with two papers at each sale and wound up with two double sales. Thirty minutes later I was down to my last newspaper. I was desperate to get it sold and count my money. Gilbert sold his and came across the street.

"All right. One more and its time to buy candy," I said.

Our brothers walked over, having sold theirs. Spooky pedaled down the boulevard with three papers tied to his rack. He dropped his bike in the parking lot behind the store, untied his unsold papers, tucked them under his arm, and came over to talk to Gilbert. I stood ready for my last customer. A man honked and made eye contact with me. Before I had a chance to run out, Spooky dashed and made the sale and pocketed my dime.

"Hey, that was his customer," my brother said. "So what?" Spooky said as he walked back.

My face flushed again. "You do that again and I'll knock your block off," escaped from my mouth.

Spooky turned. "What did you say?"

Uh-oh.

He walked toward me and stopped within spitting distance. With all eyes on us, I had no option. I opened my mouth and forced myself to repeat. "I said, do that again and I'll knock your block off." I managed to say it without wavering.

Robert and my brother stepped back. Spooky and I stared at each other. I focused on his dark eyes. I could no longer see or hear traffic just feet away. My mind fixed on the fight I was about to get into, a fight I didn't want. A fight I was probably going to lose.

"Go ahead, Spooky," Gilbert said. "You want to know how tough he is? Fight him." Gilbert said it matter-of-factly. He walked to me and took the newspaper from my hand and stepped back next to our brothers. I held my ground. My clenched fists lay at my sides ready to go. Spooky held on to his two papers. The confrontation developed so fast I didn't have time to think. I was scared and wanted to back down but couldn't. I stared hard into his face. I saw the face of a hood that probably had a switchblade knife in his back pocket. In a fog I saw my ashen corpse lying in a casket and my mother crying at my funeral.

Spooky blinked. He looked down, then back toward me. This time he didn't look me in the eye. He walked to his bike and murmured, "Nah. My mother wants me." He set his two unsold newspapers on the sidewalk next to his bike, mounted and rode away. The confrontation was over as fast as it had started. Relief washed over me; my legs shook slightly inside my pant legs. I couldn't believe my luck. For all of his tough-guy act, he was a chicken.

My brother stood mouth agape. Robert and Gilbert smiled. *Better be careful what I say in front of Gilbert from now on.* Armando and Robert walked over to me. "Aw, man, that was cool. Too bad he chickened out," Robert said.

"Yeah," I said, "too bad." Our brothers turned away, talking excitedly as they walked to the grocery store.

Gilbert patted me on the shoulder. "Hey, you're tougher than I thought." He walked over smiling and picked up the two newspapers Spooky had left. He handed me one and kept the other. I hoped Gilbert didn't notice the tremble in my hand as I took the paper from him.

"Come on. Let's sell Spooky's papers," Gilbert said.

Within five minutes Gilbert sold his and I my last one plus the one I earned from my face-off with Spooky.

"Man," Gilbert said, "this is the most I've ever sold."

I counted out two dollars and ten cents and gave it to Gilbert. Incredibly, I had ninety cents in my pocket plus one paper sold at one hundred percent profit, for a total of one dollar, a dollar that I didn't have at the beginning of the day. All I had to do now was figure out what I was going to do with this windfall. No longer would I envy the white kids whose parents spoiled them with extravagant allowances. I was now among the working elite.

Aside from the occasional soda bottle deposit returns, the most money my brother and I made was when Pa arranged for us to weed our neighbor Mr. Cary's yard. The old cheapskate paid us a paltry twenty-five cents each for an hour and a half of hard work. Today I earned four times that amount in half the time.

Gilbert and I headed for Cheney's Market. He talked excitedly about the standoff. I shrugged. "Aw, it was no big deal." It became apparent that the twins tolerated more than liked Spooky.

"I wish he didn't back down, you coulda knocked the caca out of him." I didn't respond, best to leave well enough alone.

I followed Gilbert into Cheney's. I bought an orange soda and Gilbert got a grape. As we walked Gilbert pulled two red licorices from his back pocket and handed me one. He showed me how to use the licorice for a straw. Life was good. Very good.

When we got to the house, Vangie and Marion were on their front porch talking.

"Hi, girls," I said as we approached, trying not to sound too excited about seeing the pretty sisters. We stopped as we neared the first stair.

Gilbert wasted no time and began to brag. "Fernando raised his fists ready to take him on and when he walked toward Spooky, you know what Spooky did? He turned and ran away like a big chicken. He was so scared he just threw his papers on the ground. Fernando chased him; I never saw Spooky pedal so fast." It was Gilbert's story, who was I to interrupt? I was embarrassed, but proud.

"About time someone stood up to that little punk," Marion said.

"Yeah," I said, "he better not let me see him on the street again."

I awoke late Saturday morning lying next to Gilbert. Our brothers were in Robert's bed. We had stayed up late and watched The Friday Night Frights. My brother and I were too embarrassed to tell them that we were afraid to watch scary movies. Fortunately, the low-budget movie Robot Monster was about an alien in a gorilla suit with a deep-sea diving helmet on his head. Bubbles spewed out of his cave dwelling whenever he came out. We laughed through the entire movie.

I was anxious for four o'clock to come and make more money but was also afraid Spooky would muster his courage and decide to challenge me. *Darn it, I should have kept my mouth shut in front of the girls.*

Saturday afternoon came and we went back to the corner to get copies of the Sunday paper. "What are you going to do when you see Spooky?" Gilbert asked excitedly.

"Not sure," I said, not wanting to dig myself into a deeper hole. I looked nervously to the corner as we neared. Spooky wasn't there. When we walked around the front of the market and to the parking lot I held my breath but only saw Augie and Porky's bicycles lying on the asphalt.

"Hey, Augie, where's Spooky?" Gilbert asked.

"Don't know, he's usually here by now." I was beyond relief.

Gilbert looked at me and our brothers, "Maybe he'll show up later."

The Sunday edition was three times the size of Friday's. Sales were slower as there was no rush-hour traffic, but we were netting ten cents a copy. The Sunday edition sold for a quarter. We asked for fifteen copies each.

Incredibly, my earnings were a dollar and fifty cents. I counted and recounted the money to make sure I hadn't made a mistake. Robert and Gilbert took the earnings in stride. My brother had his hand in his pocket and couldn't stop shaking it.

Gilbert and I walked past Cheney's to the malt shop. Porky's overworked bike lay on its side beside the front entry. Porky and his dogs walked out of the shop. He was drawing on a straw from a chocolate shake he held in one pudgy hand and two burgers and an order of fries in a paper tray in the other. A Baby Ruth candy bar stuck out of his shirt pocket. He had a wet brown stain on his shirt. Archie and Tonto scampered about him on nervous feet looking up expectantly. He let the straw out of his mouth.

"Hey, guys. How you doin'?"

"Good, Porky. Did you sell all your papers?" Gilbert asked.

"All fifteen of 'em. I was real hungry by the time I got done."

He walked to the white metal table with matching chairs outside the malt shop. He chose the chair in the shade of the umbrella and set his feast down. He pulled two pieces off a burger and dropped them to the ground for his children. They snapped up the food, swallowing it whole, then licked their mouths and shuffled their feet, waiting for more.

"Archie, Tonto, that's enough." The dogs didn't seem to understand. Porky took a colossal bite out of a burger. In this moment, Porky could not have been happier had he inherited a fortune.

When we stepped through the screen door of the shop, the sweet scent of hamburger grease and fries welcomed me. A large, white menu board with bold red lettering was attached to a sidewall. Four soda taps with a stainless-steel drain grate on the counter faced the kitchen. Three booths with attached benches with seating for four ran along the entry wall. Each table had a small steel-and-glass case mounted at the end of the booth. The cases had plastic-coated cards with the names of the latest rock and roll songs printed on them. A juke-box with soft yellow lighting sat in a corner. A teenage couple ate at a booth. "Rock Around the Clock" by Bill Haley and His Comets was playing. Gilbert tapped his toe.

A lady in a white apron with red lace trim smiled at us. Her blonde hair was tied in a bun on top of her head. An order pad peeked out from her apron pocket; a pen stuck in the bun. The top two buttons of her white blouse were undone.

A man in a short-sleeve white shirt, paper military cap, and apron stood farther behind in the kitchen.

"What'll you boys have?" asked the lady.

"Root beer float, please," I said, feeling like a big shot.

She looked at Gilbert, "What about you, hon?"

"A frosty, please." For once Gilbert followed my lead and said please. She seemed impressed with our politeness. She took a scooper, leaned into a floor freezer, and rolled out a generous ball of ice cream. I tried not to stare at her ample bosoms as she leaned. Gilbert nudged me and smiled. She plopped the ice cream into a tall paper cup and filled it with soda from one of the taps. My mouth watered. She put a long-handled white plastic spoon and paper straw in and handed it over.

"Thank you, ma'am." She smiled, grabbed a wafer cone, held it under the frosty dispenser, and gave Gilbert a man- sized portion. I reached into the mound of coins in my pocket and handed her a dime. Gilbert gave her a nickel and we turned to leave.

"You two come back and see us real soon, now."

"Okay," I said. I had the feeling this was the beginning of a long, beautiful relationship with the malt shop.

We stepped out just as Porky turned the paper tray and let the last few fries drop to the ground. His dogs jumped on them. "See you Monday, Porky," Gilbert said as we walked by.

Porky nodded.

I savored the float purchased with my own money. Thanks to Robert and Gilbert I was now a man of means. As we started for home, I walked with my head held high.

When we neared the porch Ricky came out of the house. "Oh, boy. Can I have some of your frosty?" He looked to Gilbert. "Okay, but just three licks." Gilbert held out his ice cream.

Ricky tried to sneak a fourth, but Gilbert pulled it back. "That's enough."

I felt sorry for Ricky and handed him my float. "Here, Ricky, have some."

"Gee, thanks." After a long pull a white foam moustache graced his lip.

We met our brothers at the toolshed, they were playing darts. Ricky walked with us, eyeing the frosty and my float. A dartboard was mounted on the outside wall of the shed.

"Hey, Ricky. You know what Fernando did to Spooky today?" By the time Gilbert got done telling Ricky, Spooky had a bloody nose and was crying.

"Can I play darts with you guys?" Ricky asked.

"No," Robert said, "you're too little."

"Aw, come on, Robert. You never let me play."

"No. You can't even hit the dartboard."

"Please?"

"No."

"I'm telling Ma," he said, nearly in tears. He turned toward the house.

"Okay, okay. But pay attention when it's your turn and don't cry if you lose," Robert said exasperated.

I was glad Robert let Ricky join us and shared more of my float with him. Gilbert gave him three more licks from his frosty. We began to throw darts. Ricky was thrilled to be part of the brotherhood. His talk was animated, and he laughed when he not only hit the dartboard but actually made a point and didn't pout if he missed and embedded his darts in the wall.

After the first game, Robert and my brother finished their candy and made for the malt shop. Ricky stayed with Gilbert and me. We played doubles when our brothers came back with their treats. Ricky rotated partners in between games.

My brother and I were evenly matched in skill, as were Robert and Gilbert. I was able to plant all three of my darts on the board most of the time. Like every activity we did with the twins, we competed. We were patient with Ricky, knowing that whoever was matched with him against the other two was probably going to lose. Screams rose on the rare occasions when one of us haphazardly managed to hit the bull's-eye.

My root beer float was long gone after the second game, and I wanted another treat. A quarter of my float had gone to Ricky. Change sat restlessly in my pocket.

"Let's go back and get something else," I said to Gilbert.

A few minutes later we walked back into the malt shop. The nice lady behind the counter looked surprised.

"Well, what would you like this time?"

"We want to split an order of french fries, please." The man back in the kitchen shook his head smiled and began to prepare our order. In minutes a small mountain of steaming fries lay before us in a white-and-red oblong cardboard bowl.

The lady pushed a plastic ketchup bottle toward us. Gilbert uncapped the bottle and drowned the fries. She laid two paper napkins on the counter.

"You two sure like your treats, don't you?"

"Yes, ma'am."

"Are your moms okay with you eating so many goodies?"

I reached for a fry, gently pinched it, and slid it into my mouth. A wisp of steam oozed out as I broke the skin and chewed with an open mouth; I felt a burn on my tongue.

"This is only our second one," I said.

"No, this is your third. I hope you don't get stomach aches."

I reached for another fry when it dawned on me that she was confused. I explained. "Me and Gilbert, here, came in first, then our twin brothers came later, and now we're back. So we've only been here twice."

"You have twin brothers?"

"Yup."

"You gotta be kiddin' me."

"No. It's for reals."

She looked back at the cook, who shrugged, and turned back to us. She leaned toward me, a hint of a smile on her pretty red lips.

"Tell you what. If you can prove that you both have twins, I'll give you all a free snow cone." My eyes perked. I looked over at Gilbert.

"We'll be right back," he said. We walked home as fast as passing the fries back and forth allowed and finished them by the time we reached the yard and broke into a sprint when we got to the path.

"Robert, *cuate*, Robert, *cuate*," we yelled running to the toolshed.

"The lady at the malt shop didn't believe that we have twin brothers. She said if we come up and prove it, she'll give us all free snow cones." We fumbled our words over each other and had to repeat ourselves before they realized the prize that waited for us. Their faces lit up. We ran back to the malt shop with Ricky arriving seconds behind.

The cook at the grill looked up as we walked in, shook his head, and laughed. The counter lady beamed. The four of us and Ricky stood panting with expectant looks, much like Porky's dogs.

"Okay. Line up for me," the lady said. We stood at attention. Ricky got at the end of the line. "So you two are brothers and you two are brothers and it looks like you're all twins. So what are your names?"

Robert made the introductions. "And that one down there is Ricky. He's our little brother."

"Boy, he sure is your little brother."

No longer able to contain himself, Gilbert asked, "Do we get snow cones?"

"Yes, you do."

"Can I have one, too?" Ricky pleaded.

"Well, you aren't a twin, but I guess we can get you one, too."

We talked excitedly as we waited. The lady couldn't stop smiling as she handed us our cones.

"Thanks a lot, ma'am."

193

"You're very welcome."

When we got home, we walked into the kitchen holding our cones. We told Mrs. Maestas about our great fortune. She laughed loud and hard. "Hey, viejo, come in here." Mr. Maestas walked in from the living room. "Tell him what happened." He laughed, too, obviously delighted with the story. When Lillian, the oldest sister, came home an hour later, Mrs. Maestas had us tell her what happened. Mrs. Maestas laughed again as if it was the first time she had heard the story. It was nice seeing her so tickled.

We went back out to competing on the dartboard. My brother and Robert were matched up against Ricky and me. My brother planted his third dart near the bull's-eye. Ricky stepped up hoping to hit the dartboard. He pitched his dart hard and did the impossible. His dart stuck in the center of the plastic feather of my brother's dart. We all stared at the board for a second at what Ricky had just done. There they stood— one dart planted in the end of the other. A miracle if ever there was one. Screams erupted.

"I did it, I did it," Ricky yelled. He did what we saw Robin Hood do in the tournament when he split the end of his opponent's shaft with his own arrow. The twins ran to Ricky and lifted him onto their shoulders and carried him around the driveway pumping their fists in the air as we all cheered. Ricky looked intoxicated with the attention and his well-deserved glory. His chin jutted out, his shoulders straight. Having witnessed the absolute apex of dart throwing that professionals not dare dream of, we retired into the house emotionally exhausted.

We walked up the stairs to the boys' bedroom and lay on the three beds. We talked about the events of the day. Gilbert brought up my standoff with Spooky again but couldn't exaggerate much since our brothers had witnessed it.

After dinner we watched *Gunsmoke* on their black-and-white TV with Mr. Maestas, who like Pa, never missed an episode. He and Mrs. Maestas went to bed afterward and we stayed up and watched a movie called *Them!* The movie was about giant ants that terrorized the people of New Mexico. By ten o'clock we were exhausted from the day's adventures and went up to the boys' room. I fell into a deep, dreamless sleep.

When Ma came to pick us up Sunday morning, Mrs. Maestas came out of the house and asked Ma to get out of the car. "Hey, boys, come here," she called. "Tell your mother what happened with the malt shop lady yesterday." Ma smiled and seemed more amused by Mrs. Maestas's reaction than to the story.

My brother and I got into the car and waved good-bye.

Going to the Maestas house was better than going to Disneyland. It seemed that everything they had was better than what we had. They lived in a two-story house with a really big yard, malt and taco shops a short walk away, and an unlimited source of making money. And I was the toughest kid in the world. Life at the twins' house was great.

19.

4th Grade Summer – Candy Slugs and a Car Wash
Fernando

"He who laughs last, laughs best."
Teddy Wayne

IT WAS JULY. THE SUN ROSE EARLY and set late. Armando and I had just been dropped off for a weekend sleepover with the twins'. The boys were engaged in their latest business venture. They were making lead slugs and using them on old man Cheney's gumball machines.

"Come on in," said Gilbert as soon as we got out of our car. Armando and I were about to be introduced to the fine art of counterfeiting. We walked into the toolshed. A single-burner camp stove sat on the workbench. A small, blackened pot rested on the stainless-steel grill.

"Hi, *cuates*," Robert said with a smile. We sidled next to Gilbert, who was busy on the next batch of slugs. He pinched a small tab that stuck out of the side of the stove reached below the tab, grabbed a knob, and pumped air into the chamber.

"I give it forty pumps." His lips counted silently as the knob moved in and out. "Now we gotta light the stove." He took a stick match from the box and turned the burner knob. The compressed air and fuel mix hissed. The burner lit with a poof.

Robert set the pot over the flame and put a lead bar in it. "In a minute the pot will get hot enough to melt the lead."

"You mean the lead will melt and not the pot?" I asked.

"Lead is softer than other metals so it melts easier." In less than five minutes the lead began to liquefy as the heat did its magic. I watched, fascinated. The hissing flame was the only sound in the shed.

"Hey, it's melting," I said.

Five minutes later the lead was ready. Robert grabbed a shop rag, put it over the metal pot handle, and carefully poured the molten lead into an old cookie tin beside the stove. Heat waves shimmered out of the pot. Sweat droplets formed on Robert's forehead. He set the empty pot on the workbench, wiped his brow, and turned the camp stove off.

"The lead in the bottom of the tin box needs to be the thickness of a penny," Gilbert said. While the lead was still hot, he put the open end of a short metal tube the diameter of a one-cent coin on the lead. Gilbert tapped the top of the tube with a hammer, lifted the tube, inserted a small wooden dowel into the top of the tube and pushed out a slug. While the molten lead in the pot was hot, the twins worked fast and produced six slugs.

Gilbert laid a penny next to the slugs to check for thickness. "Too thick and they won't fit in the candy-machine slot." He showed us how to finish off the slugs with a metal file. The process was slow, but time was not a consideration, summer days were long.

Robert smiled. "Let's do some shopping," We set off for Cheney's corner market.

Gilbert gave us instructions on our way up. "We have to wait until there are a lot of customers in the store before we get the gum. When it's time, don't walk too fast to the machines. We don't want Cheney to get suspicious.

We stood outside watching the entry. The store had a metal sliding door that was left open during business hours and locked at night. I was nervous and excited as we waited for the right moment. An array of bright red, green, yellow, and blue gumballs sat in their glass prison waiting to be released.

Gilbert looked into the store, several customers were lined up with groceries in hand waiting to be rung up. "All right, let's go." We casually walked to the gumball machines. Gilbert squatted, put in a slug, turned the small metal handle, and miraculously a big beautiful blue gumball rolled down the little metal chute and into his palm. We took turns. Each of the slugs worked perfectly. We walked home and competed along the way to see who could make the biggest bubble. Robert won.

The following morning, we made a few more slugs and walked back to the store but Cheney was waiting. He came out before we had a chance to use any of them. The process had been working well for the twins, but they got overconfident and got careless. I was the unlucky one closest to Cheney.

He glared at me. "Hey, kid."

"Yes, sir?"

"Some little shit has been using slugs in my machines." He was a big, balding man in need of a shave. He wore a stained white long-sleeved shirt under a dirty green apron. One of his two front teeth had a silver veneer. Thick dark hairs exploded out of his nostrils and ears. "Do you know who's doing it?"

"No, sir."

"If I find out who he is, I'm gonna call the cops." He set his ham hock-size fists on his hips.

"Yes, sir." He looked at the four of us for a moment, then turned and walked back to his cash register.

"Little assholes," he muttered on his way in. He stood behind the counter two steps from the store entrance taking glances at us as he rang up customers. We were forced to walk away with the fruits of our labor lost.

"Man, we were lucky he didn't ask us to empty our pockets," I said.

"I would've run for it," Gilbert said. Dejectedly, we walked back toward the house.

"The Thrifty drugstore by our house has better gumball machines than old man Cheney's," my brother said indignantly. Robert stopped. "Hey, we should go to the new Safeway. They got nice machines up there." We turned on our heels and with renewed spirit headed for the supermarket. We discussed whether we would buy our candy bars and sodas from Cheney's anymore. We felt insulted by his accusatory tone. After all, we were all altar boys and deserved respect.

Two blocks up National Avenue sat the new supermarket. A variety of new machines to choose from sat at the entry. Cheney's only had two old ones. The store was a lot cleaner. Besides candy and gumballs some of the machines offered small prizes in clear plastic oblong cases, while others gave you cool-looking stick-on tattoos or a handful of salted peanuts.

"I think we'll be happier here," Armando said. The new machines were off to the side of the front doors away from meddling store owners. We used all eight of the slugs. Gilbert got a red dragon tattoo and applied it to his left bicep.

Later in the summer we heard that Spooky hadn't got word about Cheney's threat and got caught using a slug he had borrowed from Robert. True to his word, Cheney called the cops. The police put him in the backseat of their patrol car and drove him to his house. "Spooky got the crap beat out of him by his dad," Robert told us. I couldn't help but smile.

We built tree forts during those warm summer days, played football with Augie, Porky, and Ricky in the twins' weedy yard. Porky had to scold his dogs when they tried to bite whoever was trying to tackle him. Some nights we camped out by the toolshed.

One morning the four of us and Ricky sat on their porch dreaming up money-making strategies. We were engaged in a fly-killing competition. Gilbert was in the lead, I was two kills behind him.

"We should try shoe shining." Gilbert said.

"Where would we set up?" I asked.

"How about in front of church on Sunday mornings?"

"Probably most guys would already have shiny shoes before going to Mass."

"How about at the gas station?" said Ricky.

"Nobody is going to wait to get their shoes shined while they get gas. It would take too long," Gilbert said.

"Let's do a car wash," Robert suggested. "We can charge a dollar a car." We perked up. "I can hose off the cars and everyone else can soap them, and then I can rinse them when they're done."

"Then we can all dry them off," I said. The brainstorming began to pick up momentum.

"Gilbert can collect the money and make change. Ricky, you can wash the hubcaps and tires."

I thought the idea brilliant.

"But where could we do it?" Armando asked.

"Not sure but it would have to be a good place where there are a lot of cars coming in and out."

"Hey," my twin said, "how about the new supermarket? A lot of cars go in and out of there all the time."

"Good idea," Robert said. "Let's go up there and see who we have to talk to."

We half-jogged to the store talking excitedly about the possibilities. We pushed the metal-framed glass doors open, walked in, and asked the cashier closest to the door who we needed to talk to. The lady told us to talk to Mr. Carter, the manager. She looked down the main entrance aisle and pointed. "There he is. He's the man talking to the woman in the red dress."

The checker lady looked at us. "Are you boys all brothers?" she asked.

"Yes, ma'am. He's my brother," I said, then pointed to Robert, Gilbert and Ricky. "And they're brothers."

"You all look so much alike."

"Yeah, we're all twins, except for Ricky." She smiled as we walked to the manager. I heard her excited voice call out to the lady at the next cash register.

"Hey, Marge, look, two sets of twins."

Mr. Carter was a well-groomed man about six feet tall and slim. He wore a dark blue tie, light blue long-sleeved ironed shirt, and black soft-soled shoes. His name badge read, STORE MANAGER in bold letters with his name underneath. He looked at me as we approached, then looked to my brother and Robert and Gilbert. He smiled, too.

"Well, what can I do for you boys?"

"Sir, we would like to have a car wash in the parking lot if it's okay," I said.

He paused. "Gosh, son, no one's ever asked to have a car wash on the store property before. I don't know."

"We'll be polite with the customers and maybe some of them would like to get their cars washed while they buy stuff in the store," Robert said.

I looked directly at the manager as we negotiated, then received a divine inspiration. "We're raising money for our Boy Scout troop."

Gilbert picked up on the ploy, stood at attention, and gave him the three-finger Boy Scout salute.

"Tell you what, if you want to set up behind the store so you don't get in the way of traffic and you promise to behave, I'll let you do it. But if I get one complaint you boys will have to leave."

"Thanks a lot, sir. We'll be really careful."

"When are you thinking of having this car wash?"

"Today."

He paused again, "Well, I guess it's like they say, there's no time like the present." He chuckled and followed us to the door.

"Remember our deal."

"Yes, sir, we will."

"They're doing a carwash to raise money for their Boy Scout troop." Mr. Carter said to the nice checker lady.

"How wonderful. Hey, boys, wait a minute." We stopped. "How much are you charging?"

"A dollar a wash, ma'am."

"Well, you got your first customer."

"Gee, thanks a lot. We'll be right back."

"We already got a customer," Gilbert said as we ran out of the store entry.

Robert strategized. "Armando and I will make a sign. Gilbert, you and Fernando find us buckets, rags, soap, and two hoses."

"What can I do?" Ricky asked.

"You can get the hoses," Gilbert said.

Once home Ricky ran toward one of the yard spigots, unscrewed the hose then went around the other side of the house to get the other hose.

Gilbert and I burst through the back door of the house and found Mrs. Maestas in the kitchen. She had her apron on and was putting chunks of meat into a manual meat grinder. A pile of hamburger lay on a sheet of waxed paper.

"Hey, Ma, we're going to have a car wash at the new supermarket. We need some rags and soap." His voice louder than necessary.

"You boys are having a car wash?"

"That's right, Ma. And the store manager said we could do it behind his store." She looked to Gilbert, then to me.

"Well, let me see what I can do." She wiped her hands on her apron, walked to the laundry room, handed us a pile of rags, and gave us her dish-washing soap and some advice. "Put plenty of soap in your buckets, use the small rags for washing and the big ones for drying."

"Thanks, Ma." She seemed pleased to see her young entrepreneurs willing to work hard. We ran out to the toolshed and found four five-gallon paint buckets. Gilbert had to empty electrical extension cords out of one and plumbing parts out of another. A black bucket in the corner was partially filled with Mr. Maestas's pee. Gilbert gingerly walked it out behind the shed and poured it on the weeds. He took it to a water tap and rinsed it, then grabbed a one-gallon bucket.

"What are we going to use the little one for?" I asked.

"It's for Ricky to sit on when he washes the hubcaps." Robert and Gilbert were really smart; they thought of everything.

Ricky had set a coiled hose by the toolshed and was walking over with another over his shoulder. Gilbert handed me a hose and gave Ricky the five-gallon bucket with the one-gallon can inside. We joined our brothers at the toolshed. They had just finished making the three-by-three-foot cardboard sign.

"All right, let's go," Robert called out. We were panting by the time we got back to the store. Mr. Carter showed us where to hook up our hoses on the rear wall of the store. Robert had Ricky hold the car wash sign at the parking lot entrance. The sign read CAR WASH 99¢ in large black letters. Three of the letters had black bleed marks running down the cardboard.

"I thought we were gonna charge a dollar for the washes?" Armando said.

"Ninety-nine cents sounds like a lot less. Besides, probably everyone will just give us a dollar. Ninety-nine cents might get us more customers." I thought it brilliant.

"Ricky, smile and wave when you hold up the sign. If someone wants a wash, bring 'em back. As soon as you're done washing the wheels, go back out to the front and get us more customers." Ricky seemed honored to be given such an important job.

My brother hooked up the hoses and ran back and forth turning the water tap on and off as needed. Robert squirted dish soap into the four buckets and half-filled them with water.

The high water pressure created a tall head of foam. Gilbert and I grabbed our buckets first. My brother took the black one.

I had to hold back a gleeful scream when the teller lady drove her white Volkswagen bug back with Ricky leading. Gilbert grinned as he waved her into position. She got out of her car. "I want a good job, now. I'll be back in a few minutes." She disappeared around the corner. We had her car washed and dried in ten minutes.

"Ricky, go into the store and tell the checker lady her car is ready." Ricky started to run back out front. "And take the sign with you," Robert yelled.

The checker lady came back and handed Gilbert a dollar. I saw him reach into his pocket and she waved him off with a smile. She got into her car and drove off. Robert's marketing idea worked.

Ricky brought our second customer, an elderly woman driving an old classic black Lincoln Continental in like-new condition. The body had a light coat of dust. I walked over to the car. She smiled and rolled her window down. The lady was neatly dressed. A beehive hairdo rested on top of her head.

"Should I get out or should I stay in my car?" A heavy mix of beauty powder, strong perfume, and hairspray wafted out of her window.

I yelled to Gilbert, "She wants to know if she should stay in her car or get out?"

"Tell her she can get out or stay in."

"You can get out or stay in," I said to her confidently.

My brother ran to the tap. Gilbert and Ricky approached with soap buckets. Robert stood near the passenger side of the car and pointed the hose-end gun, turned, and yelled to my brother, "Okay." He turned the spigot on. Robert squirted the car top just as the lady was stepping out.

"Robert, wait!" I screamed. He jerked the hose back too late. The lady got a face full of water.

"Oh, my!" she yelped.

My heart dropped. Robert turned his head to keep her from seeing him laugh. "Are you okay?" I said, asking her the most stupid question possible.

"Of course," she said forcing a half-smile.

I ran to our rag pile, picked up a clean hand towel and handed it to her. She took the towel and stepped away. *Darn, I hope she doesn't tell Mr. Carter.* I noticed she had groceries in her car so maybe she won't bother to go back in the store and complain. I closed the door for her and she stepped away.

"Okay, Robert," I yelled. The five of us descended on her car like hungry vultures. The huge car with large tires and hubcaps took us twice as long to wash as the Volkswagen.

When we finished Gilbert and I approached her. She opened her purse, took four quarters out, handed them to Gilbert. She handed the white hand towel smudged with makeup to me.

"Thank you, ma'am," Gilbert said. She stood and waited for her one-cent change before getting back into the car. Gilbert handed her a wet penny. She drove to the front of the store. I sneaked along the side wall to see if she was going to complain, but to my relief I saw the car exit the parking lot.

"Next time be more careful," Gilbert yelled to Robert with a chuckle.

Mrs. Maestas drove in and parked her Ford station wagon. "Hi, Mrs. Maestas," I said, happy by the surprise.

"Hi, boys." She got out of the car, walked to the passenger side, pulled little Patricia out, and stepped away. She giggled as she saw us work with purpose. When we finished, she put Patricia back in and handed Gilbert two dollars.

"Ma, the wash is a dollar."

"I can read, honey," she said with a smile, got back in her car, rolled her window down, and handed me a bag with five cans of soda.

"Gee, thanks, Mrs. Maestas."

"You boys did a great job." I handed the sodas around; we waved as she drove away.

"Ricky, get back out there and get us more customers," Robert said.

"Can I drink my soda first?"

"No. Drink it out there and keep the sign up."

We became more efficient with each car, learning to make sure all windows were rolled up before hosing and to know where the customer stood. We learned teamwork, two took one side, two the other, thus avoiding double and triple washing panels and doors. Ricky learned to wash the wheels fast and dash back out front. We had cut our washing time in half by the end of the day.

Customers were taken to see two sets of twins giving it their all. Some chuckled at little Ricky sitting on a gallon can soaping wheels and hubcaps.

Gilbert got a twenty-five-cent tip after he complimented a lady on her cool candy-apple red Thunderbird coupe. He started to compliment every customer. "Wow, those are great looking wheels. Are they mags?"

"Why thank you, young man. Yes, they are."

"That's what I want to put on my car when I'm old enough to get one."

"Ricky, do an extra good job on those wheels," he shouted. Another tip.

Ricky led in our next wash, a new deep blue Chevrolet pickup truck with mud-caked wheels and panels. A tall man in a red-and-blue plaid cowboy shirt with snaps for buttons, blue jeans, and cowboy boots got out. His heels tapped the pavement when he swaggered toward Gilbert. "Y'all do a good job now. I'm going into the store, be right back."

"Yes, sir, we will," Gilbert said. "Boy, this sure is a nice truck. I hope I can get one this nice when I get older."

"Thank you, son I expect it'll be like new when I get back."

"Yes, sir, it sure will." The cowboy walked to the front of the store.

"Let's get the top part washed first, then do the rest. Maybe the soap and water will loosen the mud on the way down." Robert walked to the back of the truck, hopped up onto the bed, hosed off the top, and worked his way down the windows.

I got on the bed and soaped the roof and rear window. As the rinse water made its way down the truck, it rolled off of the sun-caked mud. The five of us worked hard to get the packed mud loose. We had to push and smear the mud off with soapy rags. We double washed the bottom half. After twenty minutes of hard labor, the truck was clean. A slimy brown rectangle stained the asphalt around the footprint of the truck.

The man came back with a grocery bag in one hand and a small brown bag in the other. He took sips from the small bag as he approached. He walked around his vehicle, closely inspecting the windows and the truck's chrome grille. He stepped back and looked at Gilbert. "There's still mud inside the treads of the tires, son. Now, I told you I wanted a good job, didn't I?"

"Yes, sir." Gilbert looked at the treads.

"Y'all get busy now and get them treads clean."

"Yes, sir."

"Resentfully we took a tire each, soaped and scrubbed between the treads and rinsed them off."

"Well, now, that's more like it. Now how much do I owe you?" *What's the matter mister, can't you read?*

"Ninety-nine cents, sir."

"A little steep, don't you think?"

Gilbert stood looking at the truck; the cowboy looked at Gilbert waiting for a response. After a few seconds he handed Gilbert a dollar. He stood and looked at Gilbert. "I got some change comin', son."

Gilbert reached into his pocket and handed the man a penny. The cowboy took a last drink from his bag, turned it upside down, let the last few drops spill, then handed it to Gilbert. He climbed into his truck and drove off.

"That guy was a jerk," Armando said. "We should have squirted him in the face."

Robert looked at Ricky. "If you see another truck like that, turn the sign around."

After washing two more cars we were dog-tired. We had been working since eleven o'clock and it was nearly five. No longer able to keep up the frantic pace we had set at the beginning of the day, the washes were taking longer to finish.

"Can we go home now?" Ricky said to Robert, as he looked up from washing the fourth wheel of a junky Rambler.

Robert turned to the rest of us. "Are you guys ready to quit?"

"Yeah," my brother yelled from the other side of the car.

"Me, too," I said. I looked to Gilbert, he nodded.

"Okay. Let's get this car dried off and we'll quit."

Anxious to finish the day my pace quickened.

"Your car's ready, ma'am. That'll be ninety-nine cents," Gilbert said, not complimenting her on the tired old car. "Thank you, young man. My car looks great." She handed him a dollar and a quarter.

"Thanks a lot," he said and opened the door for her.

Gilbert and I splashed the soapy water from the buckets onto the mud left from the truck while Robert sprayed with the hose. My brother and Ricky collected the rags. With the clean-up done we huddled in the shady corner of the building and sat on the buckets.

"How much did we make?" I asked Gilbert.

"A lot," he reached into his front and back pockets and pulled out wads of damp one-dollar bills and lots of change, along with two slugs that he put back in his pocket. He squatted and made a stack of the one-dollar bills and the change in another. He counted the money twice. "Eighteen dollars and seventy-seven cents."

I sat stunned, not sure if I had heard him right. "Did you say eighteen dollars?"

"And seventy-seven cents," my brother said, his voice barely audible. We stared at the bankroll. It was the most cash I had ever seen in one place.

"What do we do now?" I asked.

"We split the money." Robert, my twin, and I stood and formed a circle as Gilbert began to hand a dollar at a time in our outstretched hands. He put a dollar in his pocket as he made each round. I looked at my hand. It held four dollars.

"What about me?" Ricky said. Gilbert scooped the change and handed it to him.

Ricky beamed, "Wow, thanks, Gilbert."

Car washing was even more profitable than selling newspapers. Lead slugs would be a backup business from now on.

"Ricky, stay here with our stuff," Robert said as we entered the store. We picked up a big bag of potato chips and a family-size bottle of Pepsi and got in the nice cashier lady's line.

"Well, hello, boys. How did your carwash go?"

"Real good," I said.

"We made eighteen dollars." Gilbert proudly said.

"And seventy-five cents," Armando said.

"That's great. I bet your scoutmaster is going to be very proud of you."

"Huh?... Oh, yeah,... he sure is."

We took our groceries and hustled out of the supermarket.

I walked to the candy machines and got a tiger tattoo, only this time it was with a real penny. The thrill of getting it with unlawful currency was sadly missing.

We ate chips and passed the soda around as we walked. Ricky happily jingled the pile of coins in his pocket. Our t-shirts were soaked through, the front of our jeans were streaked with mud, and our tennis shoes sloshed. It was the price we had to pay for such a profitable day.

"If we bring small brooms next time we can offer to sweep out the inside of the cars and wipe off the dashboards for twenty-five cents more," Robert said.

"And if we do this every day, we'll be rich by the end of the summer," I said. Even though exhausted and still having to lug hoses, wet rags, and buckets home, our spirits soared.

Our walk took us past the Big as Texas Bar and Grill. The small, one-story building had a roof-to-ground map of Texas painted on the side wall. We took a shortcut through the back parking lot. "Ghost Riders in the Sky" streamed its way out of the open window. Parked in the lot was the cowboy's gleaming Chevy pickup reflecting the afternoon sun.

"Hang on a second," Gilbert said. He walked with the bucket of wet rags to the unpaved border of the parking lot, scooped handfuls of dirt into the bucket, picked up the rags, and wrung them into the pail. He mixed the water and dirt and formed a sloppy mud ball. Gilbert calmly walked to the truck and set his bucket down. He spread his feet, cocked his arm, and threw a fastball. A beautiful brown mud splat covered the driver's side window and splashed onto the side-view mirror.

Adrenalin shot through my veins. I grabbed one of the hoses and lit out for home. I heard the guys huffing hot on my heels. I sneaked peeks back over my shoulder as we raced down the street, praying no one was following us. We slowed to a trot a block away from the yard, unable to muster the energy to continue running. No one said a word.

We dropped our gear when we reached the house and plopped on our backs in the shade of the porch. Robert started to laugh, then Gilbert, then the rest of us. We laughed deep and hard. We laughed until it reached a crescendo and we could laugh no more. By the time we stopped my cheeks ached and my sides hurt. We peeled our wet shoes and socks off and finished the chips. "I guess we'd better not do another car wash for a while," Gilbert said.

"Guess not," Robert said.

We did so well on the car wash that we didn't need to use slugs on Mr. Carter's supermarket for the next two weeks.

20.

5th Grade – Wrestle Mania
Fernando

"LET'S GET READY TO RUMMMBLE."
Michael Buffer, ring announcer

ONE SATURDAY, DURING MY fifth-grade year, Vangie and Marion invited Martha to come over on one of our visits to the twin's house.

The two sisters, like Martha, never missed *American Bandstand*. The half-hour music-and-dance program aired on Saturday afternoons was hosted by Dick Clark who played the latest rock and roll hits. Each week groups of teenagers from high schools in the Philadelphia area went to the studio and danced to the music. Clark's program featured live interviews with singers or bands whose records made the Top 40 hits.

While the three girls watched their program, the four of us, along with Ricky, sat on their front porch engaged in conversation. The discussion began with a simple yet perplexing question I posed. If Godzilla fought King Kong, who would win?

"Godzilla," Robert said matter-of-factly.

"No," Armando countered. "King Kong because he can fight with both hands and all Godzilla has is his mouth." He was as confident.

"I think Godzilla would win because he can breathe fire and burn King Kong and bite him, too," I said, animated.

Gilbert got into the mix with a loud voice. "King Kong would win. Remember what he did to the giant lizard and dinosaur? He grabbed the lizard by the tail and beat his head against the rocks, then took the dinosaur by his head and jaw and almost tore them apart. He has more experience fighting." My simple question devolved into a free-for-all shouting match. Ricky turned his head from one yeller to the other.

"Hey," Robert hollered over everyone, "it's time for wrestling." While the girls never missed "American Band Stand, we never missed the World Wrestling Federation matches that aired right after. We jumped to our feet and hustled into the living room.

"The wrestling matches are on," Gilbert said to the girls.

"Who cares?" Vangie said, Marion and Martha giggled. The girls walked out of the living room and into Vangie and Marion's bedroom. Moments later we heard Top 40 records playing on their record player and feet shuffling.

We sprawled on the floor and couch. Today's card included a warm-up match between Gorgeous George and Gorilla Monsoon. George wore velvet robes and grew his wavy blond hair long. Gorilla was a hairy-chested, six-foot-six-inch, four-hundred-pound monster. Gorilla wore an ear-to-ear Abraham Lincoln-like beard.

However, it was the main event that we were excited about. It featured a tag-team match with Mr. Moto and The Destroyer pitted against Haystack Calhoun and Ricki Starr. Mr. Moto was a hated Asian wrestler who cheated. In a match once, he had hidden salt in the elastic belt of his black trunks and rubbed it into his opponent's eyes. He wore black mid-calf tights under his trunks and wrestled barefoot. He sported a six-inch long goatee. His partner, The Destroyer, was a masked man who also played dirty and was known for his deadly Figure Four Leg Lock. The Destroyer's off-white mask had dark, exaggerated eyebrows and stitching around his mouth which gave him a fearsome look. They were taking on Haystack Calhoun, a behemoth six-foot-four-inch Texan who weighed six hundred pounds, and Ricki Starr, a clean-cut All-American wrestler.

We could hear The Ronettes' "He's a Rebel" through the wall. Robert got up and went to the bedroom door, banged, and yelled, "Hey, you're making too much noise." The girls turned the volume down a little.

We watched the first match cheering for Gorilla Monsoon the "good guy" in the contest. Late in the match Gorgeous George cheated when he punched Gorilla in the stomach.

While Gorilla was stunned George tried to drop-kick him, but Monsoon made a miraculous instantaneous recovery from the sucker punch and grabbed George's ankle in midair. Monsoon slammed George to the canvas and rolled on top of him. With four hundred pounds of flesh on him, Gorgeous George couldn't move, and the referee slapped the canvas three times for the pin. We jumped and cheered. Our guy won.

It was time for the main event. I leaned into the TV. The Moto-Destroyer tag team entered the ring first. The crowd booed while The Destroyer mocked the fans. The two wrestlers took short warm-up jumps and flung their powerful arms.

Ricki Starr and Haystack Calhoun entered the ring in the opposite corner to roaring cheers. Ricky clapped and bounced on the sofa.

Haystack wore his blue denim overalls, big enough to cover a Volkswagen, and a sleeveless white t-shirt with the collar torn off. A tattered, country-boy straw hat sat on his huge head, and a heavy chain, with a padlock attached, around his neck. Like Mr. Moto, Haystack wrestled barefoot.

Haystack removed his chain and hat and joined Ricki in warm-ups. The Destroyer walked to the center of the ring and taunted his opponents. Haystack took a step toward him, but the referee jumped between them, with outstretched arms and sent the men back to their corners. Hoots and hollers erupted from the crowd. The tension in the arena made its way through the TV screen and into the living room.

A trim, handsome ring announcer, stylishly dressed in a black bow tie, white shirt, and black suit, walked to the center of the ring. A microphone lowered from the ceiling. His baritone voice introduced the wrestlers to loud cheers and boos. After the introductions he yelled into the mic, "LET'S GET READY TO RUMMMBLE." The crowd went wild.

The bell clanged and the match was on. I sat on the edge of the couch next to Ricky. Mr. Moto and Ricki Starr stepped toward the middle of the ring and circled each other. Their partners stood in their corners outside the ropes, holding on to the corner post, ready to go in when tagged. Mr. Moto stopped and looked into the upper seats and pointed. Ricki looked up, Moto cheap-shot him on the chin with his forearm. Ricki reeled. Moto pounced on him and put Ricki in a headlock. With his back to the referee Moto pulled a small black bag from the top of his belt, took something out, and rubbed it into Ricki's eyes.

"I saw him do that before," Robert yelled. Outraged, we jumped up and yelled at the referee. Ricki was able to drop to the floor and spin out of the headlock and rolled to his corner and tagged Haystack's outstretched hand. Mr. Moto ran to his corner and tagged The Destroyer. The Destroyer pulled the ropes apart and hopped into the ring. He danced slow circles around the Texan taunting him. Haystack stood in the center of the ring and followed his opponent waving him in toward him. The Destroyer stopped and looked up at the top seats and pointed but Haystack was having none of the ploy. The crowd booed. The Destroyer began to circle Haystack again and lulled him into his and Moto's corner. With Haystack's back to Moto, Moto hit him on the back of his neck with a judo chop. Haystack, unfazed, turned and grabbed Moto by his beard and hair and dragged him over the ropes and into the ring. The Destroyer hopped onto Haystack's back and began to punch him. We went berserk. Ricki jumped in and ran to his partner's aid, breaking the only-two-men-at-a-time-in-the-ring rule. The referee danced from wrestler to wrestler, futilely trying to stop the infraction. The match was spiraling out of control.

Ricki pulled The Destroyer off Haystack, slipped his arm around The Destroyer's neck, and flipped him head over heels onto the center of the ring. The Destroyer lay dazed. The ref got in front of Haystack and motioned him back to the corner.

While Haystack was distracted Mr. Moto climbed onto the top of the ropes and sprang with the intention of knocking the crap out of Haystack.

"Look out!" Ricky shouted from the couch.

Haystack turned at the last instant and sidestepped. Mr. Moto landed spread-eagle with a loud thud onto the canvas, stunning himself. Ricki dragged The Destroyer by an arm and leg and put him on top of Mr. Moto. Haystack body-slammed them. The crowd erupted. The Destroyer rolled off of Moto lying motionless on his back. Ricki laid on The Destroyer and Haystack on Moto for the pins and the match was over. We jumped, pumping our fists into the air as victors. The ref stood between our wrestlers and raised their arms for the win.

"We won, we won," yelled Ricky, the program ended and Robert turned the TV off.

The three girls walked out of the bedroom. "And you said we were too loud? How can you guys watch such stupid stuff?" Vangie said walking past us to the front door, followed by Marion and Martha.

"It's better than watching a bunch of dumb kids dancing," Gilbert called behind them.

The five of us ran upstairs to the twin's bedroom, set blankets on the floor and had a tag-team match with Ricky as the referee. Ricky lost control of the situation when the only-two-men-at-a-time-in-the-ring rule was broken.

After our match Robert had an idea. "I heard Vangie say that they were going to walk up to the taco shop. Let's ambush them on the way back."

We scampered down the stairs. Mrs. Maestas smiled as we ran past. She had her ironing board set up in the living room waiting for "The Lawrence Welk Show" to come on later. She was talking with Mr. Maestas, who had come home and taken over the couch. "Hello, boys," he called to my brother and me.

We ran past, "Hi, Mr. Maestas."

Robert devised a plan. "Gilbert, you, Fernando, and Ricky hide up near the sidewalk and wait till they pass you, then jump 'em. Armando and I will hide halfway to the house in case any of them get away. This needs to be a surprise attack. If you guys knock them down, we'll come and help you finish them off. If they get away, we'll wait until they get to us, then we'll spring on 'em and you guys can catch up."

"We'll show them who's watching stupid programs," Gilbert said.

We gave the girls code names. Martha was Mr. Moto, Marion was Gorgeous George, and Vangie was The Destroyer. We saw them in the distance walking toward the house. Gilbert, Ricky, and I ran into the waist-high weeds and sat in wait near the beginning of the path. A primal urge to hunt blossomed deep inside me as I inhaled the scent of wild oats. I looked down the path and saw our brothers crouch, then be swallowed by the tall grasses.

"Which one do you want to tackle?" I whispered to Gilbert.

"I'll take The Destroyer, she's the toughest. You take Mr. Moto and, Ricky, you take Gorgeous George." I was disappointed. I was hoping to take Gorgeous George, besides being the prettiest, she would be the easiest to take down.

"I'm going to put the Figure Four Leg-Lock on Gorgeous George," Ricky whispered.

217

"I'll get The Destroyer in a Full Nelson headlock," Gilbert said.

I eased the oats aside and saw them nearing. Engaged in happy conversation, they were about to step off the sidewalk and onto the path.

"Here they come, get ready," I whispered. Gilbert and Ricky squatted. As they neared, I heard Martha say, "Oh, Dion, he's so cute."

Just as the girls walked past us Gilbert yelled, "Now!"

We jumped. They screamed. I grabbed Martha around the waist. Gilbert tried to tackle Vangie, and Ricky grabbed Marion by a leg. Martha didn't go down as easily as I thought she would. She fought me off by slapping and pulling at my hands to keep me from getting a good hold. Marion ignored Ricky, who had wrapped himself around one of her legs. She grabbed me with both hands by my collar and pulled, nearly strangling me. I grabbed a handful of the back of Martha's blouse as she tried to run, but I slipped on the dry oats and fell. Martha spun out of my grip. Marion pried Ricky's arms off and laughed as she ran with Martha down the path.

I heard Gilbert grunting while I was wrestling Martha. He wound up on his knees, trying vainly to get a grip, while Vangie twisted and turned. She rained down fists to his head and shoulders. She managed to put a hand on his forehead and push. Before running away, Marion grabbed a handful of Gilbert's hair and pulled hard. He let go and Vangie got away.

We chased them into the waiting trap. Martha and Marion screamed again when our brothers hopped out, blocking their escape. Vangie was a fast runner and had passed the other two girls. Robert stood to block her, she slammed into him at full speed. They tumbled to the ground. Gilbert, Ricky, and I caught up. I reached for Martha again. In the confusion my brother jumped to help but landed on me instead. Ricky jumped from girl to girl, grabbing at legs, arms, and waists. My brother and I recouped and got back into the fight.

While my brother locked his arms around Martha's thighs, I tackled Marion. We hit Martha on the way down and the four of us wound up on the ground. The girls screamed. Gilbert helped Robert with The Destroyer. She fought her brothers like an Amazon warrior, punching, scratching, and kicking. I heard slapping and groaning from Robert as Vangie clawed at him. When I grabbed Marion, I buried my face in her hair. She was soft and smelled like an angel. My hand rubbed across her breast as we went down. A jolt coursed through me. Ricky took advantage of my wrestling with Marion and jumped on us. He missed Marion and his tennis shoes landed on my leg. I let Marion go and grabbed my knee.

We finally got all three girls on the ground. With our mission accomplished, Robert yelled, "Let's go." We laughed as we ran away. I limped back into the cover of the grass. We worked our way behind the toolshed panting.

We claimed victory even though Robert had three nasty claw marks on his left cheek, Gilbert had the beginning of a black eye, and I had a bruise on my shoulder from when my brother tackled me and a sore knee from Ricky. My brother's t-shirt was torn and he rubbed his sore crotch where he had got kneed. Ricky was the only one unscathed.

The girls stood and patted dust and bits of dried weeds from their blouses and pedal-pushers and made their way to the house. They shook their heads and laughed, apparently, like Ricky, unharmed.

"Boy, Vangie sure is tough," Armando said. I was glad it was the twins that had to deal with The Destroyer.

"She sure is," Robert said, touching the side of his face. I sat on a soft white cloud having touched Marion's chest.

"Next time we'll all jump 'em at the same time," Robert said. "That way two of us can fight Vangie and the others can take the rest."

Thereafter, the girls scanned the yard before venturing out onto the path.

"There they are, RUN!" Vangie would yell. The girls ran like their lives depended on escaping. We took after them like hungry cheetahs, knowing it would take at least two of us to bring The Destroyer down. I always went for Marion. The girls started to use alternate paths to avoid being ambushed. Sometimes we got them, sometimes not. Either way, their screams as we chased them were reward enough.

We came out from behind the toolshed and walked back to the porch. My brother reignited the argument, "King Kong would win . . ." The conversation picked up where it had left off. With no clear consensus, we decided that one of us would write a letter to the movie studio and suggest they film a Godzilla versus King Kong movie and settle the matter. No one volunteered to write the letter.

"Do you know who's wrestling next week?" asked Gilbert.

"It's going to be Chief Strongbow and Killer Kowalski against Abdullah the Butcher and Jerry Crusher Blackwell," Robert said. "You guys should come over."

"Who do you think is gonna win?" I asked. An argument followed. No matter who would win, it was sure to be a great match. I could hardly wait.

21.

5th Grade – What Lurks in the Shadows
Fernando

"Who knows what evil lurks in the hearts of men?"
The Shadow

GILBERT TOLD ME THAT THEIR house was haunted by a pair of green hands that crawled on the floors. If you were alone, they could jump at you from behind the couch or from under a bed and strangle you.

"Let's camp out tonight," Gilbert said on one of our summer visits. The boys belonged to the Boy Scout troop at St. Jude's Parish.

I was envious. Ma didn't let us join a troop. "I have enough responsibilities without having to get you to meetings and we spend enough on uniforms."

The twins' troop went on camp outs to San Diego's Laguna Mountains. "It was really cool. One morning before everyone got up four of us sneaked out of our tents and hunted a deer. We jumped it and killed it with our knives," Robert said. I was in awe.

We used Mr. Maestas's blotted canvas painter's tarps and long scrap two-by-fours to make a tent next to the toolshed. The tent was big enough to sleep the four of us. Mr. Maestas was a carpenter, so lumber and firewood were plentiful.

They taught us to cut kindling with a hatchet from scrap wood. "Make a small teepee with the biggest pieces," Gilbert instructed. "Crumple newspaper and put it in the bottom, then the thinnest pieces of kindling on top of the paper and the bigger kindling on top of those."

My brother struck a matchstick and lit the paper. Flames from the paper ignited the smallest chips, the chips lit the bigger kindling, and the kindling lit the two-by-four teepee. It was cool to see the flames progress from a lit match to a full fire. A curtain of sparks swirled into the air when the two-foot-tall teepee collapsed in on itself. We straightened wire clothes hangers to skewer our hotdogs and marshmallows.

The twins showed us how to wrap apples in tin- foil and put them in the coals. The steaming softened apples were delicious.

We peed in the weeds behind the toolshed rather than walk to the house. "Indians and mountain men peed outside, too," Gilbert said. The idea of relieving myself outdoors gave me a sense of kinship with those brave and honorable men. If two of us had to pee at the same time, we had sword fights with our streams, the winner being the guy whose stream lasted the longest. I never won against either of the twins.

We told each other stories around our campfire. My twin drew on Tony's heroic sagas of Beowulf and Odysseus. They listened intently as my brother spun the tales.

Robert stood to tell us a story. "There was a man who got lost in a dark forest. He found this old, big two-story house. It was getting dark and big black clouds were rolling in. He knocked on the door. Nobody answered. He went in. He thought no one was home and he lay on an old couch to sleep. A storm started during the night. He heard a woman crying softly. He called out to her, but she didn't answer. He made his way to the staircase and climbed the steps." Robert's shadow danced against the wall of the toolshed as the story unfolded. "The man walked down the dark hall. He put his ear to a door and heard the crying. He tapped, a soft voice said, "Come in."' A single candle burned on a small table. A thin lady in a long black dress stood in a corner of the room, her back turned to him. Her black-and-white hair reached down her shoulders and halfway down her back. "'What's wrong?" he asked.

"'I am so hungry and there is no food."

"'Can I get you some?"

"'Please there is some food in the closet, but the door is too hard for me to open.'

"He stepped over and opened it. In the closet were two skeletons and a man's body hanging on a hook, half-eaten. The man spun around; a lightning bolt flashed. The lady had turned and was staring at him. Her face was covered with warts. Her stringy gray hair looked like spider webs. A second flash of lightning revealed big yellow fangs as she laughed."

A shiver ran up my spine. "And then what happened?"

"What do you think?"

In the tent later that night I was glad to be with the twins who weren't afraid of anything. After all, they had stalked and killed a deer with only knives. Later we turned off the kerosene lamp and stopped talking, I heard Robert cry softly, "Oh, I'm so hungry. Fernando, would you look in the toolshed? I think there is some food in there." Robert, Gilbert, and my brother laughed but I didn't.

Sometime after midnight we settled down again and we drifted into the sleep of the young.

Early the next morning I heard Mr. Maestas's truck start and the sound of the engine fade as he pulled out and onto the street. I rolled over and fell back asleep. When we got out of our bedding, the skies were cloudy, and a cool breeze blew in from the West. I put on my sweatshirt, walked to the back of the toolshed, and watered the weeds. When I got back my brother and the twins had awoken.

Gilbert got up and began to reignite the campfire. Robert went into the house and brought out a box of cold cereal, milk, bowls, and spoons.

A rare lightning storm rolled in from the Pacific, forcing us indoors. Robert turned the TV on and tried several channels, but we didn't find anything.

"Let's play hide-and-seek," Gilbert suggested. Their two-story home was the perfect place.

"Who's gonna be first to seek?" I asked.

"Everyone put your fists in the middle," Gilbert said. We stood in a circle and Gilbert began. "One potato, two potato, three potato four . . ." Armando lost so he was first to seek.

He put his head to the living room wall and counted to twenty-five.

Gilbert, Robert, and I scattered. I saw Gilbert go into the kitchen and Robert sneaking upstairs. I hid downstairs in Mr. and Mrs. Maestas's clothes closet. I always hid in a room where their mom or one of the sisters were nearby, I was keenly aware of lurking green hands in the shadows. I stood in a corner of the closet behind some hanging shirts and took my shoes off and put my feet into a pair of Mr. Maestas's boots. Mrs. Maestas was ironing just outside the open bedroom door. Vangie and Marion were in their bedroom.

Robert hid upstairs in the attic. I envied their super-cool attic. Gilbert had taken me up there once. It had a low, sloping ceiling with cobwebs in the corners where rafters met the walls. My nostrils filled with a musty lumber odor as we climbed in. The floor was strewn with Mr. Maestas's old army gear, storage trunks, fishing poles, and who knows what other cool stuff in so many dust covered unmarked boxes.

Robert told us later that he had hid in the attic and, while waiting for my brother to find him, had to go pee. He didn't want to give away his hiding place, so he knelt and peed in his dad's army helmet. He wasn't caught hiding and didn't tell anyone where he hid. I was the first one found, so it was my turn to seek.

I faced the wall, covered my eyes and counted. Gilbert hid in the attic behind some boxes and covered himself with Mr. Maestas's army jacket.

After counting I checked the kitchen pantry first and then looked under beds on the first floor. But no luck. I figured since they must be hiding upstairs, I would be safe from the green hands. I got to the top of the stairs and turned down the hall to the twins' room. I looked under their beds and in their closet. No luck. I walked back into the hall. Except for the slight creak of the floorboards under my shoes, the upstairs was eerily quiet. I decided to look in the attic. They had to be up there.

I climbed up the ladder built into the wall and pushed up on the trap door just enough to peek in. The hatch hinges squeaked like a door in a horror movie. Then I heard a loud BANG. I dropped the door, my heart jumped to my throat. "Ma, I'm home!" It was Ricky coming in the front door. I leaned against the wall, hand on my heart. Jeez. I took a deep breath and pushed the door up again and poked my head into the dark attic.

I heard a splash and panicked. I knew the green hands were coming for my neck. I squealed and ducked, and the hatch slammed on my fingers. My feet slipped off the ladder rung. I shot my hand out to grab the ladder rail but missed. I fell to the floor and sprang to my feet. I streaked down the narrow hall toward the stairs. Skinny, weird grandma cracked open her bedroom door and looked out. Her bony, blue-veined hand wrapped around the doorframe. Her stringy black-and-white hair, no longer covered by the head scarf, looked like spider webs. She smiled. I swore she had big yellow fangs. I backed away to the staircase, missed the first step, and banged my way down screaming, "Robert! Gilbert! Robert! Gilbert!" Robert and my brother ran out from their hiding places. Mrs. Maestas left the ironing board. Vangie and Marion ran out of their room. Ricky appeared.

"My god, what happened?" Mrs. Maestas asked.

"The green hands! The green hands! They're in the attic. They almost got me." I panted, terror-stricken.

"Green hands?" Mrs. Maestas said. "What're you talking about?"

I spit out the words. "Gilbert-told-me-about-the-green-hands-hiding-in-the-house."

She looked amused and said, "Calm down. There's no green hands in this house." *What about the flesh-eating grandma? I saw her.*

"But Gilbert told me that . . ." I stopped when I heard foot-steps coming down the stairs. I stepped back and turned to look, afraid of what I might see. Gilbert appeared, dripping liquid from his head and onto his shoulders and chest. We all stood in silence.

"Gilbert, were you hiding in the attic?" Robert asked. "Yeah."

"And did you put dad's army helmet on?"

"Yeah."

"I peed in it when I was hiding up there."

Mrs. Maestas looked from Robert to Gilbert, then burst out laughing, then my brother, then everyone. Mrs. Maestas put a hand to her breast, the other over her mouth, leaned against the wall and kept saying, "Green hands . . . pee," and roared.

The only ones not laughing were Gilbert and me, Gilbert because he was dripping with pee and me because I was not convinced that the house wasn't haunted.

Gilbert hung his head, turned, and trudged back upstairs. "I'm going to take a shower," he mumbled. Mrs. Maestas had to sit, overtaken by laughter.

After things settled down, Robert, my brother, and I walked out to the porch. The weak rays of the early evening sun were breaking beneath the cloud cover. "It doesn't look like it's going to rain, let's sleep out again tonight," I said.

I was happy to sleep outside and not in the haunted house. As far as I was concerned, not only were the green hands still in there, but were now emboldened by Mrs. Maestas saying she didn't believe in them.

The three of us and Ricky walked out to the tent. I cleaned the ashes and partially burned wood from last night's fire. My brother got the hatchet, chopped kindling, and formed another teepee.

Gilbert came out after showering. He and I walked to the store. We considered walking the extra blocks to the super-market to boycott Cheney's, but we compromised our moral resentment. Old man Cheney watched us come in. I felt his eyes burn a hole in the back of my head.

We put a bag of marshmallows and two sodas on the counter. He rang it up without saying a word and stuck his hand out. Gilbert pulled a handful of change out of his pocket. Mixed in with the change were two penny slugs. I panicked and said, "Hey, Mr. Cheney, how much are those?" I pointed to some small boxes on the wall behind him. He turned. Gilbert grabbed a dollar from his fist and shot the slugs back into his pocket. Cheney turned back around.

"Now, what would you two do with rubbers?"

"Huh? Oh, never mind," I said. Cheney took the dollar, rang up our order, and handed Gilbert his change.

"Do you think old man Cheney knows we used the slugs?" I said on the way back.

"Well, he didn't call the cops on us and he caught Spooky, so I guess he doesn't."

"What's a rubber?"

Gilbert chuckled, "You don't know what a rubber is?"

"I kinda do."

"Look, a guy puts a rubber over his dick so his wife won't have kids."

"Oh, yeah, I sorta knew that."

When we got back to the campsite Mrs. Maestas came out of the house with a pot of chili beans for us. Gilbert and I took concrete blocks and made a stand over the fire to keep the pot warm. We made two benches with buckets and a scrap two-by-eight. We ate the chili and passed the soda bottles around. The evening sun melted into dusk and dusk slowly into night. We stared into the yellow flames, anticipating the collapse of the teepee. The smell of burning Douglas fir was warm, therapeutic.

My brother laid out plans for our futures. "We'll all get good jobs, buy a big two-story house like you guys have, and live together."

"And we can all have our own bedrooms," Robert said. It was a novel idea to have an entire room to myself. I sat quietly trying to grasp the concept. "We won't have to share beds, clothes or underwear or anything anymore," I said.

"And we'll drive really cool cars and have pretty girlfriends," Gilbert added.

We listed qualities we would demand in a girlfriend. "She has to be a good cook," I said.

"She should wear nice clothes but never a bikini. If she tried to wear one I wouldn't let her out of the house," said Robert.

"She should go to Mass on Sundays," I added.

Gilbert broached a subject I was thinking about but too embarrassed to bring up. "She should be a good kisser."

"You want to kiss a girl?" Ricky asked.

"You'll know about that when you get older," Gilbert said.

"None of us will get married," my brother said.

Ricky furrowed his brow and asked, "Can I be with you guys?"

"Sure, as soon you get old enough you can live with us," I said. "So we'll have to get a five-bedroom house."

"But I want to be in Gilbert's room." Ricky said, "Okay. So we'll only need four bedrooms."

"We can all build the house and have your dad help us." Everyone thought that was a great idea.

Robert lifted a cheek and ripped a loud one. The chili was doing its magic. A competition started and like everything else, Robert and Gilbert outdid us.

We got into the tent and lay on our bedrolls. I was dizzy with anticipation, pondering the great future that awaited. We talked in wandering, hopeful tones. Gilbert shared that he wanted to be a dentist. Robert wanted to be a successful businessman. I wasn't sure what a successful businessman meant but it sounded good. My twin and I didn't know what we wanted to be but knew whatever it was, we wanted to make a lot of money. Being a manager of the *Green Sheet* newspaper was a strong possibility for me. I thought about all the money the manager was making at seven cents a copy.

The conversation slowly and quietly died. In the silence I prayed to St. Francis Xavier, my patron, to grant us our dreams. But Francis was a good guardian and knew better than I did what was good for me. Our visions of sharing a big house with our friends, driving fast cars, and having beautiful girlfriends never materialized. The real world dictated our futures. Eventually my brother and I stopped going to their house as the four of us drifted apart with new friends and interests. My twin and I were fortunate to have been their friends; to this day I treasure the memories of our adventures at the home of the Maestas twins.

22.

5th Grade – Fighting the Devil
Armando

"You must not eat fruit from the tree that is in the middle of the garden, and you must not touch it, or you will die. You will surely not die, the serpent said to the woman."
Genesis, Chapter 3

THE DEVIL WAS AS MUCH A PART of the Garcia family as was the Virgin Mary. I loved the Virgin Mary, the Mother of Jesus. She was good and pure, the only person who had never committed a sin. The most boring job in the world would be the priest who heard her confession.

Our teachers said that if you were in hot water with God for having committed a really, really big sin and were too afraid to ask Him for forgiveness, you could always go to Mary, and she would intervene on your behalf. The God of wrath and judgment had a tender spot in His heart for Mary and couldn't deny her anything. This was a great advantage for Catholics. Our poor Protestant brethren didn't have the good sense to pray to her.

The devil was always there, too. When alone in the bedroom, I'd beat the crap out of the devil. I'd imagine him standing before me and grab him by the collar. I'd rear back my fist and hit him so hard that he'd go flying and land on a bed. I'd jump on him, straddling him like a cowboy hero jumping on his horse. The bedsprings squeaked as I pummeled him with rights and lefts. He would plead with me that he'd had enough. But he had tempted people like me into sinning and the ones who didn't make it to confession, went to hell where he tormented them forever. Mercy? I think not. He had it coming, and more. I picked him off the bed and flipped him over my shoulder like a judo master slamming him to the ground. And like a good cowboy, I never kicked a guy when he was down. That was for cowardly bad guys like the devil. I picked him up, lifted him over my head, spun him round and round until he was good and dizzy, and then threw him through the window, shattering the glass into hundreds of pieces. He'd limp off like a beaten dog. God, it felt great giving the father of lies a sound beating. It was his fault that man had to die and not live happily forever in the Garden of Eden because he tempted poor, unsuspecting Eve.

I asked Ma, "What are the devil's favorite colors?"

"*Rojo y negro,*" (red and black) she answered. "*Y cuando esta de acercas uno huele el azufre,*" (And when he's close by you can smell sulfur). I never used red or black when coloring again. When alone in the dark I began to smell sulfur, I'd make a hasty retreat into the house, to find Ma, who was as good and holy as the Virgin Mary.

The devil possessed a lot of power. The world was filled with people who had fallen prey to his influence, people like Marilyn Monroe and Elvis Presley and the sailors from the Naval base where we lived in San Diego. Some of them would go to the Tower Theater downtown where they saw movies with naked women. My big sisters wrote letters to the degenerate owner of the Tower, explaining that morally corrupting our sailors was a terrible threat to our country's security. My sisters, under the guidance of the nuns of their high school, in union with the Legion of Decency, fought the good fight. They were doing their part to stem the nation's steady slide toward decadence. Decadence led to the fall of the Roman Empire. We were next.

"Morally weakened sailors can't defend us like those who stand on solid moral ground," my older sister told me one night. The stakes couldn't be higher; godless Russians were poised to overtake our morally weakened forces. Thank God for the nuns, my sisters, and the Legion of Decency.

I couldn't wait to be old enough to join the fray. I would become a leader in the Legion. Maybe if I talked to the bishop, he would put me in charge. I'd give inspiring speeches and help the world understand the importance of living moral lives. Millions who didn't know the truth, like we did, were being led astray. The world needed my voice. Why couldn't people understand? There were misguided souls who didn't believe in the devil, or even God. It was my Christian duty to save them.

I lay awake nights, making plans to save the world. As soon as I was old enough, I would apply for director of the Legion. It would be my job to research moral degradation intensively. I'd start at the Tower Theater. I'd carry a notepad and document every moral transgression. And in the interest of furthering my education, I would go to burlesque shows and force myself to sit through them ten, twenty, thirty times, if necessary, no detail too insignificant, no sacrifice too great. I would look at dirty magazines of all sorts. The more the degenerate, the harder I would have to apply myself. I'd have to do this in secret of course. People who saw me doing such things could understandably get the wrong impression. I would have to wear dark glasses, a hat, and a long coat to hide under and then do my undercover work.

The devil was powerless in the Garcia household. Father Gomez blessed our house just after we moved in. He used holy water and holy incantations in Latin. Our family went to Mass every Sunday, attended Catholic schools, and memorized the Baltimore Catechism questions and answers. We confessed our sins on the first Friday of every month, received Holy Communion every Sunday.

Hector, across the street, went to Gompers Junior High School. He made friends and brought them over to play one Saturday. I got to like them and didn't want them going to hell. Once, during a break from playing war, we sat and chatted. I was aghast that they knew so little of the spiritual world. I explained heaven, hell, and purgatory to them and asked them if they were aware of these facts.

"I know about heaven and hell," one said. "But I don't know what in the hell that other place is." It made my head spin to hear him use a cuss word when talking about God's justice system. I explained Adam and Eve's original sin and how Jesus came to earth and died so people like him could have a chance at getting into heaven.

Then the kid laid a bomb on me. "I wasn't baptized." *Not baptized?* I offered to baptize him right there. The poor fool declined. I warned him of Jesus's impending return to separate the believers from the heathens and what fate awaited them. He stopped me and said, "Look, preacher boy, I don't care about any of this shit."

I asked Hector not to bring him over again. One day he'd be sorry, I'd look down from heaven and shrug my shoulders.

"Told you so."

There was a lot of work to be done in the world. The devil was deceiving people at every turn. There were juvenile delinquents everywhere. It seemed as if everybody was getting divorced, even Hector's mom. She had been a good, practicing Catholic and got a divorce. The church allowed her to go to Mass, but she couldn't receive Communion anymore. The devil had to have had a hand in it.

Father McGinn, one of the parish priests, came into our fifth-grade religion class and told us just how sinister the devil was. "He can get into your mind and trick even good children like you into having sinful thoughts." I rolled this around in my head. The more I thought about it, the more sinful thoughts came to mind. I begged the Virgin Mary to go to God and ask Him to forgive me. I didn't want to have impure thoughts. I came to fully realize the awesomeness of the devil's power when I went to confession.

"Father," I said, "the devil's making me sin."

"And just how is he doing that, son?"

I was mortified having to say it out loud. "He made me think of what one of the nuns might look like naked, Father." I was so embarrassed I wanted to cry.

Father was silent for a moment then said. "Which one?"

"Sister Mary Grace."

"Oh, yes, the pretty one. Well, don't worry too much about the devil's tricks. He even plays them on me sometimes. Just pray harder."

I walked out of the confessional dumbfounded. The devil even gets to priests, the men of God who have been ordained by His Excellency, the bishop.

Ma had the family pray the rosary on our knees once a month after the dinner dishes were done. During May, the month of Mary, we prayed the rosary to her every night. On such nights Ma moved the Sacred Heart of Jesus statue from the top of the TV console and replaced Him with a statue of the Virgin Mary. Mary stood with her arms open, welcoming us to her. A golden halo, connecting her to the heavens, hovered over her head. She stood on a snake, symbolizing her power over the devil.

The rosary has fifty-nine beads with a small metal with the images of Jesus and His mother and a crucifix at the end. Each bead had a prayer recited with it and for a few beads we said two or three prayers. Ana, Carolyn, Martha, Fernando, Carmen, and I knelt on the living room floor. My brother Tony was excused since he was away studying at the seminary. Pa was sleeping before his midnight shift. My big sisters were expert at praying the rosary really fast, getting us through in time to watch "The Dick Van Dyke Show."

Ana began rapid fire: "HailMaryfullofgracetheLordiswith theeblessedartthouamongstwomenandblessedisthefruitofthy womb,Jesus." Like Olympians seamlessly passing the baton to the next runner, we answered, "HolyMarymotherofGodpray forussinnersnowandatthehourofourdeath.Amen." We kept the pace going for the Our Fathers between each of the ten Hail Marys.

After we got through one night, I walked into the bedroom and saw the devil, in my mind's eye.

"So, playing your filthy tricks in Father McGinn's mind, eh? And corrupting public-school kids, eh? Just you wait until I get old enough to join the Legion of Decency." I grabbed the devil by his collar and reared back my fist.

23.

5th Grade – The Science Project
Fernando

The Top Ten Things to Procrastinate:
Number 1 ...
Author unknown

MISS BELESARIO, WAS OUR FIFTH-GRADE TEACHER. She was about as average in weight and build as a woman could be. Her puffy dark hair was just beginning to gray. Her blouses covered her arms, her skirts and dresses reached below the knee. Her choice of wardrobe colors were gray, black, and dark blue. This unassuming woman was a great teacher.

She engaged us with stories and anecdotes of exotic places she had been: the Orient, Latin America, Europe. In my eyes, she had seen the whole world, a welcome change from the narrow worldview of the nuns and their boring stories of the Midwest. The nuns constantly compared their superior life experiences to the shallow, free-for-all California lifestyle.

Miss Belesario had a sense of humor, was patient and kind, but she had her limits, as I found out one afternoon. It was during the monthly benediction held during school hours in the parish church. I was standing next to Jules Jefferson. Jules had transferred from public school and liked making kids laugh. We were singing a Latin hymn, backed up by the children's choir and organ. The priest and altar boys burned incense during the ritual, adding to the solemnity of the service. Jules started singing loudly, purposely off-key, and making up words. He either didn't know or didn't care that the ornate bronze monstrance on the altar held the body of Christ in the form of a large host. I couldn't help but laugh at his clowning that bordered on the sacrilegious.

Sister Constance, no fan of my twin and me, sat a few rows behind with her eighth-grade class. Constance must have seen us goofing off. Undoubtedly, after the service she told Miss Belesario to keep better control of her students. When we filed out to return to our classroom, Miss Belesario pulled Jules and me out of line.

"Jules, Fernando, I'm so angry at you two I could slap you. See me after school." I walked back to class, stunned. It was a long afternoon in her classroom. I rehearsed lines I would say to her as I sat. I looked over to Jules in the next row. He seemed unfazed.

The three o'clock bell rang. I stayed in my seat while the rest of my classmates left. Jules stood and made for the door. "Hey, we're supposed to stay after school."

"I ain't stayin'," was all he said, and left. I was flabbergasted.

After the room emptied, I slowly walked to Miss Belesario's desk and stood, trying to remember what I was going to say. She was shuffling papers and looked up.

"Where is Jules?"

"I told him we were supposed to stay but he just left."

She must have recognized the anxiety on my face and softened.

"You shouldn't have been misbehaving during benediction. It's a bad reflection on you and on the entire fifth grade."

I looked to the floor. "I'm sorry, Miss Belesario. I'll never do that again."

"I accept your apology, Fernando. You may leave." I walked to my desk, picked up my books, and slinked out the back door.

I don't know if Jules ever got in trouble with her but as for me and my teacher; we were good for the rest of the year.

Unlike the dogmatic nuns, Miss Belesario was keen on science. When she found out one of the students had a pet snake, she asked him to bring it to class. When we filed in Monday morning, an aquarium with dirt, rocks and leaves sat on her desk.

"Class, I asked Freddy to bring his pet snake in this morning." Miss Belesario reached into the case and took out the reptile. She told us that she could tell it was a garter snake by its stripes and color pattern. The snake's tongue darted in and out as it wrapped itself around her arm. It gave me the creeps.

"Garter snakes help keep nature in balance by eating leeches, rodents, and toads. All of God's creatures have a purpose." After the brief show-and-tell, Miss Belesario put the snake back into its home. "Just settle back in there, honey." The fifth graders laughed. I didn't, and was glad my desk was near the back of the room.

"I want you to think of a science project. You must create it yourself and give a presentation to the class. It may be anything one would find in the natural world; an animal, present or extinct, a mineral or an element, or something from modern science. Use your imaginations. Have them ready to present next Monday. That gives you a week to prepare. I look forward to seeing them."

I was excited by her challenge. Armando and I brainstormed on our walk home. "It'd be really great to build a big display and get an A," I said. Maybe this time I'd have something cool to show off on parent night.

"I think I'll do mine on rockets," my brother said.

"Rockets? You don't know anything about rockets."

"I know I don't, but I can look it up in the encyclopedia and do a report. That's how I'm going to learn about rockets, you idiot."

I hadn't thought about it that way. I guessed he was right. "What're you going to do?"

"Don't know yet."

Whatever it was, it was going to be better than rockets. I changed into my play clothes as soon as I got home and ran across the street to Robert and Chucky's and played until supper time.

After dinner Ma had us do homework: catechism, math, geography. I slogged through the work until we gathered in front of the TV. I didn't mention the science project to Ma. Monday turned to Tuesday, Tuesday to Wednesday. Next thing I knew it was Friday, the best day of the school week. The only nagging concern was the science project that would be due on Monday, but I had Friday afternoon and two more days to get it done.

We played with our friends until dusk and then came home for dinner. While my sisters and Ma cleaned up the kitchen, I thought about starting on my project but was distracted by Pa and the Friday Night Fights. There was a Mexican boxer on the ticket. "Come on, boys. Watch the fight with me." The temptation was too much. I sat as Pa coached from his easy chair, "Hit him, Mexican! Hit him!"

Pa was super-excited when his *Sinaloan paisano* hit the hard-fighting gringo with a devastating left and knocked him to the canvas late in the tenth round. Pa jerked his leg out to jump off his chair and kicked the leg of the coffee table. He groaned and cheered at the same time. He hobbled to the bathroom and came back out with his little toe wrapped to the next toe with medical tape. Pa hobbled in but was still excited.

I was happy for Pa and his boxer, but the impending science project weighed on me. It was too late to start it now. I promised myself to take time on Saturday to work on it.

Pa went to bed happy, and our older sisters came into the living room and tuned in the "Friday Night Frights," the weekly monster movie. My twin and I went to bed not wanting to spend a sleepless night afraid of monsters lying in wait in dark corners. *I'm going to work on the science project first thing in the morning.*

Pa roused us out of bed the next day with a job for us to do. He tried to instill in us the value of hard work. We hated working with him because it was boring and we wanted to play with our friends. I didn't want to tell him about my science project because he might tell Ma and I knew she wouldn't let me do anything until it was done. I would work on it in my own time.

Pa had us go to the lower yard, gave us a bucket each and half-filled them with a water hose. We carried the buckets and poured them into the basins of our six fruit trees, three buckets on each tree. After watering, Pa showed us how to cull the fruit.

"If you remove some of the fruit, the remaining ones will get more water and nutrition and you'll get bigger, better fruit." Pa knew a lot about fruit trees, he had been a farm worker in Northern California.

After watering, he worked with us weeding under and around the trees. Twenty minutes of work seemed like a week in a POW camp. Pa got disgusted with us over our lack of effort and dismissed us. "Okay, you two can go now," he said with a huff.

We ran off lest he change his mind. We crossed the street to see what Robert, Dave, and Chucky were up to.

Saturday evening was fill-the-bathtub time. We took turns and scrubbed a week's worth of dirt and grime off. An impressive gray-brown ring adorned the tub when we finished.

Afterward we joined Pa and our sisters in the living room to watch *The Twilight Zone*. Then it was bedtime and church on Sunday morning.

When we got home from the ten o'clock Mass, Dave and Chucky were waiting for us on our front porch. We hopped out of the car and ran to them.

"Hey, look what my dad got me," Dave said. He held up a plastic magnifying glass the size of a sheet of notebook paper.

"Come on." We followed him into Ma's flowerbeds and found a trail of red ants. He lifted the magnifier at just the right height and focused the super-bright light beam on individual ants, instantly cooking them. Each of the tiny ants vaporized in a small wisp of smoke.

"Can I try that?"

He handed it to me.

"Armando, Fernando, get out of your good clothes," Ma said.

"Hang on, we'll be right back." We hustled into the house, changed, and ran back out to spend the rest of the day cooking bugs and starting paper and small twigs on fire. This was really, really cool.

Sunday evening, I forced myself to do the math and geography I meant to do Friday. I chose not to think about the project. I hurried so I could tell Ma that my schoolwork was done and could I please watch "Disneyland." I was anxious to see Davey Crockett fight at the Alamo.

I agonized in bed that night about what I should have done and hadn't. Maybe I could tell Miss Belesario that I got sick over the weekend and couldn't do it or that on my way to school I had to jump out of the way of a speeding car and my project wound up getting run over and that I was lucky to be alive. I could rub some dirt on my uniform. Or maybe I could fake being sick, but Ma was too smart for that.

My brother had commandeered Carolyn to help him. Always ready to help us, especially with schoolwork, she had him look up rockets in our encyclopedia and told him to make notes and write a report. He plagiarized a few paragraphs while Carolyn worked on the construction.

She used a picture from the encyclopedia as her model. Carolyn took the cardboard tube from Ma's waxed paper for the fuselage and cut several fins from a cereal box. She cut a piece of construction paper to form the cone and taped it to the top of the tube. She glued on the fins and had him spray paint the rocket white. Carolyn had a small, plastic letter stencil. She drew U.S.A on a rectangle scrap of construction paper and glued it on his rocket.

"*Cuatito*, you can't take your notes on ordinary notebook paper."

"Why not?"

"Because it won't look right. You want to get a good grade, don't you?"

She sat at our typewriter and rewrote his notes, with correct spelling and grammar. In no time she had his one-page typed report finished.

"Now, isn't this better?"

"Heck yeah, thanks."

"Hang on *cuatito*, I'll be right back." She went back to her bedroom and returned with a shoe box. "Put your rocket in here. That way it won't get damaged when you carry it to school."

"Oh, man, Carolyn, thanks a lot."

She smiled and went back to her own homework.

Monday morning, he was excited to go to school, I left in dread. My brother happily carried his project, ninety percent done by Carolyn. *Darn, I should've done mine Friday instead of playing with Robert and Chucky.*

Miss Belesario had the janitor set up two tables in the classroom where the science projects were to be displayed. Cindy Johnston, took a cue from our teacher's example and brought in a glass box with a big ugly, green iguana. The box had sand, stones, and small branches of greens arranged to mimic the lizard's habitat. I couldn't look at it without shuddering.

John Maloney had a large cardboard panel mounted on a dark wood stand. The lower part of the panel was painted a cool shade of green, the upper part, sky blue. He had neatly drawn and colored shrubs and trees on it. He cut out pictures of animals from the African Savannah from an old *National Geographic* magazine and pasted them on. Lions skulked among shrubs stalking antelope. Wildebeest grazed at the foot of Mount Kilimanjaro. Next to his display lay a page-and-a-half typewritten report. John's mom worked in a doctor's office.

Philip Kajawa had a two-foot-by-two-foot piece of plywood with green napped fabric giving the effect of grass. He had made a volcano out of plaster. Red and orange flames painted on glossy enameled construction paper erupted from the caldera. Bright lava flowed down the side of the mountain. A blue glass lake sat in the center. He had attached plastic dinosaurs, meticulously painted to resemble their skin color.

Project after project, the fifth graders had done some impressive work. No one noticed that I hadn't brought one in.

Science class followed the noon recess. I thought about walking home but knew I'd only get in trouble with Ma. I sulked at my desk, ready to be humiliated, but the first set of presentations took the entire afternoon. To my great relief Miss Belesario announced, "Those of you who didn't get a chance to present today will present tomorrow."

I was spared. I resolved to do a great project tonight and be ready to impress everyone tomorrow.

When I got home, I decided that a little playtime with the boys would help me focus better once I settled down to some serious work. A little time turned into more than I planned. Hector had learned how to light a fart with a match and said he would give us a demonstration. There was no way I was going to miss that.

Hector's bedroom was a remodeled garage, detached from the house, away from his meddling mother and annoying little sister.

"Co...co...come on in," he smiled as he opened the door and locked it behind us.

"Do you think you can do it?" my brother asked.

"Watch." He took his shoes and pants off and set them by his dresser and lay on his bed in his socks, underwear, and T-shirt. We waited patiently while he cooked one up. As my brother and I sat, he gave us a tutorial.

"Your body produces methane gas when it digests the food in your stomach. Methane is flammable as you will soon see." He sounded really smart, and I learned a new word, methane. My brother and I sat on edge of his bed.

"Are you sure this is going to work?" my brother said. "Yeah, just give me a minute."

"Have you seen somebody do this already?" I asked. "

Sh—sh—shut up. I gotta concentrate."

"Okay, here it comes." He spread his legs, we leaned in.

"Almost here." He lit a stick match and held it close to his butt. We leaned in closer.

"Watch this." Whoosh!

We jumped back from the big, beautiful blue flame. A second of astonished silence, "Oh, man, that was boss." Then I saw more flames.

"Oh crap your socks are burning!"

The fart flame had ignited the lint on one of Hector's socks. He beat at it but the lint quickly burned off. Hector was momentarily shaken but regained his composure as fast as the lint flame burned out, "Wh—what did you guys think about that?"

"That's the coolest thing I've ever seen."

Hector beamed. He was learning skills we never would have been exposed to in our sheltered Catholic school. We walked back across the street just in time for dinner.

After dinner I sat at the kitchen table and did the homework that was due the next day. As of yet I hadn't come up with an idea for my project.

"*Estas terminado con su tarea*?" Ma asked.

"Yeah Ma, I got most of my homework done, but I have a science project due tomorrow and I'm not sure what to do it on. Got any ideas?" I spoke nonchalantly as if it were no big deal, but nothing got past Ma.

"You have a project due tomorrow and don't know what you are going to do yet?" she said incredulously. She went into another one of her rants about my brother and me not doing well enough in school. While Ma ranted, I fantasized how cool it would be to for me to give the class a demonstration on how methane burns. There would be no phony flames in this one.

Ma continued on about how my brother and I would not be able to support ourselves when we grew up because we were such boneheads in school. As she talked, I noticed a large dead fly lying belly-up on the kitchen windowsill, no doubt another casualty of Ma's Black Flag pump-sprayer attacks. The insecticide had a nasty dull odor that permeated the rooms she sprayed. There's no telling what damage Ma's hand-pump massacres were doing to our developing nervous systems.

"I've got an idea," I said. "Let me work on it and I'll show you later."

Ma walked off muttering, "*Van estar resurando antes que terminan la primaria.*" (They'll be shaving before they get out of grammar school.)

I opened the F encyclopedia book and flipped through the pages to the section on flies. And there it was, a beautiful picture of a fat horsefly the size of a big beetle. I tore a sheet from my notebook and paraphrased a page on horseflies. Our older sisters were gone to a school function so I couldn't get them to type my report. I cut a piece of cardboard to fit the size of my report, taped the paper to the board. I mounted the fly to the top of the board with two pins from Ma's sewing drawer. I stuck one pin on each wing. As I lay in bed I envied the kids that had done such great science projects. I admitted to myself that I wasn't happy with my hastily done project but at least I would have something to show.

On our walk to school the next morning Armando dampened my spirits even more when he told me how lame mine was.

Miss Belesario started the presentations again after the noon recess. My brother was first up. He stood his rocket on the teacher's desk and turned it so the bold USA letters faced the class. The bright red cone and fins contrasted nicely with the white fuselage. He had rehearsed his lines well and his rocket looked good. Like all the other students, he got a thank-you from Miss Belesario when he finished. Walter was next; he gave his on water.

I sat low in my desk, hoping our teacher wouldn't see me. I hadn't put my project on the display table but hid it under my desk. Philip's erupting volcano with dinosaurs and blue lake followed Walter.

"Thank you, Phillip. That was a wonderful project," Miss Belesario said with a broad smile. Philip tucked his report under his arm, lifted his project off the teacher's desk, and carefully walked it back to the display tables.

"Let me see. Who is next?" She looked down at her roster. "Ah, Fernando Garcia." She looked at me.

I reached for my project and slowly walked to the front of the class. I felt like a death row convict taking his last lonely walk to the electric chair. I stood behind the teacher's desk. "Horseflies," I began, then turned my cardboard for all the class to see my fly at the top of my board. My fly's delicate wings had become brittle and broke loose from the body. Its corpse slid unceremoniously off the cardboard and onto Miss Belesario's desk. Not sure what to do, I reached down, picked it up and put it in my shirt pocket.

I hadn't had time to rehearse my lines and stammered through my report, trying to decipher my hasty handwriting while praying that my project would sound better once I began to read. When I finished, I looked up and saw a room full of blank stares looking back at me.

"Ah—well—thank you, Fernando."

I stood, cheeks burning, eyes downcast. I didn't bother to put my project on the display table. I made for my desk, my brother gave me a hearty double thumbs down when I passed him. *Think I'll slip my fly into his dinner tonight.*

John with his African display was next and was the last of the presentations.

I couldn't wait for the end of the school day. Shortly before the three o'clock bell rang Miss Belesario reminded us of book reports that were due at the end of the following week. *I'll get to the library and find a thin book, get it read, and get busy on the report as soon as I get home.* The bell rang and my brother ran toward the back door. I stuck my foot out, he fell. His books spewed onto the aisle, his shoebox opened, and his project rolled onto the floor. He gathered his things, grumbling. I stepped around him and accidentally stepped on his rocket.

"Oops, sorry." He glared at me.

WORD GOT AROUND THE NEIGHBORHOOD of Hector's show and he agreed to stage another demonstration for all the guys. I couldn't wait. *I'll get to the library first thing in the morning.*

24.

6th Grade – The Fight
Armando

"What makes a king out of a slave?
What makes the flag on the mast to wave? Courage!"
The Cowardly Lion

IT WAS LATE OCTOBER AND THE NOVELTY of the new school year had faded. Fernando and I were back in the routine with our classmates we hadn't seen over the summer and well acquainted with our new teacher and the students who had transferred from other schools. School was just a part of our daily drudge again.

"*¡Levantense!*" Ma gave her usual call one morning. I lay only long enough to repeat the same prayer I said every morning, then rolled out of the top bunk. We dressed into our uniforms and made our way from our bedroom to the bathroom and then to the kitchen. Our older sisters were on the city bus in route to their high school.

My twin and I ate cold cereal and toast. Ma had our lunches ready and reminded us to bring the bags back for reuse. We walked out the front door with Army Surplus backpacks stuffed with books strapped to our backs.

"Every day the same stupid thing," I said

"We could be in reform school where they treat kids really, really bad," Fernando said.

"I just wish something different would happen."

"Like what?"

"I don't know, something interesting, something that would make life less boring at stupid school."

We got to the front of the church. Dominic Aquino and his goon Sean Kelly were hanging out to the side of the entrance. Dominic was my height and weight, his black oily hair was combed straight back, and he wore his pants low on his hips like the tough guys. They liked to spit on kids' shoes and laugh. If the kid said anything about it, Dominic would hit him.

"Hey, it's the beaner boys," Dominic said. I was afraid of him. He intimidated guys he thought he could take.

Every student knew they were supposed to be in church. Dominic and Sean defied the rule.

Fernando and I looked to the ground, quickened our pace, and walked in. I looked to see where pretty Patricia was sitting. Even though everyone's head faced the altar, I knew where she was by her short-cut blonde hair. I got to sit next to her once. I found it hard to concentrate on Mass. I took sideways glances, her hands folded in prayer, how gracefully she stood, knelt, and sat. I even caught her scent.

We filed out of church to the playground after Mass where the classes gathered in military- like formations, faced the flag, and said the Pledge of Allegiance. We were to maintain silence the entire time although I always heard whispering.

Once in the classroom we put away the books, faced the front of the room and recited the Moring Offering. Then lessons started. Studies included religion, math, English, history, and geography.

Church bells tolling at noon meant that it was time for our teacher, Sister Catherine to lead us in saying the *Angeles* a pre-lunch prayer that had been recited by Catholics since the Middle Ages. An eighth-grade girl came in as a monitor and sat at the teacher's desk while Sister left for the convent. We were given ten minutes to eat before recess. After recess we slogged through the last two hours of school until the much anticipated three o'clock bell rang and the day was finally over. Fernando and I then faced the long walk home and the homework assignments that too often were left uncompleted.

One day was a carbon copy of the last. Tuesday was like Wednesday that was like Thursday. Monday was different only in that it ushered in another week of tedium. Fridays were happy days when even the crabby nuns and teachers seemed to be in good humor.

THERE WAS NOTHING TO LOOK FORWARD to on these autumn days. Our first class of the day was catechism. Every Catholic grammar school kid had to memorize answers to the questions posed by the Baltimore Catechism. The book contained a litany of questions and answers pertaining to Catholic dogma, sort of a do's and don'ts manual.

Q. Who made you?

A. God made me.

Q. Why did God make you?

A. God made me to know Him, to love Him, to serve Him, and to be happy with Him forever in the next life.

Blah, blah, blah.

Geography followed catechism. We were studying South America and specifically Peru where one found good old Lake Titicaca. On the years when we studied world geography I looked forward to hearing teachers say *Titi-caca*. It didn't get any better in my miserable little Catholic school kid world. Except Sister Catherine cheated and pronounced it *Lake Titicac*. I was robbed.

I raised my hand. "Sister, do the Inca Indians of Peru fish in Lake Titty-caca?" Most kids cracked up. She didn't react, maybe she hoped that it would end there. But I pressed on. "So, do the Inca Indians of Peru fish in Lake Tee-tee-poo-poo?"

Sister Catherine put on her you're-going-to-get-it face and opened her mouth, ready to let me have it, when the ear piercing fire alarm bells went off scaring the Titicaca out of me. The bells rang over and over at two-second intervals.

"You know what to do children," Sister said.

Everyone stood and filed out quickly, one row following another. The alarm bells echoed off the hallway walls making them sound even louder. A lot of us covered our ears as we hurried to the staircases and down to the playground.

I liked fire drills. They got me out of class for half an hour. I wished that just once it would be the real thing. It would be cool to see the school burning, see big red shiny fire trucks race up the street and onto the school grounds. I could see it, sirens screaming, firemen running and yelling in their big heavy jackets, helmets and rubber boots snaking their hoses all over the playground. Then they'd shoot tons of water on the building and let the school have it with their axes. With all the commotion, no one would notice me sneak out of line and turn the wrench on the fire hydrant, cutting off the water, and then sneak back. Patricia would fall and hurt her leg. She would yell for help but somehow the firemen wouldn't notice her. I'd run in and carry her out of the building with flames and smoke billowing out windows. I'd set her on the ground. Everybody would cheer and then I'd get a medal for bravery.

When the drill ended, we got back to our classroom just as the lunchtime church bells rang. We prayed the *Angeles* and Sister left for the convent. Students who ate at the cafeteria were dismissed. The rest of us stayed at our desks. And today our monitor was Barbara Callaway, my classmate Mike's really pretty eighth-grade sister. This was turning out to be a pretty good day after all.

I took the bean burritos from my sack and dug in. Ma also put in two pineapple guavas from the tree in our front yard. We were never lucky enough to get Twinkies or Hostess Cupcakes like a lot of the kids.

We played fighter pilots with the boys on the playground. With my arms outstretched like a fighter jet's wings, I ran at full speed, zeroed in on John, and attacked him from his right flank. He didn't see me coming. I tapped his midsection with my hands and yelled, "Rata-tat-tat-tat," and got my first kill. I soared over the upper end of the playground on the lookout for enemy aircraft to engage in a dogfight. Besides being ace fighter pilots, my brother and I were also the fastest runners in our class, able to escape enemies or overrun them at will.

The upper end of the playground had five or six fighter pilots engaged in combat. One zeroed in on another and opened fire. I took a wide turn, gave my engine full throttle while I looked over my shoulder. My right wing hit Dominic who was walking with Sean. The two were strutting with their hands in their pockets.

"Hey!" Dominic flashed his yellow teeth. "Watch it, punk!" he yelled as he shoved me. I reacted by shoving back. His fist came out of nowhere and hit me in the chest. My fist caught him in the shoulder. In a flash we were on the ground.

"Beat his beaner ass!" Sean yelled. My twin and the other fighter pilots came running.

"Get him," my brother yelled, "get him!" In seconds we were surrounded by dozens of kids. I don't know how it happened, but I wound up on top of Dominic sitting astride his stomach. He lay on his back cussing, wildly swinging his fists upward, and rolling side to side. I cocked my fist ready to bring it down, but someone grabbed my arm.

A woman's voice yelled, "Stop! Stop!" My friend Donny's mother, a playground monitor, pulled me off Dominic. "You boys stop right now or I'm sending you to the principal, understand me?" she said as she pulled me off of Dominic.

"Yes, ma'am," I panted, heart pumping, fists clenched. Dominic got to his feet.

"You go over there and you go that way."

Dominic walked away, the back of his uniform shirt dirty.

He turned and pointed a finger. "After school."

"Yeah, after school," Sean said.

I stuck out my chest. "After school."

"He'll get you, punk," Sean said.

"My brother'll take him," Fernando fired back. The bell rang, recess was over.

We made for our classroom. "Wow. That was cool!" my brother whispered. "I wish you could've finished him off. He thinks he's so tough, but he's just a jerk, man."

"Yeah," said Donny, "Dominic and his public school friend, Leonard, the big seventh-grader at the junior high, threw rocks at me and my friend James last Saturday when we was exploring the West Park Canyon. He yelled 'niggahs' at us and laughed when we ran off."

"That punk Dominic's always doing crap like that, but this time you'll show him" John said.

Donny patted me on the back. "Man, you're gonna cream him."

"Yeah, you'll beat the heck out of him," Fernando said, eyes wide and excited.

"Uh, yeah," I answered, looking down with my hands in my pockets.

"No, really," my brother said. "You'll pound him, you'll see. Don't be afraid of him."

"Sure," I whispered, imagining Dominic pulling a knife on me. Patricia and her friend Debbie were looking at us when we walked into the school building. I heard from Debbie that Patricia liked me. *She must have seen the fight. I hope she doesn't show up after school and sees what happens.*

I went back to my desk wondering how I ever got myself into this mess. Dominic was a dark-skinned half White/half Filipino. He used the F-word whenever the teachers weren't around, and he didn't think twice about giving the finger. Last year he hung around with Frankie Santana before Frankie got expelled for punching Sister Mary Lucille in the stomach, knocking out her wind. She was trying to stop him from beating up a kid. I wondered if Dominic would be waiting on the playground after school with some of his goons to gang up on me.

I remembered an incident last summer when I saw him cry. I mean really cry. I was walking to the store. I had to pass Dominic's house and decided to walk on the opposite side of the street. He was in his front yard with Sean. Sean was pitching rocks to Dominic who was hitting them with a baseball bat. He hit a foul ball that crashed through a house window. Mr. Aquino burst through the front door and pounced on him, grabbed him by the back of his shirt and beat him with his fist. Dominic screamed as the blows came down on his back, shoulders, and chest depending on how Dominic jerked around. Mr. Aquino dragged Dominic into the house and slammed the door behind them. Dominic would probably do that to me, now that he's so mad.

I could never have imagined an afternoon in school when I wished that it would not end. This afternoon the second, minute, and hour hands of the clock raced.

I'd look at the clock every day following the lunch recess, frustrated that it didn't seem to move. The long, thin red second hand crawled from dot to dot. The minute hand didn't seem to move and forget about the hour hand. There were afternoons when I swore that the clock was running backwards. But today the final bell rang two minutes after recess. If you are waiting to get the crap knocked out of you, Old Man Time becomes a sprinter. A few minutes before the final bell we recited the

Act of Contrition, a prayer asking God to forgive us our sins; it's also the last prayer one says before dying. If you were in a life-threatening situation and said this prayer sincerely, your sins would be forgiven even if they were serious. I was finally able to grasp the significance of this lesson and prayed it with reverence. The bell rang. Fernando jumped out of his seat, slapped me on the back as he ran past with Donny and John right behind him.

I approached Sister Catherine shuffling papers and asked if she needed help. Sister looked up. "You want to help me?"

"Yes, Sister."

"I don't need help today, maybe tomorrow."

"I'll be happy to sweep floors, carry your books, anything."

"No, thank you Armando, I don't need help," she said in a tone of finality. I lowered my head, walked out the door, down the hall, and out of the building. From the top of the staircase, I could see my brother and friends talking excitedly. Fernando caught sight of me and pointed. The three waved me down excitedly.

Patricia and Debbie stood outside the schoolyard fence looking toward the guys. I began to walk down the stairs hoping she wouldn't stick around. It could be horribly humiliating, and she might not like me anymore if she saw Dominic sweep the floor with me like Bluto did to Popeye before Popeye ate his spinach.

I looked around. Could Dominic be down there with his gang? No, they weren't, or at least I couldn't see them yet. They must be waiting for me under the stairwell, itching to get at me. I thought about the Christians the nuns told us about that were fed to lions. I got to the playground on weak legs. Dominic and his gang weren't under the staircase either. Where could they be?

When I got to the guys, John slapped my back, "You're gonna pound him."

Yeah, it probably wouldn't be a fair fight. Why don't you fight him?

"He isn't here yet," Fernando said. "But he'll show up any second." He looked across the yard. "Hey, he's over there by the bus with Sean. Come on." Everyone but me ran to the bus.

"Hey, Dominic we're over here," my stupid brother yelled. Dominic turned. He didn't say anything but climbed on the bus that was quickly filling with kids happily chattering away.

"Hey, Dominic, come on back. Aw, come on," my brother begged. But my would-be adversary was walking to the rear seats. Sean Kelly looked out at us, and then jeered Dominic when he sat down. Dominic spit out the window and gave us the finger.

"You're kidding," Fernando said, his voice laced with disappointment. He and the guys looked at me with sad eyes.

I fixed my eyes on Dominic. "You act tough but you won't come out here," I said just loud enough for the guys to hear.

"You'll get him tomorrow," Fernando said on our walk home.

"I think I'm getting a cold."

25.

6th Grade – Philip, Portrait of a Rose
Armando

"Blessed are they that mourn for they shall be comforted."
Jesus Christ

PHILIP KAJAWA, MY BEST FRIEND in sixth grade, would be dead by the end of the day. Mrs. Kajawa would not get his daily phone call after school where she worked. She would call Danny's mother to see if the neighborhood friends were together. But Danny, uncharacteristically, would not be home from school either, though he should have been. Unbeknownst to their mothers, Philip and Danny would have been crushed and suffocated under tons of drenched earth. The firemen would pull their mud-slick bodies from the collapsed cave.

I saw Philip lying in the casket at the memorial rosary the night before his funeral. Was he really gone forever? We were laughing really hard the last time I saw him at school. The Philip lying in the casket didn't look like the Philip I knew, but some kind of cold, still mannequin in a suit, hands folded at rest over his chest holding a rosary.

When the service ended Fernando and I joined our classmates Keith and Hal. Keith said that we should say something to Philip's mother. I didn't want to go but a voice inside me said that I needed to. The four of us walked to the pew where Mrs.

Kajawa sat, body limp, head at rest on Mr. Kajawa's shoulder. She straightened when she noticed us. It looked as though she was barely able to hold up her head.

"We're sorry that Philip had to die," Keith said scarcely over a whisper. "We liked him a lot."

She put a trembling hand to Keith's cheek. Her soft voice quavered through the black lace veil shadowing her face. "You're nice boys," she said then put her hands to her face. "My baby, oh my baby," she said over and over. I stood staring transfixed and aching for her. I'd never seen a person so drained, so completely filled with pain. I could make out her face under the veil. Her eyes were red and swollen with dark circles under them.

My mother, not one to show much emotion, took a tissue from her purse and wiped her eyes. Ma tucked my brother and me into bed that night for the first time that I could remember.

A week later our teacher, Sister Mary Catherine, told the class that Philip's mother had lashed out at the nuns and the church, and even God, for the loss of her only child. Later she asked them to forgive her. As young as I was, I understood that Mrs. Kajawa's grief must have caused her to lose her mind.

I went to my younger neighbor Chris's house to play. His mother invited me in for cookies and milk.

"I heard the news of your classmate's death," she said. Chris's mom pulled him toward her and wrapped her arms around his chest so the two were facing me. "I can't imagine how much the poor woman is suffering."

"My teacher, Sister Catherine, said that Philip's in heaven," I said.

Chris's mom slowly shook her head. "I know that your family is religious and you have your beliefs, but I don't understand how a loving and merciful God could allow something so terribly tragic to happen."

I didn't know what to say to her, then it came to me. "Sister said that God has a plan for us, and sometimes it's hard to understand."

"That may be so, dear boy. I will never be able to understand these kinds of tragedies. A big part of being a woman is to have children in order to keep the life cycle going. All animals from fish in water to birds in the air to animals on land, even plants, are born, mature, reproduce, and die. The reason for being created is to recreate. Your friend's mother procreated but her offspring would not. The reason for her existence, of having known the pain and joy of motherhood was stolen from her. Now she's a childless mother. What a terrible irony."

I lay in bed that night thinking about what Chris's mom had said. I didn't know what irony meant, but it couldn't be good. And how could a God that loves us take Philip like that? I'd have to ask Sister about it and if she didn't know, then I'd ask our pastor.

I HEARD THAT PHILIP AND DANNY removed the supports from their cave. Why? And it never rained much where we live, but it rained hard just when Philip and Danny dug their cave. And poor Philip's mother. All that was left for her was to blame someone: the church, the nuns, priests, even God. Hard as I might, I could not understand.

Danny Cortez's father said that God gave His only son for us, and if God wanted one of Mr. Cortez's children, then who was he to question.

"Philip never told those silly snot jokes or played those dumb games with the girls like some of the other boys do," Fernando said on our walk home from school.

"Phil and I were laughing yesterday," I said.

Since it had been raining, we weren't able to go out on the playground at recess time. The class was playing seven-up, a pointless indoor game that I detested. Sister as usual left during recess, leaving behind an eighth-grade girl to monitor the class. The monitor chose seven kids to line up in the front of the room. The rest of us laid our heads on our desks, hiding our eyes. The seven walked down aisles and each touched a kid's head, then walked back to the front of the room. We raised our heads and tried to guess who it was that touched us. If you were lucky enough to guess the right person, then you got to take their place at the front of the classroom and then touch a kid's head so they would have to guess who it was. Dumb; really dumb.

It was like a broken record playing over and over again. Every time it rained Sister would ask, "What would you like to play?"

"Seven-up! Seven-up!" shouted the indoctrinated simpletons. The nuns liked the game because it was nice, quiet, harmless (and stupid.) Anyone with even the slightest bit of imagination, like Philip and me, found the game mind-numbing boring.

Philip and I put our own spin to it. When it was time for us to put our heads down and hide our eyes we'd listened for one of the chosen seven to pass then we'd shoot out a foot to trip him or her. We kept score. Making contact with a person's foot was a point. Making them stumble was two. And a full fall down trip was a bingo and five points. Now we were having real fun and sharing good hard laughs. Philip tripped Matthew who should have fallen to the floor, but caught himself on Sharon, almost taking her and her desk with him. I gave Philip four points. We were having great fun timing our tripping attempts and laughing hard whether or not we had successfully tripped somebody.

Philip had a long, wide forehead that made him look like he was balding. He also had a friendly, comical face that one couldn't help but like, and had a great sense of humor.

One morning while we were filing into the school after Mass he took a set of large ears out of his backpack and put them on. He stood straight-faced as if there were nothing unusual and looked around as if to see what all of the laughter was about. Even strict Sister Mary Catherine chuckled when she told Philip to put them away.

A couple of weeks later he came to school with a nail through his index finger wrapped in blood-stained gauze. We looked at the injury with skepticism.

"My doctor couldn't remove it. See?" He tugged on it. "I've got to go back tomorrow." He took me in. One of the girls covered her mouth. It became a distraction in class and Sister made him remove the bandage and the nail that curved around his finger.

Philip had a curiosity and love of the natural world. Last year in fifth grade, he created an elaborate dinosaur display for our science project. His entry was voted the best.

It was Philip's love of science that caused him to die. He and Danny dug a cave in an undeveloped plot of land in their neighborhood to look for specimen rocks for a rock and mineral fair. They worked on the cave after school and on Saturdays.

Their digging produced few specimens and so they dug deeper into the hillside. Why did they crawl into the cave when it was raining? Wouldn't it have been cold and damp? And why did they remove the braces?

During the funeral Mass Father Vidra told the story of a gardener who took much pride in his work tending the famed gardens on an estate. He became angry when he noticed that someone had taken a perfect blossom from the most beautiful of his prized roses. Later he was told that the owner of the mansion was so moved by the beauty of the flower that he could not help himself but to take it into his home and display for his dinner guests to admire. The gardener was pleased to hear that his employer so appreciated his work.

261

Our class stood outside the front of the church after the Mass as pallbearers loaded Philip's shiny copper-colored coffin into the hearse.

All that was left for his grieving parents and longing friends were precious memories of our rosebud, Philip. I stood with my class looking on as the hearse, followed by a black limousine and a procession of cars, disappeared into the morning fog.

26.

6th Grade Summer – The Flying Flexy Brothers
Fernando

*"Be brave, even if you're not, pretend to be.
No one can tell the difference."*
Jackson Brown Jr.

SCHOOL WOULD BE LET OUT TODAY at the twelve o'clock bell. It could not ring soon enough. It was the last day of the school year. I was anxious to get home and start summer vacation. Little doubt, the teachers were in the same mood. A few minutes before the bell Sister Mary Catherine, our sixth-grade teacher, gave us her last instruction for the year. "Stand and say the parting prayer."

Like fifty-eight programed robots, we stood at our desks as we had at the end of every Friday. We made the sign of the cross, folded our hands, and said the Act of Contrition. "Oh my God, I am heartily sorry for having offended Thee, and I detest all my sins because of Thy just punishments . . ."

The skinny nun took out a vial of holy water from the top drawer of her desk and uncorked it. She cocked her bony arm back and sprinkled us as we prayed. Her long, black habit swayed with each fling.

"I bless you in the name of the Father and of the Son and of the Holy Ghost. Amen. Be careful over the summer. I want to see every one of you back here next September," she warned. Sister Catherine must have been thinking of our deceased classmate, Philip, when she warned us to be careful.

Most of us had already attended the daily 8:15 Mass that morning and all of us had said the Morning Offering at the beginning of class. I didn't like praying so often, but at least I knew that if I was killed on my way home my eternal salvation was guaranteed. I found much comfort in that. The challenge was to stay sinless; even thinking of committing a sin, was a sin. It was hard not to sin.

Like nervous racehorses at the starting gate, the boys sprinted for the door as soon as the bell rang. "Good-bye, Katzenjammer Kids," Sister said, smiling as Armando and I flew by. Her smiles were as rare as her admonishments were abundant. We should have been flattered but didn't have time to think about it. We were on a mission to start summer vacation for three whole months.

"Bye, Sister," I said over my shoulder. "See you next year."

Katzenjammer Kids was her nickname for my twin and me. She took it from a newspaper comic strip about two high-energy boys who were constantly getting into mischief.

The school yard was alive with kids chattering and making their way to the bicycle rack, waiting cars, or the school bus at the curb. Our last walk home for the year was actually pleasant. The June air was still, cool, the sun warm on our faces. Traffic, unlike on our walk to school, was light and we didn't have textbooks to carry, allowing for a brisk pace.

"What do you want to do when we get home?" my brother asked.

"Burn our uniforms."

He laughed. "Do you think you got any D's this time?" I asked.

"Don't know, I think I got a C minus in math and C's for the rest."

"Remember that time I got a B in English?" Armando said, my brother would never let me forget his one B. I resolved to get one in seventh grade and even the score. It would be hard earning one from Sister Jane, though. She, like Sister Catherine, was a hard grader. But that was something I wouldn't have to think about until September.

"Do you ever worry about being smart enough to get a job when you get older?" I asked.

"All the time."

"We should think of a job that wouldn't be too hard," I said.

"Like what?"

"Do you remember when Pa took us to the circus?"

"Of course, that was really cool, what about it?"

"There was a guy inside of a metal cage, he was on a motorcycle."

"Oh, yeah, I remember him. He rode his bike in loop-de-loops. I liked that a lot," Armando said.

"Well, maybe we could be like him, like Evil Knievel."

"Great idea, we wouldn't have to have good grades and we might become famous and make lots of money."

Summer was off to a great start.

Once home we changed into play clothes, threw our uniforms into a corner of our bedroom, and walked into the kitchen.

"*Que quieren comer?*" Ma asked.

"I don't know. What do you have?" I asked, as if I didn't know.

"*Frijolitos con tortillas.*" "Okay."

In seconds she served us bowls of hot whole pinto beans in broth spiced with onion and oregano with her homemade flour tortillas on the side. Ma sliced an avocado and gave us a half each. Amazing how good Ma could make a simple meal taste.

When we finished eating, Ma gave us a line we must have heard a hundred times over the summers. "*Andale, para afuera.*" (All right, outside.)

With five neighborhood buddies, it wasn't hard to find things to do. Adventures abounded.

"Let's take the Flexy and see what Chucky's doing."

"Bye, Ma."

"*Adiós, y portansen bien.*"

"Why does she always have to tell us to behave?" my brother said.

We had inherited a red Flexy Flyer that our sister Carolyn's boyfriend had outgrown. Before we got the Flexy, we modified Carmen's old tricycle and raced it down the dirt slopes in the canyon behind our house. We also nailed our older sister's abandoned skates onto the bottom of scrap two-by-fours and rode them up and down our uneven concrete driveway. Scrapes, scabs, and bruises were constant companions. The Flexy was a tremendous boon to our insatiable appetite for adventure.

A Flexy was suicide on four wheels. It was a one-man sled, ideal on sidewalks and streets, and just low enough for drivers to not be able to see you. It had two hand grips at the front for steering. To stop, the driver turned the steering handles downward to make contact with two metal tabs on the small, solid-rubber front wheels. The brakes were effective on flat surfaces but useless on steep slopes.

Our neighbor, Chucky, was a portly kid with perpetual snot rings around his nostrils. Ma's nickname for him was, *Mocos* (Snots). He was two years younger than us. His close-cropped dark hair stood on end, like a brush. He was easygoing and was always up for adventure. He wasn't the brightest kid but did teach us how to add a little water to our Nehi orange and grape sodas to make them last longer. Ingenious, I thought. We crossed the street and walked the half-block to his house.

I knocked on the door. "Can Chucky come out and play?" I asked Mrs. Price when she answered. We heard him yell from in the house.

"Coming."

Mrs. Price chuckled and walked back in, her house slippers flapped, and her extra-large robe swayed off her ample hips. Chucky came out wearing our unofficial play uniform: a white t-shirt, jeans, and black high-top tennis shoes. His face lit up when he saw the Flexy. Chucky went to the public school two blocks down Euclid Avenue and had started his vacation a few days before.

We walked off his porch and onto the sidewalk. "Where do you guys want to ride?" he asked.

My brother suggested that we take the Flexy to the dirt hill across the street from our house. We set off with Inky Price, Chucky's black mutt following. Inky was scruffy, like his owner. The happy little high-strung black dog skipped more that walked and was obsessive about keeping his genitals clean.

We got to the hill and looked down the long rough road. I was excited by the challenge. Chucky looked down the hill, shifted his feet, and said, "Let's try half- way down first."

Six tennis shoes and four small paws kicked up dust as we made our way.

"Let me go first," I said and lay on the Flexy before they could object. I turned the handles down and locked the wheels. Chucky and my brother stood on either side. I released the hand brake and bumped my way down. They chased after, with Inky Price happily yipping, chasing them. I would have outdistanced them had I not applied the brakes. I hit the dry, sandy wash at the bottom of the hill and came to an easy stop.

"Man, that was cool," I said, with a big smile. Chucky and my brother took their turns.

"Let's do a double-decker," my brother said.

My brother and I took turns steering with either Chucky or the other twin on top. Double-deckers were a lot more fun.

"Okay. Let's try it from the top of the hill," I said.

"It's awfully high," Chucky said.

"Let's go up and then decide."

We trudged up, taking turns carrying the Flexy. We sat when we got to the top of the hill, our foreheads were beaded with sweat. A light breeze blew up the hill and picked up dust from the surface of the road.

As we sat, I was struck with an idea so brilliant it must have been divine in origin.

"A triple decker," I said excitedly and confident as a daredevil.

"Heck, yeah," my brother said. Chucky stood quietly looked down and scratched his fuzzy head.

"I'll get on first," I said, "my brother on top of me, and Chucky you get on top of him."

"Gee, I don't know."

"Aw, come on, it'll be great. After all, it's a long way up here and whoever goes first will have to carry the Flexy all the way back up. This way we can all take turns."

"What if we crash?"

"We won't. I'll keep the brakes on. It'll be easy."

"Well . . ." Chucky hesitated.

"Ha, that's the spirit." Before he could say anything, I lay on the Flexy and turned the hand grips down. My brother got on top of me. Chucky stood looking at us.

"Just get on top and see how it feels," my twin said.

"If you're still not sure, you can get off and my brother and I will go down." Visions of Armando and I performing death-defying acts in front of huge crowds filled my head. I looked at Chucky and nodded my head, inviting him to get on.

Reluctantly, Chucky stepped up and laid on my brother. I turned my head back and released the brakes. We were off. I realized how heavy they were at the first bump. The hill looked a lot longer and steeper from my prostrate position.

My brother rode with his hands clinging to the steel rails on either side of the wooden bed. Chucky panicked and shot his arms around our necks and pulled tight.

"Chucky, let go, I can't breathe," I yelled. But he didn't. The breeze blew dust in my face and made it nearly impossible to see. The combined weight of the guys pushed the air out of my lungs as we bumped over embedded rock. I struggled to keep control of the Flexy, steering with all my might to keep us moving in a straight line, lest we swerve to the side, topple, and roll to our deaths.

Halfway down the hill we were racing faster than I could have imagined. The vegetation on the side of the road was a blur. A raging dust trail followed in the Flexy's wake. I hit the brakes with all my strength; they were useless. My brother whooped and hollered in one of my ears as Inky Price yapped in the other.

"Slow down! Slow down!" Chucky frantically yelled.

"I'm trying," I yelled back. We hit a rut in the road and went airborne for an instant. I was nearly crushed when they landed back on top of me.

We were three-quarters of the way down, my body tense with anxiety. I struggled to keep the Flexy true.

Dust and sweat formed a dirty film on my face. I tasted mud. I dug the toes of my tennis shoes hanging off the back of the Flexy onto the road surface. Saying a final prayer of salvation flashed through my mind but I had to concentrate.

The sandy wash was coming up fast. We might make it. I braced for the impact. We hit the sand. The wheels dug in. The Flexy stopped dead. We didn't. The three of us shot forward. With the weight of the guys on top of me, my head and arms scraped on the abrasive surface. My brother slid off me,

Chucky off him. They rolled before coming to a stop. Clouds of dust enveloped us. They lay on their backs howling in delight and jumped to their feet laughing. I rolled over and opened my eyes. Chucky wiped muddy snot from his nose and upper lip. Inky Price, still barking, ran in happy circles, then sat and started licking his dusty balls.

I raised my arm and saw nasty scrapes wrist to elbow. My forehead stung. I willed myself not to cry. I forced a smile, pretended to have enjoyed the ride.

"Let's do it again," Chucky yelled.

"Heck, yeah," my brother said.

"I think I should go home," I said weakly.

My brother looked at me and winced at the sight of my forehead as beads of scarlet blood started to form. The skin on my forearm was smeared with blood and dust, forming a red paste. We started the walk up the hill. The two boys took turns carrying the Flexy as they talked excitedly. I felt woozy. The touch of the breeze on my wounds stung.

When we got home, I walked through the front door. My brother and Chucky left the Flexy on the front porch and went back to Chucky's house.

"*Ay, Madre Santa de Dios, que te paso?*" Ma said when I walked through the door.

She took me into the bathroom as I started to explain what happened. She sat me on the edge of the tub. "*Ay, es un milagro que no se mataron.*" (A miracle you didn't kill yourselves.)

Ma took a washcloth, wet it, rubbed soap into it, and with a gentle hand wiped the sand and grit from my wounds while telling me to stop writhing and complaining.

"*Pues quien te mando tonto?*" (Well, who made you do it, dummy?)

After washing my wounds, she applied one of her ointments and bandaged them. Ma allowed me to lie on the couch and watch TV. *The Price is Right* gave me some temporary distraction.

At dinnertime Pa came out of his bedroom from his afternoon sleep before his shift and joined us at the table. He looked at me as he took his seat.

"Fernando, what happened to you?" I told him the events of the fateful ride. Pa listened as he began to eat. "How come your brother isn't hurt?"

"Because he and Chucky were on top of me."

He paused, then slowly shook his head and took another bite. Not looking up from his meal and still chewing, raised a finger, wagged it, and said, "No more Flexys."

Pa's word was law. The Flexy Flyer was retired. Sister Mary Catherine would not have to worry about the Katzenjammer Kids coming back after summer vacation.

27.

7th Grade – Chato's Steal
Armando
"In springtime Christ and baseball are risen."
Armando Garcia

I NEVER UNDERSTOOD THE SIGNIFICANCE of this hallowed sport until the day that my father squatted to call balls and strikes for my twin and me. We had signed up for St. Rita School's baseball team and were practicing for tryouts. My father. The same man who only sits, smoking Pall Malls, and drinking Bulldog Ale when he wasn't sleeping, watching sports on television, or working. But he gave up his precious free time to umpire and coach his boys who wanted to play organized baseball.

All seventh and eighth-grade boys were encouraged to try out for the team. Mr. Rodriguez, the father of one of the boys, was enthusiastic about putting together a winning club and agreed to be our coach. He had played high school baseball, making him the best choice of the fathers.

Tryouts were held on the Saturday after Christmas vacation. My brother and I were excited about the possibility of making the team and playing real baseball, as opposed to the informal pickup games we were used to. Although we had plenty of fun in our games with friends, there were no umpires, no fans, and no baseball diamond. We had never been able to field two complete teams. We played a hybrid game called work-ups, that allowed a minimum of players. We had to be careful not to lose one of the two baseballs or break either of the bats we were able to muster from the neighborhood, forget about catcher's equipment, bases, or batting helmets.

Fernando and I made the team and got real uniforms: green-and-white baseball caps, jerseys, knickers, white under socks and stirrups with St. Rita's School in bold lettering across the front of the jerseys. We saw our first jock straps and wondered what happened to the rest of the underwear. Pa bought us baseball gloves and cleats like major leaguers. I dreamed of the glories I would have on the baseball diamond. I could hear the roar of the crowd as I rounded the bases after hitting homers time and again and made game-saving catches in the field, delighting girls and crushing our opponents.

"Do you think girls in our class will show up?" my brother asked.

"I hope so," I said. "Maybe Patty will show up and see me in my uniform, and then maybe I could walk her home." I could hardly wait.

We lay on our bunk beds, excited, on the eve of our first game and plotted on how to show off in front of our fans without looking like we were showing off. The opportunities for fame were endless.

The importance of baseball became more apparent as Pa devoted afternoons driving us to practices twice a week and watching our games on Saturdays. Pa even volunteered to be the equipment manager and was assigned duffel bags filled with gear. Games and practices became part of our routine, like church on Sundays, except that Ma and our sisters weren't involved. They only heard from us about our teammates, coaches, and the descriptions of the games that we lost week to week.

" It's only a game," Martha consoled. But what did she know about competition?

Pa, the eternal optimist, seemed to find a silver lining in every loss and never gave up encouraging and coaching. "If only that kid hadn't hit that three-run homer, you guys could have tied the game."

Pa showed us how to field ground balls and to use our bodies as a backstop. He helped us with batting by instructing us not to try and hit a home run with every swing and to be patient for the right pitch while in the batter's box.

"Just meet the ball with the bat," he coached. He taught us a batting trick one afternoon.

"Duck when a pitch is close; it can make an inside strike look like a ball," he said from the pitcher's mound he had made in the backyard.

"Ready? Here it comes. Oh, Jeez. You're stepping in the bucket. You're taking a step back because you're afraid of the ball. Don't be afraid. Stand closer to the plate and swing, *Chato*."

Chato, I hated that name. It meant flat nose. Pa gave it to me after I broke my nose, causing a slight deformity.

"It's okay to have that name," Pa said. He explained that in Mexico people call each other nicknames like that and don't think anything of it.

"Remember the man in your mother's hometown with one leg? They called him, *Mocho*." (Stump). And there was a man who had to have one of his balls cut off because it got cancer. Guess what they called him? *Huevo*," (Egg). My brother and I laughed.

"The gringos are ready to fight you if you find something peculiar about them and then give them a nickname over it. Mexicans don't get angry, it's just your street name. It's also saying that you are one of us. Almost everybody in Mexico has a street name."

"I wasn't born over there," I told my brother when we lay in our bunks that night. "I still hate it when he calls me *Chato*." Fernando tried consoling me but to no avail. Dad called my brother *aguzado* (the sharp one), adding to my frustration. My brother was a little bigger and stronger than me and outdid me at most everything, wrestling, running, even schoolwork. Baseball, however, was the one area in which I was better.

Our rookie coaches made innocent mistakes like the time our assistant coach, Mr. Hernandez, was warming up the guys before a game. He hit ground balls to the infielders. He smacked a smoker to his son, Cruz, who was playing second base. The ball took a hop and hit him in the mouth. Mr. Hernandez grasped Cruz's bleeding mouth as he carried his son, crying uncontrollably, off the field. John Maloney and I found chunks of Cruz's teeth at his infield position. Cruz showed up to our next practice with a set of gleaming silver front teeth that reflected the sun.

Despite so many losses, our coach put up a good front and encouraged us, trying to get us to believe that we were on the cusp of turning our season around. But it became obvious that he was frustrated. I was bored in left field once and took to making designs in the dirt with my cleats. My concentration was broken by a ball speeding between my legs. Spectators screamed as I ran the ball down and threw it back to the infield.

The batter wound up with a triple and knocked in all three base runners. He should have only gotten a single.

"What the hell were you doing out there, *Chato*?" Pa said on the drive home. "You're not paying attention to the damn game."

I sat looking down at my cleats. Not paying attention. The same thing my teachers always said.

We became the door mats of the Catholic grammar school baseball league. We made other teams and their fans happy. Blessed Sacrament and Holy Redeemer crucified us, St. Jude's and Our Lady of Angels martyred us, the St. Bridget Lions ate us up. They all gave us holy beatings. Our frustrated coach lost control after a game and let us have it as we sat on the bench in the dugout.

"It's a goddamned embarrassment. You're playing like dead men out there. Get your heads in the game!" I heard that word of his outburst got around the parish and that monsignor had a talk with him about setting a good example for the boys.

We hadn't won a single game. My brother and I had long abandoned the notion of one day becoming stars in the major leagues, we just looked forward to our final game to put the season behind us.

St. Rita's rose from the dead for one glorious moment. It was our final game of the year. We played each school twice during the season, and St. Jude's was our final game. Although we played well against them in game one, we still lost by four runs. St. Jude's had not lost a game all year. All they needed was one more victory against the door mats for a perfect season.

"Let's get this over with," coach said before the game.

The brief pre-game meeting was held between coaches and the umpire. After sweeping off home plate, the umpire took his position behind the catcher, put on his mask, and shouted, "Play ball."

Dad stood on a dirt slope overlooking the field where he got a better view of the game than did the people who sat below on the bleachers. We went into the bottom of the final inning, miraculously tied at three runs each. I even managed to get on base and score once, something I had not done for a while.

Although the team was playing well and we had a call or two go our way, I don't think that any of us could help but doubt ourselves and wait for the inevitable outcome of an inevitable season for a bunch of rookies. There were two outs when I got my last ups. I worked the count full, three balls and two strikes.

The next pitch caught the inside of the plate but I ducked away and fooled the umpire.

"Ball four," he yelled." Take your base, batter." It should have been strike three and the end of the game. I jogged to first base hiding my smile. I didn't dare look at the pitcher, Frankie Santana.

I was afraid of Frankie. Besides being big for his age, he had failed two grades. I could have sworn he had already started shaving. Frankie was being recruited by the two Catholic boys' high schools.

Louie, my best friend on the team, was next at bat. He was one of the few bright spots on the team. He was the fastest runner, could hit, catch, and throw with accuracy. On a two and two count he grounded a single to right field, advancing me to second base.

Scrawny little Mikey was next, and likely be the last out of the game. He made the team because his father, a radiator shop owner, provided the team with our uniforms. Poor Mikey was a nice kid but not an athlete. He reached base only four times all year and three of those came by way of fielding errors. He was the strikeout king, and everyone knew it, including Frankie.

Frankie threw the first pitch, a fastball right down the middle of the plate. The umpire raised his right arm, "S-t-e-e-r-i-k-e one." Cheers came from the St. Jude fans.

A lone voice was heard from the St. Rita's stands, "Come on, Mikey, you can do it." I stole third base and didn't even draw a throw from Frankie. He wasn't paying attention to me. Why should he? He sneered at Mikey. The strategy was obvious: intimidate and strike the little *pendejo* out.

Coach Rodriguez curled his fingers through the chain-link fence of the dugout, staring down, shifting dirt with his toe, waiting for the end of a season. He looked up, "Let's go, Mikey, keep your eye on the ball, he said half-heartedly.

I took a lead from third base. Frankie aimed his next pitch, a screaming fastball, right at Mikey. Mikey flung out of the batter's box. His batting helmet flew off his head and tumbled up the third base line.

"Back in the batter's box, son" said the umpire. Frankie's plan worked. Mikey stood as far away from the plate as possible, leaving home plate a wide-open target for him. Mikey's bat trembled in his hands.

I took a long lead from third base and could have easily been thrown out, but Frankie was focused on throwing strikes.

Dust exploded from the catcher's mitt. The umpire raised his hand. "S-t-e-e-r-i-k-e two."

St. Jude's fans clapped.

Frankie is going in for the kill, I thought. all he needed was a final strike. I remember seeing a kid steal home once. He waited until the catcher was about to throw the ball back to the pitcher, then bolted for home plate. The catcher smiled, casually cocked his arm from his squatting position, and what felt to me like slow motion brought it forward, returning the ball to the pitcher for the last pitch.

Now! Now! Now! a voice screamed in my head. I blasted for home. The catcher saw me, but it was too late, the ball was out of his hand on its way to the pitcher. Like a cat, the catcher jumped to his feet, landing between home plate and me. Frankie was caught flatfooted when the ball reached him. He fumbled the ball in his glove, got control, and threw to home. I closed my eyes, sliding feet first. The catcher stretched his mitt high over his head reaching for Frankie's frantic throw. My cleats collided with the catcher's. His body flew sideways and landed on me. The momentum took us both sliding over the plate, raising a cloud of dust. Everyone sprang from their seats, craning their necks, witnessing the collision at home plate.

Did he catch the ball? Was I out?

I opened my eyes to see the umpire crouched over me, his arms outstretched like a bird on the wing." S-a-a-f-e!"

Safe? Safe? I was raised from the earth by coach. He put me on his shoulder. Screams and cheers filled the air. He set me down to the backslapping and head-slapping of my teammates. Frankie slammed his mitt to the ground. His lower lip quavered in anger and frustration.

"I got you, *cabron*," I whispered.

Pa laughed and patted me on the knee several times on our drive home. "That was heads-up ball, *mijo*. That was heads-up ball." He stopped for a can of ale and bought my brother and me candy bars to celebrate the victory.

Later that afternoon I sat on the back porch with Chris, proudly showing him the large red burn on my left thigh from the slide over home plate. "It's what major leaguers call a strawberry," I said. Chris was impressed and asked to hear the story again. I gladly obliged. Dreams of the Major Leagues resurfaced.

I heard Pa's excited voice in the house. He was telling the story to Ma and my sisters and then again later to my *tios, Flaco* and *Chencha*. His voice grew with each retelling.

"There we were, tied in the last inning with two outs. He was on third and then he ran like the wind for home. He slid into the catcher. And ha, ha, he knocked the ball out of the catcher's mitt! And Armando won the game! Our Armando won the game!"

28.

7th Grade – The Saint's Jewels
Armando

"Not everyone who says 'Lord, Lord' to me
will enter the kingdom of heaven."
Jesus Christ

"THE INFIDEL GANG," LAUGHED ST. IGNATIUS when he heard that John, Donny, Fernando, and I had failed to honor our Lenten fasts. Ignatius was average height, chubby, and had thin, cropped brown hair that stood like a porcupine's. The four of us were huddled on the playground during recess when St. Ignatius happened by. He wasn't *the* St. Ignatius, who was martyred in Northern Africa while converting pagans to Christianity, but he did want to be a saint.

Ignatius listened in distant-eyed wonder whenever nuns or priests told us heroic tales of the saints. He fantasized himself converting entire countries to Christianity or giving his life for the faith like those who martyred themselves for the church. Our St. Ignatius, like the rest of us, had no idea what it took to be a real saint. He probably pictured himself on a holy card wearing velvety robes, Jesus-style sandals, and a golden halo hovering over his head.

Holy cards of saints were given to Catholic school kids as rewards for excellence. My twin and I never earned such cards. Ignatius acted pious, received communion every morning at Mass, and carried a rosary in his pocket. He tried preaching to us during recesses. We tolerated him until his proselytizing disrupted our basketball game. "Ignatius, will you shut up?" I yelled.

"God will judge you if you aren't ready to die for him like I am."

"Well, then go die for him somewhere else."

Ignatius scoffed and walked away. Later I saw him preaching to second-graders on the playground. But his resolve came into question on the dreaded polio vaccination day.

"In a few minutes you will be going to the hall to get your polio vaccinations," Sister Mary Jane, our seventh-grade teacher, announced. The class became deathly quiet. I tensed. I heard a groan from Cindy Smirker behind me.

The piercing and frightening odor of rubbing alcohol accosted me as I passed through the doors of the school hall where nurses had set up a clinic. I heard sobs in the room from the kids of the lower grades as I entered. We lined up at the injection tables. As my turn came, I heard whispers and looked behind me. Cindy was saying a prayer. Ignatius was in front of me. "I hope it doesn't hurt too much," I said into his ear. He turned, "I have faith in Our Lord that He will deliver me from this test of faith." His voice quavered. I realized he was scared like the rest of us.

I stared ahead past the tables, not wanting to see the syringes. Ray East, a small, quiet black kid with toothpick arms was ahead of Ignatius. Ray pinched his earlobe when he got his shot. Someone must have coached him to do that as a distraction from the painful prick. I turned away. When I looked back Ray was getting the small Band-Aid put on his arm. He walked out as if nothing had happened. Ignatius was shaking like a Christian about to be fed to the lions when his turn came.

I stepped up, closed my eyes, the nurse wiped the cold alcohol against my skin and then came the sting. Ouch, it hurt, but at least it was over. And it wasn't as bad as I'd imagined. I opened my eyes to see Ignatius drop. Sister Jane and a nurse rushed to him and lifted his fuzzy head off the floor. I stepped over him. Good luck with the natives in Africa, Iggy.

Donny, one of my friends, got mad at Ignatius once because he said that Donny was going to hell for saying *shit*. Donny wanted to fight him after school but when they met Ignatius pulled a crucifix from his pocket and pointed it toward Donny. Unfair. Who would take a swing at Jesus? Ignatius undoubtedly dreamed this act would become one of the legends told of Ignatius Signorelli, the Saint of St. Rita's School.

Ignatius also invested in hell insurance. It was Catholic lore from centuries past of the significance of wearing a scapular around your neck. The scapular was a small, square cloth with the image of a saint on one side and the Sacred Heart of Jesus on the other. It was attached to a thin brown shoestring-like twine. If you wore the scapular, the Virgin Mary would guarantee that you would get one last chance to confess your sins, especially big ones, before dying, thus avoiding being damned to hell. And get this, a scapular only cost fifty cents!

This was way beyond a good deal. Commercials on late night TV had ads that sold these really cool knife sets, and "if you order today," they'd throw in a knife sharpener at no extra charge, but "if you order right now," you'd get a free block of wood to hold your new knives. This scapular deal was the knife deal to the tenth power. Fernando and I begged Ma for fifty cents to buy a scapular. She kept promising but the money never came. What if we were hit by a car and died with a mortal sin on our souls? We'd go straight to hell forever and all for the lack of a lousy fifty cents. Then an idea came to me. What if next time I served a Sunday Mass, I could borrow fifty cents from the collection basket, get me the scapular, and I would be a shoo-in for heaven. Of course, if I didn't pay it back, then I'd have to deal with a sin of sacrilege for stealing from the church. A sin of sacrilege was worse than a mortal sin with unimaginable consequences in the afterlife. But with the scapular around my neck, I'd be given a shot at making a sincere confession. But how genuine would my confession be if I stole the money for the scapular knowing I'd be able to confess? I resolved that I'd have to gain heaven the poor man's way: be good and hope if I wasn't that I'd make it to confession in time. I envied people who would live lives of drunkenness and debauchery and get to heaven because their mothers were able to give them fifty cents. Life wasn't fair for Catholic kids of modest means.

My classmate John, told the gang that he was sitting next to St. Ignatius on the school bus when the driver almost got into an accident. The Saint frantically tore his shirt open to get to his scapular. He clenched it so hard that his fist shook, as he prayed with his eyes shut.

"What possible sin could he have ever committed?" Donny wondered.

"Maybe he said *caca* once," Fernando said.

"Jesus gave His life for your sins," Sister Jane said to our class. "He died for all of the sins that we have committed and ever will commit. How can we show Him our gratitude?"

"Pray and say thanks?" Peggy said.

"Well, yes, that's one way."

My brother offered a suggestion. "Maybe we should commit some sins so Jesus wouldn't have died for nothing."

"It's never okay to sin," Sister Jane said.

"I know, I know," I said. "Give more money at Sunday's collection. My dad says that monsignor is always asking for more money at church." My classmates murmured excitedly in a shared experience.

Kenny spoke up, "Yeah. Dad asked how the monsignor could afford that new Buick." Sister crossed her arms and gave him the not-another-word stare. We got the message. We were talking about a subject that was taboo. Grown-ups had mysterious ways about them.

Sister gave up on asking for suggestions. "Lent begins one week from today on Ash Wednesday. We nuns abstain from desserts during Lent. Think you could give up desserts?"

Yes, I could, but it would be cheating because we rarely got them. It was all our parents could do to keep the family fed.

"Think you could give up TV or candy?"

TV would be impossible. Between Pa and my sisters, it was on every night at home. But candy? It would be tough but doable; after all, it would only be for forty days. Yeah, that's it, I'll give up candy.

"It's important that you sacrifice something that you'll be able to do. Don't get too excited and try to give up more than you're able."

The monsignor must have sent this message to the nuns because of an incident that happened last year.

Mr. McIntosh and Mr. Sanchez, a couple of heavy smokers, had given up cigarettes. It was the first Sunday after Lent had started and they hadn't had a smoke for four days. After the eleven o'clock Mass they were caught in the weekly traffic jam leaving the church parking lot. McIntosh was in the car behind Sanchez, who had allowed too many cars to pass in front of him when no-nicotine-since-Ash-Wednesday-Mac gave an irritated honk. Sanchez, who normally would have smoked half a pack by this time, got back by allowing three more cars to pass. McIntosh put his bumper to Sanchez's new Impala and gave it a shove. One stupid act followed another.

The two ended up in the monsignor's office with him admonishing them. One had scrapes on his face, the other the beginning of a black eye. "What example does this set for your children? And humiliating your wives in front of everyone. And, my God, what the Lutherans across the street must have thought." The men sat quietly in front of monsignor's desk looking down at their hands. The old patriarch suggested to them that they give up their Lenten fasts. Sanchez agreed to replace Mac's broken glasses, while McIntosh paid to have Sanchez's dented bumper straightened. Moments later they were seen outside the monsignor's office bumming cigarettes from a parishioner, shaking hands, and courteously lighting each other's smokes.

Ash Wednesday, the kickoff day of Lent, came. We went to kneel at the Communion rail after morning Mass. Priests had small brass bowls filled with palm ashes. They put a thumb into the bowl and made the sign of the cross on our foreheads with the black ash.

"Remember man that thou art dust and unto dust thou shalt return. Remember man that thou art dust and unto dust thou shalt return." The mantra was repeated over and over until everyone had a smudge cross on their foreheads. Four hundred school children and their teachers, all duly marked, marched to their classrooms. I wanted my ashen cross to last until after school so my public-school friends would see it, but it didn't survive the sweat from the morning recess.

The Saint went to the evening service to get another cross on his forehead, then went visiting. "I'm giving up candy *and* television for Lent."

"Oh, that's very good, Ignatius," said Mrs. McCarthy, the head of the altar society and a real living saint if ever there was one.

"Yeah, it won't be easy, but Jesus did die for us."

"I'm sure Jesus is grateful to you." The Saint marched off proudly. And the little pendejo kept his damned fast for all of Lent and jeered when he heard we had failed to keep ours.

"Infidels. I'm surrounded by Infidels," said the little saint with a laugh. We didn't know exactly what an infidel was but knew enough to not want to be one. We couldn't help it if we weren't able to keep our Lenten fasts. We had fallen victim to false information. One of our older sisters heard from a friend that during Lent one could take Sundays off from their abstinence. Craving our candy habit, we embraced the good news, shared it with John and Donny, and ate a week's worth of candy on Sundays.

Our birthday fell during Lent, a time of sorrow, so we could not have a party until Easter Sunday. We took to self-pity in front of our Ma.

"*Pueden comer un dulce por su cumpleaños.*" Our soft-hearted Ma allowed us to have one candy on our birthday. Cool, Lent wasn't quite so hard after all.

But Father Vidra informed us that Sundays and birthdays were no reason to break our Lenten fasts.

"Did Jesus break his fast during His forty days of sacrifice while He was in the desert?"

"Well, what's the use now?" I said. "Since we've broken our fasts, what's the point in continuing? Darn that person who misinformed our sister anyway."

"Next year we'll know," Fernando said.

"Yeah, next year for sure. And if one of us cheats, then the other can hit him without the cheater getting mad, okay?"

"Deal."

We sealed our sacred pact with a handshake and Snickers candy bars. St. Ignatius was not so understanding and named us the "Infidel Gang." And he called us that until the beginning of June when we went to the annual school picnic at the park and swim center.

It is said that vengeance is the Lord's but on this day, vengeance belonged to the Infidel Gang. Ignatius loved to swim. His family was the only one in our parish that had a swimming pool. We were not among the kids that he invited over during the summer. He was a good swimmer and diver. He relished the attention at last year's picnic when he displayed his skills from the low- and high-dive diving boards.

"Show-off," my brother grumbled.

Ignatius pinned his scapular to his bathing suit, taking no chances while swimming, and probably used it as an excuse to show off his piety.

Normally we steered clear of the Saint, but this year my brother sat on the bench next to him while they changed clothes in the pool locker room. The Saint stripped down to his underwear, then rolled up his scapular and set it on the bench. He stood, bit his towel so that it hung in front of him hiding his privates, then took off his briefs. Quicker than a cat my brother snatched the scapular and threw it out the window above their heads.

"Naked ladies, naked ladies," my brother yelled.

"There, now you've thought of them so you have a sin on your soul. If you drown, you'll go to hell."

Ignatius turned white. The bathing suit fell from his grasp. He yanked the towel from his teeth, tied it around his waist, and sped out to redeem his hell insurance. John, Donny, and I waited outside the door.

"Ooooh," we yelled, drawing all eyes, including the girls', at the pool.

What happened next became an unresolved point of contention. On Monday the Infidel Gang was called to the principal's office. We stood in silence as Sister Mary Constance demanded explanations.

"How could you do such a thing to this poor boy? And, Armando, was that you who pulled off his towel in front of the girls?" She glared. I could only stammer that the towel must have gotten snagged in the doorjamb.

"I want to see you all at confession on Friday! Do you understand me?" We all nodded our heads in well-acted remorse.

We pooled our pennies on our walk home for a victory treat. All we could afford was a bag of M&Ms. We sat on the curb and split them up evenly, throwing away the two remainders. They tasted better than any Lenten candy.

Ignatius could no longer meet eyes with Gail, Christine, or Laura without hearing them giggle.

"I thought the Saint's balls would have halos," Donny said to raucous laughter.

"Saint's balls," cheered another. We settled on "The Saint's Jewels," and only had to threaten to call him that once for St. Ignatius Signorelli to quit calling us the Infidel Gang. We knew we had probably committed a sin and probably should confess it and probably would, but it was well worth it. It would be forgiven anyway, so we figured that we might as well have some fun and took to describing what the holy card would look like of "St. Ignatius and His Holy Jewels."

29.

7th Grade – The Pendulum
Armando

*"And throw them into the furnace of fire: where
there will be wailing and gnashing of teeth."*
Matthew the Evangelist

KISS-ASS IGNATIUS SIGNORELLI WAS THE MONITOR. He was always the monitor and left in charge when the chosen sixth, seventh, and eighth graders went to choir practice on Friday afternoons. Practices were held in the church choir loft. The children's choir sang at the nine o'clock Sunday Mass.

If Fernando and I could have joined, we would have been able to leave the classroom for the hour-long rehearsals.

Sister Mary Jane, our seventh-grade teacher, who played the organ, was short and portly. Her dull-white complexion contrasted starkly with her black habit and she had dark circles under her eyes. We nicknamed her Uncle Fester. About the only positive thing I could say about the children's choir is that they were not as bad as the adult choir that sang at the twelve o'clock High Mass on Sundays. They were awful.

"You two birds can lower your hands right now," Sister Mary Constance said to my brother and me when we raised our hands hoping to get selected for choir. Constance was in our classroom recruiting for this year's choir. She selected every other student with their hand in the air, nearly half of the kids in the class. I sat dejected.

Why didn't Sister Constance choose Fernando and me for the choir, or at least give us a chance to audition? Could it have been because of what had happened last year?

My twin, our friend John Maloney, and I sneaked up the staircase to the choir loft during the Mass before school. We crawled on our hands and knees to the rail and raised our heads just enough so as not to be seen from below. We had a bird's-eye view of the entire church. All eyes looked toward the altar.

Couldn't the priests and nuns understand that we were bored with the routine sanctity of the endless rites of the church? From the daily Mass to the High Mass sung in Latin to monthly benediction to Holy Days of Obligation; on and on they went. The nuns had explained the various services to us in religion class but I never truly understood what they all meant.

I decided a harmless little game would make the forty-minute service pass faster. I sneaked on all fours, hid, and sprang like a cat, surprising John and my brother, causing them belly laughter.

It was a good move. I not only surprised them but risked making too much noise. I liked pushing things, especially if it meant making people laugh. John put his hands over his mouth to contain his laughter, but a muffled snort escaped.

We entered a part of the service when there was total silence. Fernando had sneaked into the pew in front of me. His head popped, I covered my mouth, convulsing, and ripped a ceiling-echoing fart. Fernando lost control. Panic overtook his face as he shot his hands over his mouth. Compressed air exploded through his hands, sounding much like my fart. Snot burst from between his fingers. I opened my mouth wide, allowing me to laugh hard but quietly. John lay on his back doing the same. Fernando took a handkerchief from his back pocket and used it like a muffler while he wiped himself.

The choir loft door hinge squeaked. I looked over. Sister Constance stood at the entry. Her girth took up most of the doorway, a scowl on her round face. I froze. We were dead. There would be no explaining our way out of this one. She narrowed her eyes and spoke in a hoarse whisper. "I hope you don't die before you confess this. I don't know if God would forgive this desecration of His house. I expect to see all of you at confession Friday. Now, get down to your class. I will be talking to your teacher."

We picked up our books and lunches and slinked past her looking to the floor. Mass was almost over.

On our way home from school that afternoon Fernando said if what we did was unforgiveable and a sure sentence to hell, then we might as well sin all we wanted since we were doomed anyway. He confided that he couldn't muster the courage to confess it and how heavily it weighed on him.

That had to be the reason we were not allowed to join the choir.

The following Friday afternoon, Sister Constance and Sister Jane waddled their way across the playground to church for choir practice. The choir members followed them like so many ducklings. Sister Catherine, the sixth-grade teacher, stayed behind to wander the halls as backup support for the monitors.

Sister Catherine was frail and sickly. The habit around her thin face was loose, unlike Constance and Uncle Fester's, whose ballooned cheeks bulged out of theirs. Sister Catherine was a stick in a habit. It seemed to me that she was too young to be so ill all of the time. A sickly odor permeated around her. When she lectured, dried saliva collected into small globs of white paste at the corners of her mouth. She missed a week of school once. We were told she was under a doctor's care and needed our prayers. Though small in stature, she had a strong spirit and was the best of the upper-grade teachers. Even if she was able to make kids genuinely laugh on occasion, everyone knew that you did not fool around in her class. It was rumored that her icy stare, feared throughout the school, had once frozen solid a kid's eyeballs.

"God knows everything you do, even your thoughts," Sister Jane reminded us before she left for choir practice. I anguished over this. Like an un-jolly Santa Claus, God always knew when you misbehaved or when you were thinking of misbehaving or having impure thoughts.

We were taught to say ejaculations as a mental exercise to keep the devil from planting sinful thoughts in our heads. Ejaculations were short phrases that one would mentally recite.

"Jesus, Mary ,and Joseph, pray for me, Holy Family help me, St. Rita guide me." When I saw Sister Constance at the choir loft door last year, my ejaculation was, "Holy crap!"

Monitors like Mr. Paper-route, straight-A student, parents- involved-in-every-church-and-school-function, Ignatius Signorelli were designated to sit at the teacher's desk. He got to choose who would read the next section of the *Children's Catholic Digest*. The nuns had us read the *Digest* to keep us occupied in their absence. Ignatius not only relished his role of authority but belittled those of us who weren't favored by Sister Jane.

Ignatius had a dark side. He took great pleasure in taunting John Paulson, who had a condition that made him extra nervous and got frustrated easily, especially when taunted. I saw John running while Ignatius gleefully harassed and chased him after school.

A staple of the *Digest* were stories of martyrs who died for their faith and were canonized into saints. The *Digest* had a section called "Modern Catholic Life" describing sticky situations that Catholic kids might find themselves in and what action he or she should take. In one story a girl had been eating hamburgers at a Protestant friend's home when she realized it was No-Meat-Friday. Catholics had to abstain from meat on

Fridays as a form of sacrifice. To knowingly eat meat on Friday was a mortal sin. If not forgiven, it meant eternal damnation to the fires of hell upon death. If she threw the hamburger away, she could be guilty of wasting food and committing a venial sin. Mortal sins left huge black spots on your soul and just one was enough to get you damned. Venial sins sentenced you to time in purgatory where you were punished until you suffered enough to get your sins purged and earn a pass to heaven. While purgatory was a place of shame and suffering, it had no demons and one day you'd get out and join the saved.

We were encouraged to pray for the poor souls in purgatory since they were in there doing time and could not help themselves. They needed us, the living, to pray for them. If we prayed or offered up sacrifices on their behalf, we would reduce their time.

Purgatory didn't have the huge clock that existed in hell that Father Vidra told us about. The clock's pendulum swings to one side ringing out the word ever. The damned ask, "Ever?" Will I ever escape this place of fire and suffering and torment? The back swing answers, "Never."

The answer to the dilemma for the hamburger-eating girl was obvious to me. Never risk a mortal sin. Toss the burger, it is better to have a venial sin on your soul in the event that you die before confessing it. Further reading suggested that she was guilty of no sin because she forgot that it was Friday.

I wondered, however, since she should have known that somewhere in catechism memorization the answer was to be found, so she probably committed a sin for not having done the required memorization to begin with. Catholic kids were faced with a myriad of no-win situations.

During a religion class the question came up, "Do non-Catholics who eat meat on Fridays go to hell?"

"No," answered Sister, "because they haven't been exposed to the truth like we have." It wasn't fair, those lucky kids. Just because no one told them, they could sin and get away with it.

We were on the final page of the Digest that ended with a cartoon that was supposed to be funny but was stupid. I could have identified with jokes asking how many nuns does it take to screw in a light bulb? However, making fun of nuns or priests could well have been a sin of sacrilege, damning not only the person who told it but anyone finding it funny. These issues were too heavy for me to be thinking about. Perhaps it was time for a little fun. In today's cartoon, a mother told her children not to make so much noise in their play. They replied that they needed rackets to play table tennis.

I slapped my knee. "Oh jeez, oh gosh, that was a good one. Oh jeez." Only a few kids laughed. I put my face in my hands laughing louder.

"Okay, that's enough," Ignatius said. He didn't like riffraff like me taking control.

I was bordering on getting written up but it was important for me to get a better response. My reputation was at stake. I pushed it to the limit. Overcome by the hilarity of the *Children's Catholic Digest* comic strip, I fell from my desk to the floor, kicking and pounding my fists. This was turning into real work, but all the kids broke out laughing, even the ones with spotless souls. Bingo! My friends cheered me on. Then, as quickly as the falling axe that silences the squawking chicken, the room went deadly still. Feeling nervous, I opened my eyes. My nose was an inch from the toe of Sister Mary Catherine's shiny black shoe. Reflected in Sister's shoe was the image of a fallen Catholic boy burning in the fires of hell. It wasn't purgatory because there were demons and a rather large pendulum.

I looked up. My eyes followed the black cotton of her skirt, up past the rosary that hung from her waist, past her pure white starched bib, thorough her thick wire-rimmed glasses an into her frozen stare. She stood, arms folded, looking down at me.

The small frail nun looked giant. I awaited my fate. Then, god of gods, the corners of her purplish thin lips began quivering upward. She was fighting off a grin. She tried her icy stare but, Jesus, this was a funny scene. She tried again to look angry, but a frown just wasn't coming. Taking immediate advantage of this teetering opportunity, I sprang back into my desk, bowed my head, and tried my damnedest to look remorseful, likely fooling no one.

She stammered, "St—stay in your seat," and a made quick exit into the hallway. I could hear the heels of her shoes tapping swiftly down the hallway. I shifted my eyes side to side. They still worked.

Good God, I escaped the stare. I escaped Sister Catherine's frozen stare. I looked to Ignatius, who sat in open-mouthed astonishment.

The punishment for this grievous sin was anticlimactic. After choir practice when Uncle Fester came back into the classroom, she admonished me in front of the class. "Armando Garcia, do I need to take you along with me to choir practice and have you sit alone like a child?"

"No, Sister," I answered remorsefully from my desk.

"If you don't behave better . . ." Blah, blah, blah.

"Yes, Sister."

"Now, act like the seventh-grader you are supposed to be."

"Yes, Sister."

I felt obliged to act humiliated but knew that some well-deserved back slaps were coming after school. Maybe there is a merciful God after all. Hell, I even forgot to confess it.

30.

7th Grade – The Kiss
Armando

"The best part about a first kiss is right before the first kiss."
Brett Davern

IN A SATURDAY AFTERNOON'S MOVIE, the cowboy hero grabbed the beautiful woman who had been wandering the prairie in a covered wagon. He pulled her into him and kissed her. She didn't like him and tried to fight him off by pounding her fists against his chest. He kissed her all the more until she went limp. Then, she wrapped her arms around his neck and out-kissed him, kissing him harder than he was kissing her. By the end of the movie, she couldn't live without the handsome, gun-slinging stranger that had ridden into her life.

I took the glass of strawberry Kool-Aid from Fernando and finished it off. We got up from the couch and I turned off the TV.

"Ever wonder what it'd be like to kiss a girl?"

"Only about a thousand times a day."

"I'd sure love to kiss Patricia," I said. "But how could I get myself in a position where it could happen?"

"If you did get in that position," Fernando said. "Think you'd have the guts to actually do it?"

"Don't know."

Patricia had been in our classes since my brother and I transferred to St. Rita's School in the third grade five years ago. I'd always noticed her and thought that she was okay, but something happened to me this year in the seventh grade. She looked pretty, really pretty. Patricia had short, sandy-blonde hair, and blue eyes.

I started taking the mile-long walk to church for the Saturday morning Mass just to say hi to her. I think that she liked me, too, because whenever something funny happened during class we'd look at each other and laugh. It felt really good. So, I walked to church on Saturdays, waited at the entry, and looked down the street until I saw her walk around the corner and come my way. I heart palpitated. When she got near, I'd avert my eyes, too shy to look her in the face, then I'd wait until she was at the church door and glance up. She'd shoot a quick look, smile, and we'd both give a soft "hi." I'd wait until she entered the church and followed her in and sit a few pews behind, daydreaming of kissing her. I'd make her mad at me then wrap my arms around her. She'd pound her fists against my chest, then melt in my arms and out- kiss me. Wow. When Mass ended, she'd step out of her pew and pass me on her way out. Our eyes would meet, and we'd smile. I'd follow close behind. She never looked back, probably too shy like me. Why couldn't I get the guts to say something? Instead, I'd just stand there looking at her walk away, wishing that we could talk. Then came the mile-long walk home.

I got a call from my friend and classmate Roger toward the end of our seventh-grade year. His house was across Euclid Avenue a quarter mile up a hill where people with more money than my family lived. Roger said that his parents agreed to let him have a dance party on Saturday and he wanted Fernando and me to come. He was inviting, among other girls, Patricia. Roger said that he knew that I liked her and that he had heard from her girlfriend Cathy that Patricia liked me, too.

I lay in my bed all week playing the scene over and over in my mind. I'd start off at the party dancing a few fast dances with Patricia, then I'd ask her to slow dance. And that's when it would happen. We'd kiss, she would go limp for a moment, and then the fireworks would start. The heavens would open, we'd levitate, spinning slowly, and the more and harder that she would kiss me, the faster we'd spin until we ascended to the stars in a sparkling swirl. A kiss that would change our lives forever.

"I'm going to try and kiss Patricia at the party," I said to my brother that night as we lay in our beds.

"No fooling?"

"Yeah. I've been wanting to kiss a girl for a long time, and we like each other. So if I can pull it off, I'll try."

"Man," Fernando said. "You've got guts."

"I'll only have guts if I can actually do it."

I asked Ma to wash and iron the clothes that I wore for Sunday Mass the day before the party. I shined my shoes and asked my sister Martha if there was anything she could come up with that would help me be at my best. She had gone to lots of dances in high school and told my twin and me about them and the kinds of boys that she thought were cool. She was also a good dancer and taught us the latest moves. Martha went to the bathroom and came back with Pa's aftershave. She shook a few drops into her palm, rubbed them together, and tapped my cheeks. "You sure that's enough?" I asked.

"A little is nice," she said. "Too much is gross, and don't go to the party early. Be stylishly late."

"What's that mean?"

"Everybody notices the kids that come in late, and they'll be excited to see you, especially if they thought that you might not make it."

I gave up on trying to understand how the world worked and asked Martha, "So how long should I wait?"

"At least a half hour, but an hour is better."

The party was to start at 6:00. Fernando and I left at 6:30. We walked across the street, down the dirt road to the bottom of the flood control channel, and then started the climb up the hill toward Roger's house. It had been a warm June day and the breeze felt cool against the sweat on my face. "So are you going to try and kiss her?"

"I'm going to try, and don't say anything."

"Okay, I won't."

When we got to the top of the hill and approached Roger's house I could hear Jimmy Soul's song, "If You Want to be Happy," coming through the garage door. I rang the doorbell. Roger's mom answered.

I'd always thought that she looked too young and pretty to be a mother. She was nice. She fed us whenever we came to play with Roger. She gave us a warm, welcoming smile.

"Come on in boys, the kids are in the garage." She led us through the house over a gold-colored shag carpet, by a dark wood dining room table that shined brightly, and a piano against a wall. Roger played piano at a school talent show once and wowed the audience. Fernando and I followed her to the kitchen where Roger's father was standing at a counter mixing lemonade in a big plastic pitcher.

He looked up. "How're you doing, guys?" He nodded toward a door. "Party's in there."

Roger's mother opened the door. The garage ceiling was hidden by balloons butted up against each other. A table along one side of the room had two record players and a chair where Roger's older brother, Danny, sat with music albums and 45-rpm records in stacks. A second table had bowls of potato chips and cookies and stacks of paper cups. "Easier said Than Done," by the Essex, started playing. A few couples were danc-ing neither fast dancing nor slow as the tempo of the song was somewhere in between. A dozen or so kids stood apart talking, boys with boys, girls with girls. Patricia and her best friend, Cathy, stood in a darkened corner.

"The twins are here!" somebody yelled over the music. Most everybody ran up and surrounded us. Guys patted our backs. *Martha knew what she was talking about*. I glanced toward Patricia. Our eyes met. I smiled. She smiled back. Danny, maybe feeling the positive vibes in the room, played "Heat Wave," by Martha and the Vandellas, a great song for fast dancing. Kids partnered up and danced. Some were well coordinated and danced with grace, others looked like they were in an epileptic fit. But no matter, everyone gave it their all. Except for Patricia. She wasn't one of the popular kids because she was too shy and her mother never allowed her to go to private parties for kids. I later learned that she had lied to her mother and told her that she was going to spend the night with Cathy and got into trouble when found out.

I really, really wanted to kiss her, but how? I thought of my plan to do a couple of fast dances with her, then a slow one, and then see if I could make like the gun-slinger and kiss her. I was nervous about asking her to dance, and I'd never really had a conversation with her, it was mostly glances and smiles during classes or at church. Other girls like Maria, Cynthia, Lulu, and Ginny were good friends and easy to dance with.

The garage was dimly lit and the light softened more as evening set in. Most everyone danced after the ice was broken with Fernando's and my entrance. The garage was warm from the summer sun beating on it all day and even more so from the heat created by the roomful of gyrating bodies. I danced with the girls that were my friends and got a good sweat going. I talked and joked with my guy friends between dances. It was a lot of fun. Everybody danced and talked and laughed. How I wanted to dance with Patricia, but why was it so hard to go and ask her? It didn't make it any easier that she was a wallflower.

I had to raise my voice to ask Danny what time it was. "Eight-forty," he said over the din. The party was to end at nine. Darn, just twenty minutes left. I asked Danny to play two fast songs and a slow one. He nodded okay.

He played "Surf City" by Jan and Dean. I walked to the table with the treats and took a couple of napkins and wiped sweat from my face and then made my way over to where Cathy and Patricia were. I smiled awkwardly. Patricia smiled and looked down. I put out my hand. "Would you like to dance?"

Patricia kept her eyes downcast. I felt the fool standing there with my hand out. Cathy tapped Patricia's elbow and said in a voice loud enough to be heard. "Armando asked you to dance."

Patricia looked up, surprised. She waited a moment before taking my hand and gave a weak, "Okay." She was not a good dancer. She looked embarrassed. She held her hands to her front against each other in fists while stepping from foot to foot and not at all to the beat of the music. The look of embarrassment turned pained. God, I felt sorry for her, but what could I do?

"The party's fun!" I yelled over the music wanting to distract her from her feeble attempt. She forced a smile and nodded her head, but it was obvious that she was suffering. I took her hands, made eye contact and held her eyes with mine, then did a simple side-to-side step. She was able to follow. I felt the tension in her hands ease. I kept her eyes locked with mine and added a little bounce with each step and she followed. She smiled. Not a shy smile but a "this is fun" kind of smile.

The dance came to an end. I asked her to stay on the dance floor with me. I had just enough time to grab a few napkins from the refreshment table and wipe sweat again. It felt warmer. Danny then played "Denise" by Randy and the Rainbows.

Patricia put her hands in mine and danced as we had the first time. Now she was really smiling. I noticed perspiration on her forehead. This time I added a back step. It threw her off. I tightened my grip on her hands and went back to the simple side steps, then gave her a little tug when I back stepped.

Again, she followed my lead with little effort. From that point on she did everything I did. The smile never left her face.

I stared at her lips. Would, could I kiss them? I didn't think so, but I had worked so hard to get to this point and I'd never forgive myself if I didn't at least try. The dance came to an end.

"Will you dance one more with me?" She gave a happy nod. Trickles of sweat ran down the sides of her face.

I looked to Danny. He winked and played "Our Day Will Come" by Ruby and the Romantics. I took her hand and put my arm around the small of her back, brought her into me. She rested her head against my shoulder. Patricia was wearing a pullover sweater. Our bodies were hot; uncomfortably hot.

How do I maneuver her to get a shot at her lips? I gave her head a little shove with my shoulder hoping to get her face in front of mine, but she stayed pasted to my shoulder. Now what?

And jeez, was her body hot.

"This party's fun," I said. She didn't answer. Was she too shy?

"Are you having a good time?" I asked and felt her head pressing against me. I guessed that she was nodding her head. The dance was coming to the end. "Hey," I said into her ear. It worked. She backed her head from my shoulder and looked at me.

Okay, stupid, this is it. Don't chicken out! I closed my eyes, puckered up, and leaned into her. My lips hit her sweaty nose. I dropped down an inch or so and felt the softness of her lips. I also got the perspiration between her nose and lips all over me. God, it was hot and stuffy. I pulled back from the kiss and was glad to get a little distance from the heat and sweat. The kiss wasn't anything like in the movies, didn't even feel all that great. I looked around. Everybody was looking at Patricia and me and whispering. My stupid brother blabbed.

Somebody turned on the overhead lights and the room lit up. Roger's mom's voice rang out. "Thanks for coming, kids. I hope that you had a good time."

Thank-yous from thirty kids filled the room.

I turned to look at Patricia. "See you at church next Saturday?"

She grinned and nodded and walked to Cathy.

Fernando and I followed them and the rest of the kids out of the garage, into the kitchen, and out the front door. Cars with engines idling waited for kids.

"You had to go and open your big mouth," I said on our walk home.

"What're you talking about?"

"You told everybody that I was going to try and kiss Patricia."

"I didn't tell everybody. I only told Donny."

"Boy," I said stiffly, "that went well, didn't it."

"Sorry," he said, "it won't happen again."

"No, it's not going to happen again because I'm not telling you anything anymore."

"Okay, so I'm really sorry."

I didn't talk to my brother for the rest of the walk home. Later when we lay on our beds with the lights off he asked.

"How was it?"

"How was what?"

"The kiss, man. How was it to kiss a girl?"

"Hot and sweaty."

"Hot and sweaty?"

"Hot and sweaty."

"Didn't she melt in your arms?"

"The only one who was melting was me, it was so darn hot, and she had a sweater on."

I lay in the dark and couldn't get to sleep. I kept a little transistor radio by my pillow for times like this. I turned it on. "Then He Kissed Me" by the Chrystals came on. I turned off the damn radio.

31.

8th Grade – It's Not a Lie, It's a Sales Pitch
Fernando

"Lying lips are an abomination to the Lord."
Proverbs 12:22

A. THE CREW

MINISCULE DROPLETS OF WATER from the fog formed on our brown uniform sweaters as Armando and I made the daily trek to school. The only saving grace on this Monday was that it was December and Christmas vacation was two weeks away.

"Did you get the three religion questions memorized last night?" my twin asked.

"I got two memorized. I figure I have a pretty good chance she'll ask me one of them."

"Which one didn't you memorize?"

"The long one, something about 'What evil happened to us because of our first parents?' How about you?"

"I memorized the short one," he said.

"You mean the one about Original Sin?"

"Yeah, that one."

A delivery truck a few feet from the road shoulder sped by causing a wave of frigid air to penetrate my sweater. I shuddered.

"Your chances of her asking you the one aren't very good."

"I know, but I didn't have time to do all three of 'em. I was barely able to get our math homework done."

"We should have worked on the questions on Friday," I said with resignation.

"Please stand, class," Constance said from her desk. The Baltimore Catechism book lay opened on her desktop. It was the same routine every Monday morning. It marked the start of another grueling week beginning with religion class.

Please God, I promise I'll memorize all three next time.

She asked the first student in the first row one of the three questions. "Ignatius, what happened to Adam and Eve on account of their sin?"

"Adam and Eve, on account of their sin, lost innocence and holiness and were doomed to misery and death." As usual, Ignatius got his letter perfect.

"You may be seated, Ignatius." She looked to Patricia, the next one in line. "Patricia, what evil happened to us through the sin of our first parents?"

Patricia answered correctly and sat.

"Armando, what is the sin called which we inherit from our first parents?"

He answered his question like an A student. "The sin which we inherit from our first parents is Original Sin."

"You may sit down, Armando."

"Fernando, what evil happened to us through the sin of our first parents?"

Darn, the one stupid question I didn't know. I furrowed my brow and looked down at my feet. I opened my mouth, but nothing came out. I looked to the ceiling as if lost in thought. Someone coughed.

"Fernando?"

I gave the answer to one of the questions I had memorized.

"That is not the question I asked." Her eyes narrowed. "Now, please answer the question: 'What evil happened to us through the sin of our first parents?'"

I blurted out, "God got mad at them because they were naked in the Garden of Eden, and He threw them out."

I heard a girl gasp. Ignatius chuckled.

"You may not sit."

I had to stand humiliated at my desk for the rest of religion, along with the other two losers, Louie Sablan and Steve Kreber. We were allowed to sit when the last student answered his question marking the end of religion class.

I hurried out the door at the ring of the ten o'clock recess bell. When I got to the basketball court, Louie approached me.

"Hey, Fernando, would you like to make some money?"

"Heck yeah. How?"

"Selling newspaper subscriptions."

"Selling subscriptions?"

"Yeah. A crew manager from the newspaper picks me and my brother Joe up along with our cousin Benny and a few other guys, and drives us to neighborhoods and drops us off. Then we go door to door trying to sell one-month subscriptions."

"Do you sell any?"

"I usually sell ten to twelve a week."

"How much do they pay you?"

"A dollar a subscription."

"A dollar!?"

"A dollar. So, the more you sell, the more you make."

"You mean I can make ten to twelve dollars a week?"

"Even more. My cousin Benny usually sells twenty-five to thirty."

"I didn't know you had a cousin."

"Benny's parents came from Guam the same time mine did."

"Louie, I would love to get on. What do I have to do?"

"I figured you would want to, so I already told Gary."

"Who's Gary?"

"The crew manager."

"What do I have to do?"

"Be ready around 4:00 tomorrow. Gary will honk when he gets to your house."

"How will he know where I live?"

"He picks me up first, I'll show him."

"Gee, thanks, Louie."

I felt lightheaded as I walked back to the classroom. Maybe God felt sorry for me after I was embarrassed in class this morning.

When I told Armando about my bonanza, all he said was, "Lucky."

At fourteen I would have my first real job. Mom and Dad were as excited as I was when I told them the good news. More money would be coming into our home.

"I will pray that you sell many orders," Ma said.

When the three o'clock bell rang the next day, I speed-walked to the door. Sweat formed on my forehead on my way home.

"See if you can get me on," my brother said as he jogged to keep up.

"I'll try."

When we walked into the house, Ma had my dinner ready.

"Do your homework, *mijo*," she said as I finished my meal. I raced through my homework as I glanced out the window. Thankfully, I didn't have any catechism questions to memorize.

A few minutes after four, the crew manager stopped in front of our house in his Ford Country Squire station wagon and honked. I grabbed my jacket.

"*Tienes quidado, mijo*," Mom said.

"I'll be careful, Ma." I got to the curb, pulled the door open, and stepped into a new phase of my life. Joe, Louie and Benny smiled. I sat next to Benny in the middle seat, Joe sat next to him, and Louie was in the front with Gary.

"Gary, this is Fernando Garcia," Louie said.

The driver turned and smiled. "Hi, Fernando. Good to meet you."

"Hi, Gary," I said retuning his smile.

Gary appeared to be in his early twenties and had an easygoing air about him. His neatly combed light-brown hair was parted on the side with a hint of a wave over his forehead. He turned back towards the front, put the shifter into drive, and accelerated into traffic.

"Hi. I'm Benny," Louie's cousin said. He stuck his hand out and we shook. I was flattered.

Benny was barely five feet tall, had a large forehead, thin black hair, a small, pointed nose and little square yellow teeth that were chipped from opening soda bottle caps.

Benny was a hell of a salesman. I learned about his technique a few days later. He would charm the potential customer with his smile, quick wit and easy laugh. He claimed to be their newspaper boy and told them that he was Hawaiian.

"My family is going to visit the islands next week. If you sign up, I'll bring you a pineapple," he would say, beaming. Since the morning paper was delivered at dawn, the new customer wouldn't know they had been scammed until the real newspaper boy came to collect at the end of the month. Needless to say, no customer ever got the promised pineapple.

To Benny's credit, his homely looks didn't deter him from selling orders or dating girls from his high school. He claimed to have petted a few. No doubt, girls found his gregarious personality and humor attractive.

Gary drove to Linda Vista, a neighborhood five miles north of downtown. He stopped at a WWII-era duplex and honked.

A short chain-link fence with sagging crossbars ran across the front yard. Two boys walked out of the front unit to the car and hopped in.

"Hi, Gary," the shorter of the boys said. He took the front seat next to Louie.

"Looks like we got a new guy," the taller boy said with a smile. He sidled in next to me, held his hand out and said, "Hi, I'm Johnny, and that's my brother Jimmy." Jimmy turned and gave me a salute.

Johnny was just shy of six feet, good-looking and trim. At seventeen he was one of the two oldest boys on the crew. He combed his thick, wavy black hair backwards with a small waterfall cascading down his forehead. He resembled Fabian, a teenage heartthrob singer. Johnny's fifteen-year-old brother was also genial and was obsessed with all things sexual. Jimmy, along with Benny, were the top salesmen on the crew.

Pete Goings, eighteen, was the next pickup. Pete moseyed his way to the car, apparently in no hurry. Pete was as tall as Johnny but had a hefty layer of fat over his man-sized bones. He wore a loose-fitting gray trench coat and had a slow, easy pace. Pete also lived in a duplex, along with his fat little brother and their parents. Pete had an impressive array of blackheads on his face. He kept his thin bristle-like hair short. Pete attacked life with the vigor of a two-toed sloth.

A few blocks over Gary came to a small two-story house and picked up Ed Wilson. Ed was my height and build and spoke with a Southern drawl. His parents had immigrated to San Diego from Arkansas. His thick, kinky blond hair refused to mind his comb. Ed wore thick, black horn-rimmed glasses. He had a quick sense of humor and a high-pitched hillbilly laugh to match.

Larry Addams, the last pickup, was fourteen, the same as Louie, Joe and me. He was as tall as me but ten pounds lighter. He had a pasty white complexion and carried a white handkerchief in his back pocket that he used regularly. Larry liked to pester Pete. Pete could have squashed Larry like a *cucaracha* had he been willing to expend the energy.

"Where are we working today, Gary?" Larry asked, as he got into the car and struggled his way to the far rear bench seat.

"We're doing Encinitas."

Encinitas is a quiet, unincorporated beach community six miles north of the famous Del Mar racetrack. It is divided in two by the two-lane north/south Highway One that runs along the California coast. Along the drive Benny entertained me with stories about the girls he dated. He took his wallet, fat as a cheeseburger, from his back pocket and dug out a picture of his latest girlfriend.

"This is Wanda McGillacuddy," he proudly said. Her looks were a good match for a kid who looked like an oversized Guamanian rat.

B. THE SALES PITCH

We arrived twenty minutes after leaving Linda Vista. Gary stopped at a corner in a neighborhood of one-story houses. "Johnny, train Fernando." Gary handed Johnny and me our rectangular Manila- colored order pads. Inside the pad were twenty-five orders with a piece of carbon paper that we were to put between the white cover sheet and the light green copy. When a sale was made, we filled out the order, had the customer sign the bottom, then gave the customer the original. We handed in the green copies to Gary at the end of the night. The pads fit into our back pockets.

Gary pointed. "Do this face three blocks down, then cross the street and do the opposite face. Work the blocks toward the ocean. I'll pick you up at seven-thirty at the top of L Street. That's the last street before you hit the highway."

"Come on, Fernando," Johnny said with a smile. "Let's get some orders."

The weak rays of the winter sun were waning, and evening was fast approaching. I slipped my order pad and pen into my back pocket.

There were no sidewalks on the narrow asphalt street. A couple of the houses had white wooden picket fences, the rest had none.

"Just stand behind me when we get to the door and don't say anything," Johnny said. We approached the porch of the corner house. Johnny knocked with confidence. A balding large-framed man in a short-sleeved white shirt answered. His body took up most of the entry. I took a step back on the postage stamp-sized porch.

"Good evening, sir. I wonder if you could help me out? My name is Johnny Constantini and I'm selling subscriptions to The San Diego Union newspaper and wondered if you would be interested in trying it out for a month?"

"No, son, I'm not interested." The man started to close the door.

"Sir, it would only be on a one-month trial basis, and it would really help my family out." The man hesitated. Johnny pounced, "You see, sir, my dad lost his job recently and we need the money from these subscriptions." Johnny's tone changed from an upbeat tempo to a pleading one.

The man seemed to soften.

"The paper would be delivered on your porch every morning before you get up and you and your wife could enjoy it with your coffee, and the paper has a great sports section."

"How much is it?"

"Two dollars and seventy-five cents."

"Just for one month?"

"Yes, sir, just a one-month trial."

"Okay, son, you can sign me up."

"Thank you very much, sir."

Johnny whipped out his pad and pen, filled the order out and handed them over. As the new customer signed, Johnny turned to me with a smile and winked. Johnny tore the white cover sheet off the order and gave it to the man.

"Your first copy should be on your porch the day after tomorrow."

"Sounds good, Johnny." He turned to go back into the house, then stopped. "Sorry about your old man losing his job. I remember when mine lost his just before the war, it was pretty tough on us. Good luck with your sales, kid."

"Thank you, sir."

We began to walk to the next house.

"Man, Johnny, sorry to hear about your dad losing his job."

"Lose his job? My dad didn't lose his job."

"Then why did you say it?

"To make the sale."

"But isn't that a lie?"

"It's not a lie, it's a sales pitch."

"Really?"

"A sales pitch is what a salesman uses to make sales." Johnny stopped and looked at me. "Most people don't think they want to order the paper. What we do is help them see that they really do, so we use the pitch. We're actually doing them a favor. You'll have to work on one."

"Like what?"

"There's lots of 'em. Since Christmas is coming you could say that your father died and your mother doesn't make enough money for presents for your little brother and sister and if you could get enough orders, you could get them gifts."

"Oh man, that's a good one."

"Or you could try, 'My little brother wants a bike for Christmas and you, sir, could help me get him one.'"

"I like that one."

"Here's another good one: 'My grandfather died in Arizona two days ago and we need bus fare for my mom to get to the funeral.'"

"That's a really good one. I'm going to use that one tonight."

"Try it out. If it doesn't work, try another until you find one you're comfortable with. But remember that when you give the people the line, you need to look like you are desperate for an order. If you're smiling, they won't believe you. Give them dog eyes." It was a lot to remember.

"My brother Jimmy told a lady that he just needed two more subscriptions for our mom to make this month's rent and you know what she did?"

"No."

"She bought two subscriptions."

"No kiddin'?"

"No kiddin'."

I followed Johnny for the next three houses; no sales were made.

"Fernando, you try the next one."

"Are you sure?"

"You got to do it sooner or later. Besides, I'll be right behind you."

"I'm nervous, Johnny."

"Everyone's nervous on their first night. Hell, when Gary trained me, I was so nervous I completely forgot what I was supposed to say when the lady answered the door. I just stood there looking at her like a damn deaf-mute." Johnny shook his head and laughed.

"All right," I said. "Who knows, maybe I'll get an order on my first try."

The cottage-sized green and white craftsman style house was on an equally small lot. A Rambler with rust spots on its trunk sat in the driveway and a girl's bike lay in the dirt where a lawn should have been. Bermuda grass grew between the cracks in the concrete sidewalk. I heard the national evening news broadcast out of an open window.

I knocked. In a few seconds the doorknob turned; the door creaked open. I tensed. An overweight woman in her mid-forties answered. A dirty screen door stood between me and the woman. She held the door open just enough to see who was knocking. She had a bathrobe and house slippers on, and a towel wrapped around her head. With her free hand she clenched her robe under her sagging chin. Strands of wet black hair peeked out from under her turban.

She looked at me. "Yes?"

I froze. She looked at Johnny behind me. He poked me in the back. My mind raced as I tried to remember what to say, "Good—good evening, sir—I mean ma'am. I—I was wondering if you might be interested in subscribing to *The San Diego Union* newspaper?"

"No," she said and closed the door in my face.

My shoulders slumped. "Darn it."

"Don't worry, Fernando," Johnny said while we walked away from the rude woman's house. "If you're going to make sales, you have to be ready to have people close the door on you. At least she didn't slam it."

"People slam the door in your face?"

"Shit, it happens all the time. It's just part of door-to-door sales. Here's another thing, start your pitch with, 'Can you help me out?' That way you're not just asking for an order, you're asking for help."

"Good idea. I'll try it next time."

Johnny took the next one, I marveled at his easy, smooth delivery. He had me do the one after that. My confidence grew as he encouraged me and helped me see my weak points. We got to the end of the first block.

"We're going to do a hand-over-hand."

"What's that?"

"While I do this house, you go and do the next one, then I'll hop over to the next house. Let's see who can sell the most orders before Gary picks us up."

With the competition my nervousness vanished. Shortly after I told a lady about my grandfather's untimely demise, she actually agreed to order a subscription. I excitedly pulled my order pad out, filled in the small form and handed her my pen and pad trying not to smile. I gave her the receipt after she signed the order.

"I'm so sorry to hear about your grandfather," she said.

"Oh, he'll be okay."

"What do you mean he'll be okay?"

"I mean, we'll be okay. I mean my mother will be okay . . . I mean we'll all be okay . . . except for grandpa, of course."

"You poor thing, you must be traumatized."

I sadly nodded my head and wondered what traumatized meant. I slipped my order pad into my pocket.

"Wait a minute," she said.

I panicked. Uh-oh.

"Hey, Margaret," she called into the house, "come here." I was tempted to run.

Another lady came to the door with a steaming cup in her hand. My customer explained my dire situation to her friend. "Give this poor boy an order."

Margaret readily agreed.

After signing up, Margaret said, "Good luck," her voice laced with pity.

"Thank you very much, ma'am." I fought the urge to skip to the street. I heard the door latch click.

"I got two at that house." I said to Johnny.

He stopped. "You got a two-fer?"

"I guess so."

Johnny gave me a fist to the shoulder. "A two-fer on your first night? Great job." My confidence soared.

At the end of the shift, I had sold one more and Johnny three more. I had the door slammed in my face only once.

"Fernando got a two-fer," Johnny said as we got into the car.

Pete turned around from the front seat and looked at me. "A two-fer on your first night?"

"Yeah, I guess so."

"Way to go, Fernando. Good job," Jimmy said.

I sat amazed when Benny told us he had sold six and Jimmy seven. The rest of the crew had sold three or fewer each.

"Not bad for you first night," Pete said.

"How did you do, Pete?" I asked.

"I blanked out."

"What's that?"

"That's when you don't get any orders."

"Pete's good at blanking out," Larry said with a laugh.

"Shut up, Larry, or I'll beat the dog shit out of you, you little dick brain."

"You gotta be able to catch me first."

"That's enough," Gary said, not bothering to turn his head from the front seat.

We were dropped off in the reverse order as we had been picked up. I was left off at eight.

"How'd you do?" Armando asked.

"I sold three."

"How did Louie and Joe do?"

"Louie got two and Joe got four. Do you remember when Louie told us about his cousin Benny?"

"Yeah."

"He sold six and another guy sold seven."

"Can you get me on?"

"I don't know yet, it's only my first day."

I sat at the table and did another half hour of homework before lying in my bunk exhausted. I explained to Armando how Gary drove us to Encinitas and how nice Johnny was as he trained me.

"So there's nine guys on the crew?"

"Yup."

"And how many orders did you say Louie's cousin sold?"

"Six."

"That's six dollars in one day. If he sells six a day, then that's thirty dollars in one week."

We lay in awed wonder. "And that's a hundred and twenty dollars a month." It was hard for me to wrap my mind around, that much money.

"But that's just during the weekdays. We're also going to solicit on Saturday, so he'll make even more."

"Why didn't you use Benny's sales pitch? You might have sold four or five."

"Because I don't know what it is."

"You should find out."

"I don't want to switch yet. Besides, I found out that some of the guys don't want to share theirs."

"How come?"

"Johnny said that sometimes we solicit the same neighborhoods a year later, and if a different guy is using the same line the people will know he's lying. So I'll use mine for now."

"You mean about our grandfather dying in Arizona?"

"Yeah."

"Hey, I got an idea. Why don't you tell the people that your grandfather died, and we can't afford the money for a funeral, and we had to put him in the closet and he's starting to stink it up."

"Maybe I'll try it tomorrow."

"What are you going to do with the money you make?"

"Don't know. I guess I should give Dad some."

Louie, Joe, my brother and I huddled during recess the next day and talked about the crew. I was glad my twin didn't divulge my sales pitch.

I was raring to go when Gary showed up that afternoon. After the last boy got into the car Gary told us that we were assigned the old established neighborhood of Claremont. "How come we gotta do that pud?" Jimmy asked.

"Because that's where the newspaper needs more customers," Gary replied. I found out that the pud referred to the parts of town that were hard to sell in. Interestingly, the economically depressed neighborhood of Logan Heights was a gold mine for sales. I hit my territory in Claremont with enthusiasm and only made one sale. Pete and Ed blanked out, the rest of the crew sold one or two, with Benny and Jimmy three each.

At the end of the shift on Friday, Gary handed us an envelope with our names on them. My envelope contained ten dollars. My fingers trembled as I handled the five one-dollar bills along with a fiver.

Dad was reading the newspaper when I came through the door carrying the five. He put the paper down, "How did you do, *mijo*?" I smiled and handed over the bill. "Good job." It was the first time that week I had seen him. "What do you say to the people to get them to take a subscription?"

"A sales pitch one of the guys taught me."

I bought my brother and me ice cream cones at the Thrifty Drug Store Sunday afternoon. I got us double scoopers.

C. ARMANDO'S ON

Three weeks after I was hired, Joe got fired for writing phonies. A phony was an order that the solicitor filled out with a house address and a forged signature. Usually, the irate customer would call the newspaper to complain that they had never ordered the newspaper and refuse to pay. The phony would be sent back to Gary, who in turn would discipline the solicitor. In the nine months I spent on the crew, I only wrote one phony on a desperate night. The customer must have paid his bill without complaint because the order never came back.

On the Friday night after Joe was fired, Gary asked, "We need another guy. Do any of you know anybody?"

No one said anything.

"My brother would like to," I said.

"When will he be able to start?"

"Tomorrow."

"Are you sure?"

"He's been bugging me to get him hired since the first day I got on."

Gary smiled. "I'll get his order pad ready."

"How many did you get?" Armando asked as soon as I got home.

"Two more."

"How many does that make for the week?"

"Nine."

"God, you're lucky."

"Do you want to get on?"

"Heck yeah."

"Gary said you can start tomorrow."

"What?"

"You can start tomorrow," I said with a grin.

"Oh man, thanks a lot."

"Atta boy, cowboy," Dad said when I told him I got Armando hired. Until now my brother had only heard of the characters on the crew and my adventures, now he would be in the mix. We excitedly discussed sales pitches from our bunks that night while we waited for elusive sleep to come.

My brother was lucky; his first day would be a Saturday. Saturdays were a lot better to solicit than weekdays since we would spend the day in sunlight as opposed to the dark cold winter nights. On this Saturday we worked Vista, a North County community twenty miles in from the coast and fifty miles north of San Diego. Gary had Jimmy train my twin. I had a good day, I sold four orders.

"How'd you do, Armando?" Johnny asked when my brother and Jimmy got into the car.

"Eight," Jimmy said excitedly.

"Eight?" Pete asked.

"Eight," Jimmy said. "He's a natural."

"How many of his orders were gimmies?" Larry asked.

A gimmie was an order that you didn't have to sell. The person at the door readily agreed to an order with little or no prodding.

"None," Jimmy said.

My brother's quick wit and conniving ways that got him into so much trouble with Sister Constance, served him well in sales.

D. THE WAYS OF THE WORLD REVEALED

ARMANDO AND I LIVED A SHELTERED LIFE in our religious home and Catholic school. Any form of vulgarity was not tolerated. Six of the boys on the crew went to public schools and their homes were likely not as devout as our mother's. These lost souls talked about sex, masturbation, drinking beer and made obscene gestures. Some of them even smoked; unimaginable to a good boy like me. In the early days on the crew Armando and my naivety were a source of amusement for our worldly comrades.

Johnny talked about an order he almost made. "I tried like hell to make the sale, but I couldn't get the bastard to sign up."

"What's a bastard?" I asked.

I heard Ed's hillbilly laugh from the middle seat.

Pete talked about another sale. "So the guy says he was already taking the *Carlsbad Courier*, and I said, 'Aw man, Mister, that paper's on the rag.'"

"What's 'on the rag?'" my brother asked.

"You mean you have three older sisters, and you don't know what 'on the rag means'?"

"Well, I kinda do."

"It means the girl is using Kotex; you know, a rag."

"Kotex?"

Gary, at the wheel shook his head, everyone except Armando and me laughed.

On the drive home one night Jimmy, Armando and I sat in the far rear seat. Jimmy explained in hushed tones, lest Gary hear about masturbation.

"What's it feel like?" my brother asked.

"It's like taking a piss only a hundred times better."

"How do you do it?"

"Grab your dick, think of a naked girl, and stroke."

"For how long?"

"As long as it takes to come."

My brother shrugged and said, "Okay."

On our way back from Oceanside the next night Jimmy quietly asked my brother, "Did you try it?"

"Yeah."

"Did it feel good?"

"It felt real good."

"Did you come?"

"Come?"

"Yeah, did you come? Did anything come out of your dick?"

"No."

"Did it get hard?"

"You couldn't have bent it if you hit it with a hammer."

Benny was eavesdropping from the middle seat and screamed with laughter.

The third month on the crew, I tried out swearing for the first time. I casually said the word damn and expected a divine reprimand, but nothing happened. A few days later I heard my brother call someone a dick. Again, no repercussions. After four months on the crew my twin began to lace his vocabulary with colorful words.

E. BANTER

DEPENDING ON THE TERRITORY we were canvassing, the drive could take thirty to fifty minutes. With the long drives, the conversations in the car would often get provocative. As long as things didn't get too carried away, Gary tolerated it. He coped by smoking Lucky Strikes and playing the radio, happily singing along with the music of the fifties and sixties.

"Hey, Larry, I met your parents the other day, couple of nice guys."

"Gary," Larry called out, "Pete's capping on my parents." To cap on someone was to make fun of them.

"Okay, Pete, cut it out. You know the rule, no making fun of parents."

Moments later, "Wow. Look at the knockers on that chick," Jimmy said from the front seat as Gary drove past a long-haired, well-endowed girl in shorts and a tank top.

"Which one?"

"The one walking the dog." We craned our necks to get a look.

"She kin walk mah dawg," Ed said.

"Wouldn't I like to see her naked. You know what I would do with that?" Jimmy said.

"That's enough," Gary said.

"Hey, Benny, you want some help jacking off?" Ed said. "I got tweezers and a magnifying glass."

"You can kiss my ass, Ed."

"Hey, Larry, I heard you were making out with Tippy last night," Benny said.

"Tippy? Tippy who?"

"Tip of my dick," Benny said to raucous laughter.

"Fuck you, Benny." Larry stuck out his middle finger.

"Goddamn it, everybody shut up," Gary yelled.

Things would quiet down until we got bored watching the scenery whiz by. Slowly inappropriate comments would start until Gary got mad again.

F. Sharing the Wealth

GARY TAUGHT US TO BE PERSISTENT IN SALES. The old adage, do not take no for an answer was drilled into us. On one particular sale, as long as the door was open, I kept prodding.

"But, ma'am, it's only for a month's trial and the Sunday paper has a ton of coupons to save you money." The lady finally caved and gave me an order.

From inside the house, I heard a man's voice. "Kid, you could sell sand to the Arabs."

On a good week I could clear the princely sum of twenty dollars. It was great when I got home and was able to tell Mom and Dad that I had a good night, and demoralizing when I made only one or two sales or blanked out. Armando consistently outsold me.

When I got into a sales slump Gary took me under his wing and helped me with my technique and sales pitch. "Fernando, it's not so much what you say that make sales but how you say it." Gary was patient and encouraging. I was grateful for his interest and his help. The following Saturday I sold nine orders.

Without realizing it, my twin and I were learning lifelong skills: the ability to approach strangers and engage them in conversation, the art of persuasion, and confidence in ourselves. We were fortunate to have a good crew manager.

Armando and I got big-talking Hector, across the street, onto the crew. He was excited with the prospect of making money and having time away from his overbearing mother. It didn't occur to us that his stuttering speech impediment could be a problem. He panicked the first time Benny, who was training him, had him ring a doorbell. Hector could barely get out, "good," to "good evening," out when a lady answered.

"Goo—goo—goo—goo. . ." Benny had to step in and finish the line. Hector lasted two days before giving up.

Our classmate Gerry got starry-eyed when I told him about my job. "I make anywhere between fifteen and twenty dollars a week."

"Do you think you can get me on?"

"I'll let you know if a spot opens up."

At school on Tuesday, I gave him the good news.

"I'm going to buy a stereo set," he said. "I should have enough money in less than a month."

"Stereos aren't cheap, Gerry."

"Don't worry, I've been working on a killer line. I'll be making a lot of sales."

"What's your line?"

"I ain't telling."

Gary had Benny train him. When they got back in the car Benny told us that at Gerry's first sale, he stood staring at the lady.

"Yes? What would you like, young man?" Gerry continued his stare. After a moment she asked again. "What can I do for you?"

Benny nudged Gerry. Gerry blurted out, "The babies need bottles, the babies need bottles," and stared back, unable to finish his line. Benny stepped up and tried in vain to get the sale.

After training Gerry for two days Benny whispered to me. "He couldn't sell water to a rich man dying of thirst in the desert." Gerry outlasted Hector by one day.

G. Terror in the Night

OUR SOLICITING CREW WAS ONE of three in the county. Due to Gary's leadership, we consistently outsold the other crews by wide margins. Our crew's territories were predominantly in the North County cities. The winter months were miserable to solicit in, with the low temperatures and the sun setting by five-thirty. Most of our sales time occurred after dark. It was common to walk poorly lit streets with no sidewalks or streetlights. We often approached a front door in darkness and interrupted people's dinner or family time.

At the end of the shift if the solicitor was not at the designated spot, Gary would slowly drive up and down nearby blocks giving two short honks to alert the boy of his whereabouts.

One evening we were working a rural part of Escondido. Escondido was known for its expansive avocado groves. Homes in the area I was soliciting had large lots, most of them with big well-established trees whose canopies reached across the roadway. I finished my territory and waited for Gary at the top of the street. After three hours of walking, I was cold, tired and had only sold one order. Other than a few dim porch lights I was in pitch blackness.

I misunderstood Gary's instructions for pickup and was a block higher up the street than I should have been. While I waited, a dog at the foot of the street must have sensed my presence and came out and barked. The bark was deep. Bored and a safe distance away, I picked up a few rocks off the shoulder of the road and threw them at the barking. I heard the rocks ricochet off the surface of the asphalt. The dog retreated into its yard. A minute later he came back out and started barking again. I threw more rocks. We established a predictable pattern.

I was relieved when I heard Gary's honk and headlights slowly coming towards me, but my heart sank when he turned right one block below. The dog came out again and barked. I didn't pick up any rocks. I heard the honks make their way down the opposite street. I stood in the middle of the road too scared to walk down. The headlights came again. I waited and just before I saw him turn, I screamed, "Gary!" He made the turn and continued honking. It was cold and the car windows were probably closed. Another lap of the car, another fruitless scream. Would Gary give up? Would he drive home and leave me out here?

I had one option. I had to run past the dog on Gary's next pass. I waited for the barking to stop. I picked up a rock the size of my fist and walked quietly down the street. I stopped halfway and waited. I saw the headlights make the turn onto my street and progress towards me. I waited until he was half-way up the block. I got to make it before Gary makes the turn. My heart pounded. Got to go now! Go, go, go! My tennis shoes slapped the asphalt as I darted into the black. The damn dog must have heard them. Dog paws scratched towards me. The barking this time was a low growl. I cocked my arm. My adrenaline spiked. When should I heave the rock? I felt the dog at my side. I screamed, leapt and threw the rock down hard. A yelp rang out. The dog tags went silent. I streaked to the headlights. Gary stopped. I flung the door open and jumped in, heaving. I shook. I had to force myself not to cry. The warmth of the car embraced me. The boys in the car were busy capping on one other, oblivious of my terror.

"Where were you, Fernando?" Gary asked, irritated.

I gulped and shook. "I thought you said you were picking me up at the top of the next block," I said with a tremble in my voice.

He must have sensed my anxiety and let it drop.

"How many orders did you get?"

"One."

I was the last pickup. Gary lit a cigarette, turned the radio on and started the long drive home.

My breathing began to normalize as I slowly relaxed.

"How'd you do, Pete?" Johnny asked.

"I got two but might've gotten more if I didn't have to go to the bathroom so bad."

"Hell, why didn't you just piss under a tree?"

"Because I had to go number two and I was too embarrassed to ask to use someone's bathroom and stink it up. I couldn't stand it anymore, so I took a dump in an avocado grove. I had to wipe my ass with leaves." Laughter broke out. "Boy, does my butthole itch."

"How many orders did you get, Benny?" my brother asked.

"Six. And you?"

"Three."

"Hey, Benny, what do you say to the customers to get so many orders?" Larry asked.

"He gives the men customers a hand job," Jimmy needled.

"Screw you, Jimmy."

"That's enough," Gary said.

"Or do you let them give you a hand job?" Jimmy persisted.

"It was your father who wanted me to play with his dick, asshole," Benny yelled.

Gary slapped the radio dial off and slammed on the brakes. Heads lunged forward. "GODDAMN IT! EVERYBODY SHUT UP!"

The car went silent. Five minutes later Gary turned the radio back on. Five minutes after that, muted conversations began. In another ten minutes the guys started jabbing again, although not as loud as before.

"Hey, Johnny, is it true you what your brother says?" Ed asked.

"What'd he say?"

"Jimmy says you go into the bathroom with a Playboy magazine and come out smiling twenty minutes later."

"Screw you, Ed."

Gary turned the volume up on the radio.

H. SAINTLY OR SATANIC

MONDAY MORNING MONSIGNOR GALLAGHER came into the classroom. He had never visited us before. I sat upright and wondered why he came.

"Class, I asked Monsignor Gallagher to come and talk to you this morning. You will soon be leaving St. Rita's and he agreed to come and prepare you for what you will encounter." Constance walked to the back of the room.

Monsignor strolled to Constance's desk. He wore his black cassock with the red buttons that distinguished him from a regular priest whose cassock had black buttons. He took Constance's chair.

"Good morning, children," he began. His eyes wandered across the room, then to the windows. He shifted in the chair. "Do not forget to continue to support the church once you leave our school." He's going to talk to us about donating?

"It is your duty as a member of the church to support our parish . . ." Blah, blah, blah.

I checked out. I had heard Monsignor's money pitch many times over. I thought about the crew and wondered what part of the county we would work today. I looked across the aisle. Lulu Hernandez had her legs crossed, her skirt rode above the knees. I wondered what Jimmy would say about her. She was the only girl in the school that actually needed a bra. Next to Lulu, sat Gail who was blossoming nicely, she had nice legs too.

Up the aisle sat Martha Herzog. Rumor had it she liked to kiss. Like Lulu, she had a nice pair of full lips.

My mind was brought back to the classroom when I heard the Monsignor say the word devil. He had finished begging for money and had gone on to other topics. "The Devil is the father of lies," he said. "He will tempt you. 'Oh, it's all right to cheat,' he will whisper in your ear. 'Go ahead and do it. After all, everyone else is doing it.' The next thing you know you will be sinning, and you all know what awaits you in the next life if you die with a grievous sin on your soul."

I raised my hand, Monsignor called on me. "Monsignor, my mother told me that when the devil is around you can smell sulfur."

Monsignor laughed. "That sounds like Mexican gibberish to me."

Constance shook her head in dismay.

That night Armando and I talked about what Monsignor had said. "Do you think we're sinning when we give our lines to customers?" I asked.

"Don't know, but if we didn't use them, we wouldn't make many sales, then we wouldn't be able to help Dad."

"I wonder if I should confess it."

The bedroom door opened, Dad came in. He walked to the foot of the top bunk and rested his elbow on the mattress. "I'm proud of you boys, the extra money you make helps your mother and me."

Dad's statement caught me off guard. It contradicted what we were doing and what we had heard in religion class. I hesitated before deciding to divulge my moral dilemma.

"Dad, do you remember when you asked me what I said to the people to make sales?"

"Sure. You said one of the boys on the crew helped you with a sales pitch."

"The sales pitch he taught me was to tell the customer that my grandfather died in Arizona and that my mother needed money to go to the funeral."

Dad chuckled. "That's a good one. Hell, why don't you throw the grandmother in while you're at it?"

"Johnny said I had to use a sales pitch if I wanted to make sales, but today in religion class Monsignor Gallagher said that lying was a sin. I'm wondering if I should go to confession and stop using the pitch." I was relieved to have unburdened myself.

Dad pulled the only chair in the room to the bunk, sat and pulled a pack of cigarettes from his shirt pocket. He took a cigarette, put it between his lips and pulled out a book of matches. He took a match from the book and was ready to light up. Then, he paused and took the cigarette out of his mouth and looked directly at me.

"Does the Monsignor have seven children to support?"

"No."

"How many children does he have to put through Catholic school?"

"None."

Dad set the cigarette and match on his lap and showed me his palms. "How many callouses does the Monsignor have on his hands?"

I flashed on Monsignor's soft hands I saw during Masses I served for him as he lifted his golden chalice. "None."

"Do you think the Monsignor ever has trouble sleeping at night because he doesn't know if he will be able to make a house payment or pay a dentist bill or put food on his table?"

"I don't think so."

"I don't think so either. Use the sales pitch, it's a tool. Hell, your mother will make sure Monsignor gets his cut of whatever money you boys bring in."

Dad stood, struck the match and lit up. He started to walk out, turned and said, "Keep up the good work, *muchachos*," and left. The smell of sulfur hung in the room.

32.

8th Grade – Pagan Babies
Fernando

*"But when you give to the needy, do not let your
left hand know what the right is doing."*
Jesus Christ

IT WAS THE FIRST FRIDAY IN MAY, the month of Mary. Our teachers encouraged us to receive Communion during the morning Mass on the first Friday of each month. Special graces were bestowed on anyone who received nine First Fridays in a row.

After the lunch recess we were marched to the parish hall. Monsignor and Sister Constance must have figured this First Friday was an opportune time to pounce.

"Your reward in heaven will be great," the gray-haired missionary said; he made an impressive figure in his white cassock. He spoke that afternoon to the sixth, seventh, and eighth grades. His soft, pale hands grasped the sides of the podium set up on the stage. Next to the podium stood a roll-down screen, a slide projector shot black-and-white pictures with each click of the trigger in the missionary's hand.

"Here is our new church and a few of our converts in the Congo." It was a small, humble, white-washed masonry structure that could have comfortably fit inside our parish church. Even its bell tower would not have touched our ceiling. Black men and women dressed in native garb smiled broadly, bright sunrays reflected off their dark faces. Half-clothed toddlers stood next to the women.

"Our brave missionaries need your help to spread God's gospel to these uneducated people. Without our help they will die unbaptized and not know the glories of heaven." The missionary had his young audience in rapt attention, except for Armando. When I turned to look at him he had closed his eyes and a small drop of saliva was about to drip from his chin. He stopped paying attention to the presentation once he saw that we weren't going to be seeing any half-naked native women like the ones in the *National Geographic* magazine Kenny had sneaked to school.

The missionary was telling us about the holy work the clergy did. "For just two dollars a month, we can feed and teach one of these people. If you are so moved, for twenty-five dollars you can sponsor a pagan baby. And as a thank-you, you may give your pagan baby his or her Christian name."

Oohs and aahs echoed in the hall; the missionary smiled. Armando stirred and yawned. "I am sure you children have been instructed on the benefits of indulgences."

Yes, we had. We were taught that one could earn indulgences in this life by doing good works. Indulgences could be redeemed upon death, lessening your time suffering in purgatory.

After the presentation, stacks of small cardboard cards were given to two of the eighth-grade boys who positioned themselves on either side of the exit door. They handed a card to each student as we left the hall.

"The Society for the Propagation of the Faith" was printed across the top, below was a picture of Pope Paul VI sitting on his gold-and-velvet throne. He probably was not a pagan baby.

The pope's hand was raised as if giving his blessing. Inside the card it said "Missionary Donation Card" with a series of slots the size of a quarter, four slots per side. Under the first slot was written twenty-five cents and progressed from slot to slot until it reached the two-dollar mark.

"Wouldn't it be wonderful if our class could raise enough quarters to sponsor an African baby, especially during this month of Mary?" Sister Constance said. The matter was settled. All she needed to do was water the evangelical seeds the missionary had planted by a mere suggestion. The hearts of her students, except for Armando's, were aflame with the zealotry of the ancients. I challenged myself to get my card filled.

"Ma, can I have a quarter?"

"*Porque?*"

"Our class wants to sponsor a pagan baby in Africa."

"And who is going to sponsor us?" I took that as a no.

Undeterred, I canvassed our neighborhood convinced that by the end of the day I would have my card filled. I couldn't wait to hand in the card and make a down payment against my purgatory time. An hour later I walked home with one quarter and stunned that so many cheapskates lived on our street. I persevered. The next day I walked to the kindly Mrs. McCarthy's house. She was a member of the Legion of Mary and a soft touch if ever there was one. She handed over two quarters.

"You're a good boy, Fernando. I am sure Our Holy Mother will bless you."

"Gee thanks, Mrs. McCarthy."

The rest of her neighbors were as tight fisted as Ma. The following afternoon canvass netted me one more coin. With my evangelical fire dampened I put the card atop my dresser and resolved to get it filled before the end of May. After all, I only had to collect five more quarters.

Armando was a better salesman than I. He didn't walk door to door but hit up our well-heeled Aunt Helen who stopped by for a visit. She was at the kitchen table having a beer with Pa.

"If our class collects enough money we can name the baby and I can put your name on the list. Just think, tia, there could be a little Helen walking around Africa because you donated." Her eyes perked." He went in for the kill. "It will earn you a lot of indulgences." Aunt Helen didn't go to Mass on Sundays or even on Easter or Christmas and if that wasn't bad enough, she was living in sin with Bergie, a bail bondsman. The lure of indulgences must have been too much for her to pass up. She dug four quarters out of her purse and handed them over.

The last Friday of May came and my good intentions went unfulfilled, but I figured three quarters were better than none. I picked my card up from the dresser and opened it hoping somehow an extra quarter I had forgotten about would bring my total up to a dollar. Not only was there not an extra quarter but there were only two and a small slip of paper in the slot of the missing coin. I took the paper scrap out and opened it. In my brother's unmistakable handwriting was written "IOU twenty-five cents." I found him hiding in the garage leafing through the *National Geographic* he had borrowed from Kenny.

"Hey, what's this?" I showed him the scrap of paper he had put in my cardboard folder.

"It's an IOU," my brother said.

"What's that?"

"Martha told me that if you borrow money, you give the person you borrowed it from a slip of paper with IOU written on it. That way you and the person know that you owe him that amount of money."

"Here, look at my card," my brother said opening it. I saw three slips of paper tucked in the slots where Aunt Helen's indulgences quarters had been.

"You mean you're only going to turn in one quarter?"

"No, stupid, you're not getting it. It's like there are four quarters because the IOUs mean that I will be giving the money back later."

"O-h-h, I get it."

If Martha said it, then I knew it was legit. Suddenly I understood how my brother was able to buy ice creams at lunch lately. I hadn't asked any questions when he offered to buy me one.

"But if we're supposed to hand in the money today, how are you going to get the rest of the money to Sister in time?"

"I'll bring it to her next year."

"But we'll be in high school next year."

"I'm sure Sister Constance will be happy to take my money anytime." His reasoning seemed solid enough.

Before going out to the afternoon recess I sneaked my brother's card from his desk, opened it, took the last quarter, and slipped in an IOU. I would be able to enjoy ice creams for the next two days and still have a nickel left.

We were encouraged to give our cards back anonymously. "Let us not be like the boastful Pharisees," Sister had said at the beginning of our campaign. "they have already collected their reward on earth, your reward will be in heaven." Anonymity had its advantages.

The day after the campaign was over, she designated the first student in each row to collect the cards.

"I know Jesus is very proud of you," she said as the cards lay on her desk. "Now, we need to come up with a name. Are there any suggestions?" She rose and turned to the blackboard.

John raised his hand, "How about Jonathon?"

"That's a nice name." She wrote it on the chalkboard "Any others?"

Terry raise her hand, "How about Theresa?"

"Another good Christian name," Sister wrote Theresa below Jonathon.

Mike raised his hand. "How about Michael?"

She stopped taking suggestions after Judy suggested Judith. "Well, thank you, these are all very good names." She paused then set the bait. Looking wistful she said, "As a nun I sacrificed my motherhood," a chill ran down my spine, "and I will never have children," another chill. "Sometimes at night as I lay in my bed after I say my prayers," a full shudder, "I so wish I could have been able to have a namesake but that is the sacrifice I have chosen." Her dog eyes looked pathetic. Her not-so-subtle suggestion bore fruit. Katy Williams raised her hand. "Yes, Katy?"

"How about Mary Constance?" With a broad smile Sister added it to the names. She wrote it in large letters. When the secret ballot was held Mary Constance edged out a win. I rolled my eyes. Little doubt Constance would flaunt our freewill decision to the nuns in the convent.

During recess my brother railed against the vote with our friends. "I want another vote."

"You got a name in mind?" John asked.

"Yeah, I do. What do you guys think about Dip Shit?" A roar erupted. I nearly dropped my Drumstick ice cream cone.

Monday morning Sister began class with a dire warning. "Be assured that anyone who misuses money meant for the poor will have to face the consequences in the next life."

"I think Sister knew the IOUs were from me," my brother said on the walk home.

"How could she? It was anonymous."

"She was staring really hard at me after she talked about misusing money. But I didn't misuse the money. I'm gonna pay it back."

"Yeah? How?"

"Well, I can become a missionary and come to school and get kids to fill out a whole bunch of the Missionary Collection Cards. And then there will be a whole lot of quarters."

I lay in bed that night mulling it over. My brother was not good at following through with his promises and obligations. If he didn't then we would both suffer in Purgatory. I would have to lean on him to become a missionary.

33.

8th Grade – Bountiful Harvest
Armando

*"The wise store up choice food and olive oil,
but fools gulp theirs down."*
The Book of Proverbs

I WAS ENGROSSED IN THE MOVIE. The Indian on the theater screen used a paddle like a rudder to keep his canoe on a steady, straight course through the turbulent currents of a river.

His canoe was mounded with layers of beaver, fox, and mink pelts to use as barter with white traders miles downstream. He'd had an unusually good season of trapping. What could he have been planning to trade for his goods? Maybe knives and axes made of hardened iron or beautiful beads in all the colors of the rainbow, clear as water, and yet hard as stone.

My eyes were glued to the screen as I ate from my large bag of buttered popcorn and sipped from my large cup of Coke. That's right, it was *my* large popcorn and *my* large Coke. Not the usual lame small size that I would have to share with my brother when we went to the movies. I swear that he always wound up eating and drinking more than me.

I had gotten paid from my very first job as a solicitor going door-to-door selling subscriptions to the newspaper. And let me tell you, I was really good at dreaming up sales pitches to sucker people into buying subscriptions and, best of all, I was paid in cash. I had walked into the theater with four one-dollar bills and a big fat fiver. Fourteen years old, a pocket full of money, and a wide, long gleaming glass snack bar case filled with candy in wrappers all the colors of the rainbow, all calling to me. For the first time I could afford to get anything I wanted, and as much as I wanted.

The poor Indian had had a hard go of it. He was thin, having barely survived an especially long and bitter winter, but now he had the ability to reap a bountiful harvest after a great season of trapping.

My popcorn was half gone, as was my Coke. I tucked them under my seat and made for the snack bar. I ordered one of those beautiful wieners that turned slowly and seductively on heated rollers. It would have been out of the question before, but today all I had to say was, "Hot dog, please," hand over a dollar, get my change, make a beeline for the mustard and relish table, and pile it on. The bun wasn't one of those slices of Wonder bread folded in half like we had to use at home that our parents would always say, "It's the same thing." But not today. I got a real hotdog bun, soft and warm. And get this, I still had lots of money. I could treat myself just like I had always seen the rich gringo kids do.

When I got to my seat the Indian had hit some rapids and almost went over, nearly losing his precious cargo, but he managed to right his canoe. *Whew!* I thought. *That was a close one.*

I sank my teeth into the hotdog and ate it in big bites. I reached under my seat for my Coke and took deep gulps. Man, this was really living. Minutes later the Indian passed a herd of deer grazing in a meadow. Seeing the deer eating gave me a hankering. No problem; another trip to the snack bar. I bought a long, thick Big-Stick Popsicle that was all the colors of the rainbow. I paid ten cents for it and I still had plenty of change and a few bills in my pocket.

Fernando and I had gone to the movies with Tony, our older brother, and sisters on the rare occasions when our Ma could squeeze out enough money for us to take the bus ride downtown and spend an afternoon at the Orpheum Theater. I'd get to choose one measly treat while I saw gringo kids really load up: Look candy bars and Big Hunks, Abba-Zabas, Milky Ways, Rolos. But today those kids were no match for me.

Back on the screen the Indian paddled close to the bank and passed bunches of wild blackberry bushes. Some of the berries were green, others red, the ripe ones were a deep purple. The colors reminded me of Jujubes. Ha! Jujubes! A quick jog to the snack bar for a box. I came back to my seat, shook a handful of the colorful beads into my palm, and tossed them into my mouth. The chewy candies had a gluing effect on my teeth. I made snapping, popping sounds when I had to force my teeth apart. Fun.

The Indian was nearing his destination. I didn't want to miss out on what was going to happen, but Flicks chocolates sounded good. I tilted my head back and emptied the box of Jujubes into my mouth and jogged to the snack bar with my teeth snapping and popping and bought a tube of Flicks. I unwrapped the beautiful deep blue shining paper at the end of the tube and shook a couple into my mouth. I started for the theater, but my tummy began to ache and then nausea set in. I went back to the snack bar and bought a 7UP, figuring that the carbonation would settle my stomach. But one sip and my stomach said, "Coming up!"

I ran to the bathroom, head spinning, with a pukey taste in my mouth. I pushed open the stall door, leaned over the toilet, and up it came in all the colors of the rainbow. The rush of adrenaline that followed made me feel a little better. I rinsed my mouth and walked out. The magnetic force of the beautiful display of the snack bar had lost its lure.

I went to my seat to sit through the end of the movie. The Indian returned to the riverbank after having been taken by the traders. He stepped to his canoe, sorely disappointed, and I walked up the aisle, out of the theater with a bellyache.

34.

8th Grade – Vocations vs. Temptations
Armando

"Temptation is the devil looking through the keyhole."
Billy Sunday

WITH HIS GROWING PARISH and limited slots for students, Monsignor added a second story to the school building. The first floor had been built with ten-foot-high ceilings likely to help keep the classrooms cooler during September. This gave the upper grades great views of the parish grounds, Imperial and Euclid Avenues and well beyond.

I was looking out the windows one morning lost in a beautiful daydream. My lips were about to touch Lulu Hernandez's voluptuous mouth. Although Lulu was not overly pretty, she possessed a lustful tone in her voice and a tempting motion in her hips as she walked. A few of us boys sought Lulu out after school to engage her in conversation. We knew as soon as she stepped off the stairs and onto the playground she would pull her skirt up a couple of inches, undo the top button of her blouse and cradled her books to her chest.

I was jolted out of my fantasy with Sister Constance's hefty voice. "Class we need to talk about your futures."

My dream vanished in a poof. "You kids are at an age now when you will be faced with temptations of the flesh." I looked up irritated, but wait; DID SHE SAY TEMPTATIONS OF THE FLESH? "You must never allow a momentary lapse of good judgment to cause your soul to spend an eternity suffering."

I sat upright. I noticed that my voice had been changing. I was growing dark hair on my arms and legs and my body was mysteriously, involuntarily becoming easily aroused around girls.

"If you find yourself in this situation, you must ask if this passing pleasure is worth it." She paused, "I want you to imagine a huge boulder and think of a tiny bird barely out of its nest, its beak is soft and supple," *hmm, I like soft and supple*, "and once a year this tiny bird manages to fly to the boulder and give it a peck. Imagine the eons of time it would take this boulder to be turned into dust." Sister paused again. "That would only be the first day of eternity." I heard a gasp behind me. It was Katy Williams, a nice girl who let it be known that she wanted to be a nun one day.

So, what exactly happened during this momentary lapse of good judgment Sister?

Then Constance got to the meat of her backhanded message. "You should consider the religious life. We nuns have sacrificed part of our earthly humanity for a divine one. Instead of marrying and having a family, we chose a higher calling, we chose to marry Jesus." *Lucky Jesus.*

"People ask me what our life is like—they want to know if we ever have fun. Well let me tell you something, you should see us on Saturday nights around the ping pong table." Ping-pong? "You will be graduating from high school in four years. Think seriously about the priesthood or the convent afterward." *Think I'll take my chances on sins of the flesh and gamble I'll get to confession in time.*

The students that Sister Constance treated nicely were the ones who kissed her ass. Armando and I refused to lower ourselves. It must have frustrated her.

342

Responsibilities were doled out to a good part of the eighth grade. Her pets got the cushy jobs. Jobs like collecting the weekly bank money from those students who agreed to open a savings account with the local bank. No doubt the Monsignor made a deal with the branch manager with some back-scratching involved.

Eighth grade girls were selected to monitor the lower classes while the nuns and teachers went to lunch. A few boys were assigned as staircase monitors to make sure students stayed in single file, didn't talk or skip steps as they climbed and descended. This job was given under the guise of a safety measure. It was probably created to give some of the less competent boys a job to do. John Maloney got flag duty, it was his responsibility to raise and take down the American and California flags every morning and afternoon.

Lulu Hernandez along with two other girls were sent to help the cafeteria ladies prepare and serve food.

Frankie DeVito was in Sister Constance's good graces, while he didn't exactly kowtow, he was overly polite in front of her and any other adult. He behaved in class and was an altarboy. In front of us boys however, the real gutter-mouth Frankie came out. He took the Lord's name in vain, gave the finger, told dirty jokes and spat like a sailor.

Frankie had average looks and height. He was heavy boned and dressed as nice as a kid wearing a school uniform could. He wore stylish white socks with the cool double red stripes at the top, wore neatly ironed white shirts with button down collars and the latest style brown leather shoes. He kept a comb in his back pocket, so his thick auburn hair always looked good.

While Frankie had average looks and build, he had an above average sex drive. During Mass one morning I saw his eyes follow Lulu as she swayed toward the altar for communion. He watched her like a hungry Pit-bull looks at a milkbone. For Frankie, to feel lust, was to do something about it.

Sister Constance assigned him to help carry supplies from the storage room under the cafeteria up to the kitchen and to run errands for the cooks. During lunch recess Frankie told Kenny, John, Armando and me that Mrs. Hardy, one of the cafeteria ladies, caught him with his hand up Lulu's blouse in the cafeteria's storage room.

"No kidding Frankie? What happened?" Armando asked.

"I sat Lulu on top of some cases of canned spaghetti and started kissing her."

"On the lips?" I asked.

"Hell yeah on the lips, where else?" he said irritated. "Then I started to pull her blouse up real nice and slow and worked my hand up and felt the bottom of her bra." I stepped in closer.

"Lulu put her hand on my arm to try and stop me but I just kept going, then she let her hand fall. She started to breath hard. Just as I was ready to go under Mrs. Hardy walked in."

"Aww, man," John moaned as he wiped a drop of drool from his lip.

"So I pulled my hand out real fast and grabbed a case of canned tomatoes. Lulu jumped off the boxes and tucked her blouse back in. I made for the door with the tomatoes, but Mrs. Hardy stopped me. Oh man, I thought I was screwed."

"What did she say?"

"She stood there for a second. Then she said, "I'll tell you what Frankie, go talk to Father Vidra about this and I'll talk to Lulu and Sister Constance needn't know anything about it.""

"Did you do it?"

"You're damn right I did it."

"What did you tell Father?" Kenny asked. "I told him that I kissed Lulu on the cheek."

"You mean like the cheek on her face?" Armando asked as laughter erupted.

"Yes the one on her face, stupid." Frankie said annoyed but knowing Frankie, I didn't think my brother's question was all that dumb.

"So what did Vidra say?"

"He told me what I did was wrong and that I should be putting my energies into sports like he did when he was in grammar and high school. He said I should keep a rosary in my pocket and grab it whenever I was tempted. I told him I would join our baseball team and get a rosary. We shook hands and he led me out of his office." We laughed when Frankie finished his story. One thing I knew about Frankie, he could bold face lie his ass off. Frankie joined the team, but he scored a lot more points during the season with Candy Monroe under the staircase behind the school than he ever did on the baseball diamond.

No girl in the seventh and eighth grades was safe from his advances. Frankie had no inhibitions nor letting his hormones do his thinking. Didn't Frankie fear the afterlife, wasn't he afraid of burning in the fires of hell forever? God, I envied him.

Constance gave me the job of collecting the absentee slips every morning from each of the teachers and turn them in to the office. My brother had to check the boys' bathrooms and make sure the toilets were flushed.

A few days later, Sister addressed the girls. "Girls will you please rise and walk with me to the library." She stood and followed the girls out. Father McGinn came in. We rose, "Good morning, Father," we said in unison.

He smiled, "good morning boys," he said in his high-pitched Irish brogue as he took Sister's chair. He had never visited our class before. When Sister closed the door he began.

"Boys you are at an age now when you will start to be tempted in ways you could never have imagined." *Not the bird and the boulder again.*

"When you go to high school next year, chances are you will be enticed to try alcohol. Can any of you tell me the effects of alcohol?"

Frankie raised his hand. "It makes you dim witted. My dad says sometimes when you drink you do things you normally wouldn't do."

"Good Frankie, I'm glad to know your father talked to you about it."

"Yeah Father, my mom gets angry at him all the time, she says if he doesn't stop drinking so much she's going to make him come and talk to you."

"Well my door is always open. Anyone else?"

Walter raised his hand. "One night my father came home with bruises on his face, he told Ma that he ran into a door but then she asked him why his shirt was torn. Then she said he wasn't fooling anybody because our neighbor Mrs. O'Malley told her that dad and Mr. O'Malley got into a fight at the bar." I heard Donny chuckle behind me. This was a lot more fun than listening to Sister talk about Saturday night ping pong.

"Thank you Walter, maybe this is something I should talk to your father about in the privacy of my office."

John spoke up without being recognized, "Father, I saw Mr. Kelly throwing up in the parking lot at the VFW hall one night …"

Father's face turned red, he curled his finger under his Roman collar and pulled. He raised his hand and cut John off in mid-sentence.

"Boys I came to talk to you today about vocations and the benefits of the religious life."

I tuned out for the rest of his talk.

WITH THE COLD WAR ON, air raid sirens were installed throughout the city, one was mounted on a telephone pole across from the school. A nuclear attack from the Russians was possible even anticipated. The city would turn all the sirens on for a few seconds every Friday at noon as a test. I lived in fear that the Russians would attack on a test day and I would be obliterated while eating my bean burrito. Ma took me and Armando to a PTA meeting one night; a government official addressed the members.

"Good evening, I am here tonight to help you plan how to keep your families safe in the event of a nuclear attack." With the aid of a series of slides on a screen he instructed the parents how to build a bomb shelter, stock it with the proper provisions and the length of time a family of four could expect to be holed up. "The shelter needs to have a foot of soil over the top to protect you from the nuclear fallout. It also needs to be well ventilated." I went to bed that night frightened and discouraged. Not only did we not have the money for a bomb shelter for four, we sure as heck wouldn't have enough for a family of nine plus a Mexican cousin or two. I wondered if I would live long enough to get to high school.

"Are you afraid of the Russians bombing us?" I asked my brother.

"Heck yeah, but the way I figure it, if we're lucky and the bomb drops close to us, we'll be killed before we even know what happened. Like the way Slim probably went."

"I guess that would be a better way to go. Wonder if I'll see him up there?"

As a follow up to the PTA meeting the teachers were told to give us instructions in case we were attacked. "If you hear the air raid siren be sure to get under your desks," said Sister Constance. This didn't make sense, what good could that do when a megaton weapon was unleashed on us? I had my own plan.

If I heard the siren and it wasn't at twelve on a Friday, I would get under my desk and try to guess when the bomb would hit then get back out and walk over to Lulu's desk. I would get under it and kiss her on the lips. I didn't want to die a virgin.

Any objection from Lulu would be drowned out by the wailing siren. Knowing Lulu though she would probably not object too loudly. Who knows she might even get generous with me like she did with Frankie. I would then walk back and get back under my desk and recite a sincere Act of Contrition. If, god forbid, the air raid turned out to be merely a drill, I would have to run and jump through the windows of the classroom.

The Russians never attacked, and I never got a chance to put my plan into action.

35.

8th Grade – Graduation
Armando

*"....and you know something is happening, but
you don't know what it is, do you, Mr. Jones?"*
Bob Dylan

"A RMANDO GARCIA," Sister Constance said, reading the
first ballot. She tossed it aside like a wad of useless paper.
Sister reached into the ballot box and pulled out the next and
unfolded it, "Armando Garcia."

Good God, I had gotten the first two.

She looked up unamused. "Is this a joke?"

Embarrassed, I felt blood rush to my head. The third ballot was for Ignatius. Sister smiled, displaying gold lined teeth.
There were fifty-four votes yet to come. She must have thought
that the first two were aberrations, they had to be. *Maybe the
votes had been his and his brother's.*

This was the major event of the year for our eighth-grade
class. The winner would be class president and give the com-
mencement speech to Monsignor Gallagher, his two assistant
priests, all the teachers, our parents and guests.

"Armando Garcia," she read.

Holy crap, three to one!

"Look," Sister said, setting the ballots down. "You are choos-
ing who is going to represent this class to everyone." But it was
too late. The votes were in and sat in the ballot box waiting to

349

be read. There could be no changing them now. What must have been going through her mind?

How could these lambs that she spent so much time molding rebel like this? She had always been able to manipulate her students, bending them to do her will. She would have to inform the other nuns of the decision of her class. Sister Marie Lucille would have to keep her elation to herself. This was an affront of the first order; for once Constance was a fish out of water in her own domain.

"Do you think this is funny?" Sister said. The class looked down at their folded hands resting on top of their desks. Some may have wondered if they had sinned. I didn't think this was funny and I'd bet that my classmates felt the same. Like me, they had to be fed up with manipulation, rules, regulations, many of which made no sense. We were given a choice, we made it, and we didn't want to be admonished for it. I shook off the embarrassment. My face was now red with anger. It was clear that she was wrong.

She must have felt my vibes and glanced my way while she read another vote for me. I stared hard at her. *I may not be anything to you, but it doesn't give you the right to belittle me in front of the class when a fair and democratic decision has been made.*

We were in conflict once again, but for the first time I knew I was in the right and she was dead wrong. This was a fair vote. Even Ignatius had read the handwriting on the wall during the noon recess campaign and succumbed to the will of the people. He even said that he would vote for me in a feeble attempt to save face.

Realizing she had no other choice, Sister's voice quieted saying nothing more about the voting and read the remaining ballots. We spent an uncomfortable afternoon in her classroom.

Fernando and I had been castigated many times in this school. Sometimes I was embarrassed, other times I wore it as a badge of honor, and other times I played along, pretending to be remorseful for having had too much fun. Hard as she tried, she never succeeded in the seven years we attended school here into browbeating me into one of her drones.

It was a given that Ignatius would be elected president. After all, he had been chosen by the assistant pastor to head up the altar boys where he was my boss. He was on time to Mass every morning before school. He had a paper route for as long as anyone had known him, was an honor student, and a Boy Scout. And of course, was appointed class monitor whenever Sister Constance left the classroom. He had an air about him and was backed up by the all-powerful authorities of St. Rita's School, who, like the pope, were inspired and chosen by God Himself. It was amazing what little lobbying of our classmates it took Fernando, Donny, John, Kenny, and me to get the votes. Even soft-spoken, shy, straight-A student Patricia was openly excited with the idea of bucking the system and voted for the class clown. Patricia lived under constant pressure: pressure from her parents to excel in school, be a role model in her Girl Scout troop, behave well and, above all, never question whatever she was told by the school and parish hierarchies. I thought it was only screwups like me that felt this way. Our crusade excited many and quickly took on a life of its own. Those who were sympathetic to the cause knew better than to mention anything to the handful of programmed students. We were on a crusade challenging the very heavens, we were sounding the horns of liberation, and the walls of Jericho trembled.

Sister stood next to Ignatius's seat with her hand on his shoulder when she announced earlier that we would be electing class president. Her political tactics were crude. She waited until the day of the election to announce it would be held. Subtleties or sophistication were unnecessary when the flock was being led.

351

Eight years of Catholic school doctrine taught us that the priests and nuns knew what was right and wrong, good and bad for us. It was their duty to ensure that their decisions were correct even when they were not

But this was 1964. Cultural and social norms were being defied. College students questioned what the church was about, what the war in Vietnam was about, what getting up every morning and spending a day in an office was about. Folk groups came into their own and penned anti-war songs bucking the establishment. Political leaders were starting to be held accountable.

"The Times They Are a-Changing'" was a huge hit and Kenny asked me if I had heard the lyrics to another new release: "Father McKinsey, writing the words to a sermon that no one will hear." These authors spoke directly to us.

The eighth-grade class was poised to shake the very foundations of the St. Rita's Grammar School theocracy by not voting for the chosen one. The final tally wasn't even close: me, the lost lamb, 44; Ignatius 15.

Cassius Clay, the young brash underdog, turned the boxing world upside down by knocking out the formidable Sonny Liston to win the world heavyweight title. John Kennedy, a forty-three year old Catholic, had beaten veteran politician Richard Nixon, a white Anglo-Saxon protestant. And Armando Garcia was elected president of the 1964 graduating class of St. Rita's School.

After school the kids who were quiet and nervous during the reading of the ballots a couple of hours earlier, were now reveling in our revolt. I heard two of the girls laughing and singing, "Ding dong the witch is dead." Kenny was walking to his father's car when we saw each other. "The voice of the people has been heard!" he yelled, and pumped his fist into the air.

I did it; I actually managed to get elected.

Many of our classmates' parents liked my twin and me. Unlike Sister Constance they recognized and appreciated our enthusiasm for life, our sense of humor, our innocence. Ma and Pa were dumbstruck when they heard the news.

"Maybe there is hope for the twins after all," Ma said at the dinner table. They took us shopping for special clothes for the occasion. I got to pick a sharp-looking dark blue suit and my brother opted for a cool sport coat and a pair of slacks. We both got to wear neckties for the first time.

Father Vidra presided over the graduation Mass. The school choir made a valiant effort to sing but as usual came up short. We wore Kelly-green graduation robes with matching mortar boards adorned with green and gold tassels and a small brass-plated "64" attached. By this age Ma didn't have to tend to her boys' appearance as it was "cool" to be neat and clean looking.

The class filed out of church after Mass in two columns side by side. I led one and Kerry Donnell, my vice president, led the other. As class president, I was able to choose my vice president and chose Kerry. He not only got good grades, but was athletic, well-liked, and respected by all of our classmates. The fact that he was black was all the more reason to ask him to be with me on the stage at the podium.

We walked to the hall where I would give my speech. A reception would follow. Chairs were set up theatre-style. The two front sections were for the graduating class. The first row of the section behind the graduates was for monsignor, his two assistant priests, and school staff. Behind them were families and guests. Constance with the other nuns and teachers sat in the rear. I was feeling anxious about having to give my speech.

When we entered the hall, we led our class down the center aisle and they took their seats. Kerry and I continued to the side staircase that led to the stage. A chair was set near the microphone for my vice president, I stood at the podium. I handed Kerry my speech before presenting it, just in case.

353

I stood in the hall packed with people. The stage lights made me squint. I felt an overwhelming urge to pee. It got funereal quiet. A man's cough echoed. Another cleared his throat. I looked out and opened my mouth, but nothing came out.

I noticed Sister Constance's big black pear shape sitting at the head of the nuns and nervously shifting in her seat from one cheek to another.

I tried to lead them to the proper choice, Sister Constance probably thought to herself. This is their president who comes from unrefined people. The one who disrupts class when his teacher is at choir practice. The one I scolded with his twin for leading the boys time and again in forbidden war games at recess. The imp I caught playing in the choir loft desecrating the church. The brat, who with his twin, humiliated Ignatius at the school picnic. A class president who can hardly maintain a C average. Now he can't deliver a speech. Pathetic, just pathetic. I should skip the speech and go straight to handing out the diplomas.

I had gotten help writing my speech from Carolyn. She took speech in high school and shared some techniques.

"Think about what you want to tell them after so many years at St. Rita's. What have you learned? Who do you want to thank?

What will you remember?" I wrote down my thoughts. Carolyn looked them over and showed me how to articulate them. This went on for a number of drafts until the twelve-minute speech was ready. Then she had me read it over and over until I had it memorized. Until now.

The words were not there. My palms were wet. My legs tingled. I could feel beads of sweat on my brow. Maybe lobbying to become president wasn't such a good idea after all. Constance stood and walked toward the stage she gave monsignor an apologetic look as she passed him. I thought of how hard my sister, and I worked to get this together. I didn't want to disappoint my classmates who had voted for me, and I sure didn't want Constance to have one last victory. I looked down at Kerry sitting at my side.

"How does it start?" I whispered. The microphone carried my voice over the speakers. A few muffled laughs and chuckles, and one sympathetic "Oh my," rose from the audience. My nervous ripple had turned into a tidal wave engulfing the room. My vice president sat frozen in his seat. What the hell was he so nervous about? I was giving the damn speech. I pointed to his top pocket where the speech sat folded.

"Come on, what's the first line?"

He pulled the text from his jacket and stared at the type-written pages shaking in his hands. "Good evening, Monsignor" he whispered.

The realization came to me that he would be there reading it along in case I needed more help. Sister approached the podium. I repeated, "Good evening, Monsignor." I turned and looked straight at her, "Good evening, Sister Mary Constance." She stopped dead. "Good evening to our teachers, parents, and to you my classmates. It is hard to believe that the journey is over, and we will now go on to high school."

Kerry had opened the tap and suddenly, miraculously, the words flowed smoothly and uninterrupted. This Mexican kid who was not worthy of unclasping the shepherd's sandal spoke with the assurance of a prophet and the eloquence of an oracle for twelve uninterrupted and glorious minutes. The years of memorizing detestable math formulas, endless history dates, complex rules of grammar, and infinite catechism questions and answers served me all at once. I didn't have to remember the speech. One word simply followed another like a beautiful song. And as Carolyn had coached, I stood erect and made eye contact with my audience.

Sister Constance looked to be in emotional contortions. It wasn't a mystery what she thought of me. I'm sure that she did not want to see this little uncouth smart-ass succeed, but she also needed to put on a good show for the assembly of guests and dignitaries. She turned, waddled down the side stairs and made a hasty retreat to her chair.

Just before the end of the speech my brother Father Tony, the newly ordained priest and talk of the parish, walked in the back door, dressed in his priestly garb. He drew monsignor and Constance's attention. He sat to hear the end of my presentation.

I was surprised when I finished my speech that the audience began to applaud. It caught me off guard, on and on they clapped. I could only smile broadly. My classmates applauded, whooped and hollered. Ma, Pa, Ana, Carolyn, Martha, and Carmen, along with the parents who a few minutes before were suffering with me, were now clapping with enthusiasm. The nuns who secretly liked my brother and me clapped loud and hard. My beloved Sister Marie Lucille stood beaming.

Should I bow? Should I do a summersault? Do the splits? For a moment time slowed as I stood at the podium and surveyed the room. Constance sat with her arms folded. As I looked at her Caesar's quote came to me, "Veni, vidi, vici."

Kerry, my twin, Donny, and I talked after my speech. They patted me on the back for doing such a good job. My twin was proud of me. "I couldn't have done that," he said.

"Sorry I didn't get here in time to hear all of your speech. I heard you did a heck of a job," Tony said. Several surprised parents said as much. Ma, in a new dress, smiled in proud silence. Pa graciously accepted compliments acting as if it were nothing but bordered on gloating.

Old monsignor motioned to me and said, "Come here, lad," in his deep frog-like voice, heavily laced with Old World brogue. I made my way sheepishly to monsignor, Tony, and Sister Constance. The monsignor shook my hand and patted me on the back. "T'was a fine job ye did, lad, t'was a fine job."

"Thank you, monsignor." His hand engulfed mine. I had never noticed how blue his deep-set eyes were and how many creases he had on his face.

"A fine job indeed. You must be very proud of such a fine lad, hey, Rose?"

"Yes, thank you, monsignor," Constance answered. "We are proud of all of our students." She could not bring herself to give me my due, but this was my night to shine and hers to sulk.

Rose? Rose? My God, the monsignor had the power to call her by her first name. But Rose? Skunkweed would be more appropriate. It was sweet seeing the old bag squirm and there was nothing she could do to me.

Monsignor turned his attention to Father Tony; they turned their backs to us and engaged in conversation. I caught old Constance's eye; she made a feeble attempt at a smile.

I made my way to Donny, Kenny, and Kerry.

"What did the monsignor say?"

"He told me that I kicked ass."

"Hey, why did Constance turn so red? The last time I saw her like that was when someone cut a stinky one near her during math class."

"Yeah. She had to pretend that it wasn't there and wait for the smell to go away. I'm pretty sure it was Mike Calloway. He was always doing shit like that."

"So what got Constance so pissed off tonight?"

"You mean Rosie?"

"Who?"

"Monsignor called her by her first name," I said. "She had to act like she liked me."

Fernando shook his head and smiled.

We exchanged small talk not sure what was next. I saw Sister Lucille in quiet conversation with Sister Alvira Marie and approached them.

"Good-bye, Sister, thank you for your helping me with my Latin."

"Good-bye, Armando. I enjoyed having you and your brother in fourth grade." She paused for a moment, then as if to give me one final gift, she said. "I was very proud of you tonight."

Something welled up in my chest and I felt like crying. I smiled, waved her good-bye, and made my way to the door. I turned to take one last look at St. Rita's. Sister Lucille stood proud, Constance sulked. I felt one with the shepherd boy David and his sling.

Acknowledgments

Fernando:

Jan, my wife of fifty years who patiently read and reread my stories. Her input was invaluable and I'm more in love with her than ever.

Ken Moser for his suggestions on an early draft of the manuscript that gave me a boost when I needed it.

And thank you Sally Asante for your hawk eye as an editor and for your suggestions.

I would be remiss if I didn't acknowledge and thank the School Sisters of Norte Dame who dedicate their lives to teaching and molding students to do their best. They expected C students to strive for Bs, B students were pushed to get As, etc. I thank them for my ability to write, know my geography, religion, and math. Although I still do struggle with my multiplication tables, especially the 7s. I am a better person today because of their dedication. My brother on the other hand ....

Armando:

Fernando whose doggedness kept the fire burning and creative juices flowing over these three years that we've worked on this project. It was his energy, excitement, and humor that sustained me through periods of doldrums and moments of doubt. I could not have asked for a better brother.

Thank you Hugo Murillo of Genesis Digital HD for doing such a fine job with the photographs, and Luis Rameño of Siker *Publicidar* for working her magic on the graphics.

And thank you, Señor Waights Taylor Jr. Your patience with us was nothing short of biblical. And thank you for producing such a beautiful product for us. U-Da-Man!

About the Authors (?)

"Mammas, don't let you babies grow up to be authors."
Waights Taylor Jr.

Armando and Fernando comprise a complete personality. While Fernando is more left brain and became a successful landscape contractor as a result, Armando is more right brain and leaned more toward the arts.

Fernando, in Armando's opinion, was the little angel of the two who did everything by the book, greatly pleasing their parents. But "Humph!" says Armando, "he was more the little angel kiss-butt." Armando? Well, not so much. He was "*el diablito*" (the little devil).

Armando, as you may well guess, takes issue with the word "devil." The way he sees it he liked "adventures." The problem was that these adventures too often landed him in trouble at school and at home.

There's no doubt though that despite their differences they share the deep love that only twins can understand.

Armando has been writing seriously for over thirty years, producing collections of poetry, stories and a novel, with a second on the way.

Fernando got bit by the writing bug in his first year living in Mexico after he and Armando retired in Ajijic, Jalisco. Armando dragged a complaining "I don't want to do this" Fernando to "Write to the Prompt" a writing group that meets weekly. The facilitator gives a prompt: "You find a box that you don't recognize in the back of your closet," or "You're walking along a cliff and come on a stranger," etc. Then everyone writes for forty-five minutes, after which people are invited to read what their imaginations concocted and the group gives feedback. Fernando was immediately hooked and has rarely missed a meeting of the group. As a result of the "Write to a Prompt" group Fernando has been flourishing as a writer. He works at it with the same energy that he did in creating beautiful landscapes. In fact his many hours of writing earned him a place in the same advanced writers group that Armando was invited to join a year and a half ago.

The two are eternally grateful for their family that have nourished their souls from the day they were born.

email Addresses

agdavila@sonic.net

ffgarcia49@gmail.com

Made in the USA
Monee, IL
10 November 2021